NET WORK

NET WORK

A PRACTICAL GUIDE TO CREATING AND SUSTAINING NETWORKS AT WORK AND IN THE WORLD

PATTI ANKLAM

ELSEVIER

AMSTERDAM • BOSTON • HEIDELBERG • LONDON
NEW YORK • OXFORD • PARIS • SAN DIEGO
SAN FRANCISCO • SINGAPORE • SYDNEY • TOKYO
Butterworth-Heinemann is an imprint of Elsevier

Butterworth–Heinemann is an imprint of Elsevier
30 Corporate Drive, Suite 400, Burlington, MA 01803, USA
Linacre House, Jordan Hill, Oxford OX2 8DP, UK

∞ Recognizing the importance of preserving what has been written, Elsevier prints
its books on acid-free paper whenever possible.

Library of Congress Cataloging-in-Publication Data
Anklam, Patricia, 1949–
   Net work : a practical guide to creating and sustaining networks at work and
in the world / by Patti Anklam.
      p.   cm.
   Includes bibliographical references and index.
   ISBN-13: 978-0-7506-8297-8 (alk. paper)
   ISBN-10: 0-7506-8297-3 (alk. paper)
   1. Business networks. I. Title.
HD69.S8A55 2007
658'.044—dc22

2006053080

British Library Cataloguing-in-Publication Data
A catalogue record for this book is available from the British Library.

ISBN: 978-0-7506-8297-8

For information on all Butterworth–Heinemann publications
visit our website at www.books.elsevier.com

Printed in the United States of America
07 08 09 10 11 12   10 9 8 7 6 5 4 3 2 1

To the most important networks of all, my Anklam, Christenson, Hutchinson, and Koontz families, and especially to my deeply emotional connectors, my mother, Marie, and my husband, Joe.

CONTENTS

FOREWORD

There is a transformation happening in business organizations today. Through my work with over 200 strategically important groups in 120 top organizations over the past decade, I've seen a growing awareness of importance of taking a network-based view of critical business issues today. Understanding key relational dimensions—such as information sharing, decision making, trust, and energy—is critical to the success of collaboration, innovation, and organizational change and effectiveness. While there are many drivers of this shift, it has been in no small part enabled by the application of network analysis software to social theory about group ties, a breakdown in the ability of hierarchical organizations to respond rapidly to change, and technical infrastructures that enabled ideas to spread and grow through an ever-expanding network of researchers and practitioners.

My own work in organizational network analysis began with an early interest in knowledge worker productivity and continually finding that most of us don't use databases when we have problems to solve but instead reach out to other people. This got me interested in network analysis as a way to visualize these critical collaborations in large distributed groups that need to work effectively together and I joined Larry Prusak at IBM's Institute for Knowledge Management (IKM) in 1999. In November 2000, I gave a workshop on the research at an IKM meeting in Santa Fe, NM. Patti had been invited to the IKM meeting by my colleague Dave Snowden whose work in knowledge management and complexity was beginning to take shape. She attended the day-long network analysis workshop and then cornered me at cocktail hour: "You have to come and work with me at Nortel!" she said. After participating in one of our research projects at Nortel Networks, Patti went on to build awareness and competence in ONA and the power of networks for Nortel's Professional Services organization. Since then, we've worked together, co-authored articles and collaborated on client projects.

Working with practitioners from across a spectrum of industry and the public sector, I continue to marvel at the cross-currents of ideas and methods that touch on the idea of mapping and understanding the relationships of people in networks of all types. We have seen the Network Roundtable at the University of Virginia grow from a zero- to an 80 top-level member organization in just two years. Patti has been an important contributor in this line of thinking as well as expanding her idea network to encompass thinking across a range of transformative business thinkers, including Dave Snowden and Verna Allee, as well as folks like Mark Bonchek and Jan Twombly who have incorporated network thinking into the businesses they have created.

What you will find in this book is an integrated view of a network of ideas about networks. I don't know of any other book that provides such an easy-to-read introduction to the fundamentals of network thinking and (as Patti puts it) net work thinking. The premise is simple enough: if you understand the basics of network structures and properties and the dynamics of complexity, you can be more effective at working with networks—groups of people—in any aspect of your life and work. Patti, who when pressed will tell you that she's still a technical writer at heart, has identified the key currents and tangents in network thinking and put them into a coherent, practical framework that will change how you think about relationships, building and sustaining relationships, and using networks to make a difference at work and in the world.

Rob Cross
University of Virginia
Charlottesville, VA

PREFACE

IT TAKES A NETWORK

We all use our networks every day. From the simplest transaction with a colleague to participation in complex multinational agreements, we are in webs of relationships that we tap into in order to accomplish something that we could not do by ourselves.

We take active part in many of our networks—a professional association, a business network, a network for buying, selling or trading farm equipment, or a church fellowship group. Some of our networks are in the background; we are barely aware of the thread of connections that bring felt-tipped pens to the supply cabinet outside our offices. We create networks to develop business: expand market reach, embed products and services with those of potential partners, and create product innovations.

Throughout my life, I have been supported by both professional and intimate networks of friends inside and outside work as well as by a large extended family. So have you. My journey has led me to try to understand these networks, to illuminate for myself and others how networks emerge and evolve, what makes them successful, how to work in them, and how to lead them. If your journey has brought you to this book, then you are also in the network of inquiry about networks. My goal is to articulate what I have learned in a way that that will accelerate your learning and understanding. Here's my story.

In my work and career, I was rewarded for being a smart independent contributor. I was a good team member, but was happiest with my head down working solo on a writing project or software or information architecture. But in the early 1990s, something shifted for me and I found myself leading a task force requested to scout for and pilot innovative methods to enhance the software product development for a large computer manufacturer. The task force's purpose was to improve the speed and quality of software development. I built a small core team, and together we built a large network of people who were inspired by the conversations we started. We reached outside the software group to talk with people in sales and marketing groups and with people in the services side of the business, and we enrolled co-conspirators from finance and human resources groups. We looked outside the company and the industry for expertise and experience. We signed up small project groups to work with us as pilots in experimenting with new approaches, coached them in effective communication techniques, and empowered them to question management's assumptions about their projects. We introduced them to powerful tools for collecting and analyzing customer requirements. One software architect/project leader got the picture so clearly from the requirements analysis that he told his manager the product would never make any money. His project team merged with another team (also one of our pilots).

Our task force was ultimately absorbed into the organizational structure, and we four team members were passed from one manager to another. Our last manager likened me to a gardener who went up and down the rows in a large garden, spotting new varieties, and making sure they had water and light. This task force was only one in a company that needed many such efforts to survive. But this company, Digital Equipment Corporation, was dying, no matter what anyone did. Digital creaked along for five more years, during which time I turned my attention to knowledge management, building web-based knowledge systems, nurturing communities of expertise, and connecting with the underground knowledge management network across Digital from my perch in systems integration services.

In my next job, at Nortel Networks, I built and directed a knowledge management group for Nortel's professional services group. Working as a network organization, the core team was responsible for connecting with one or more business or functional units. Our extended team consisted of knowledge champions from the business and functional units as well as the geographical regions. We had a two-year plan to create a collaborative, knowledge-based organization. I had the will to persuade my manager to fund membership in IBM's Institute for Knowledge Management (IKM), where I was able to learn and practice social network analysis with Rob Cross and to explore complex sense making with Dave Snowden. My KM group at Nortel was at the tipping point of success when, after eighteen months, Nortel Networks shut down its professional services group. I shifted from creating networks at work to joining networks in the world. I would not have survived without them.

 Former McKinsey & Company consultant Mark Bonchek thought carefully for some time about the business and organizational model on which professional services firms were based. In 2002, he launched an experiment to create a new kind of professional community, one in which a select group of professionals from diverse organizations and disciplines could benefit from both fellowship and a greater flow of ideas and opportunities. To emphasize his aspiration that it be generative and innovative, he named it Gennova. As a network, Gennova could solve larger and more complex client problems than anyone could manage individually, while bringing both innovative and holistic solutions to intractable business problems. That July, a "barn-raising" event attracted fifty people and catalyzed a core group of twenty to evolve and grow into the Gennova Group. In April of 2006, Gennova launched its fifth year by examining the group's purpose, membership, structure, and processes to set a learning focus for the fall meeting season.

During those four years, Gennova members thrived on conversations that first were internally focused on the group's own design, development, and growth. We experimented with network organizational forms and launched a collection of collaborative projects that enabled members to get to know and trust each other. Eventually, it became clear that what we were really doing was exploring the nature of networks, their types, how they form, what motivates people to be in them and stay in them. Gennova itself was a laboratory for experimenting with this new organizational form, the network.

This book is inspired and informed by conversations with members of the Gennova network over the past four years. The idea for this book was in fact suggested by Mark Bonchek, who encouraged me to gather a subgroup of "Gennovans" who wanted to explore the properties of networks. This team (Jenny Ambrozek, Kate Ehrlich, Gabriele Gandswindt, Rob Laubacher, Paul Trevithick, Stan Ward, and Nat Welch) gathered biweekly beginning in July of 2003 and continued for almost nine months to sketch out a taxonomy of network types, transition models, case studies, and a pair of book outlines. We ceased working in this subgroup in 2004, but I continued reading, collecting stories, and sketching the framework you'll read about here.

Throughout my work with Gennova and my professional consulting practice in collaborative network design and analysis, many people have asked me questions like, "So, Patti, what's the secret to creating a good network?" or "I want to start a network. Where is the *book*?" or "Can you *really* manage networks?" These questions centered my purpose in finally writing *Net Work*: to create a practical guide for the network entrepreneur or leader who is creating a network or facing a transition point in an existing network.

However, this book is for anyone who works in or with networks or who is interested in what makes networks work and what work is required to make the networks useful. I've come to believe that all networks, regardless of their size, shape, or origin, share fundamental properties and that insights derived from one type of network transfer easily from one context to another. I hope you'll see that, too.

The book has three parts:

- *Part I:* Throughout the gestation of the ideas in this book, I've come to rely on a set of assumptions about the nature of net work, which represent my underlying beliefs about the aspects that all networks have in common. These are discussed in Chapter 1.

    In Chapter 2, I demonstrate with examples from the past two decades how prevalent networks are as an organizational form, what we are learning about them, and what we have still to learn.

    Chapters 3 through 6 set out the still-emerging taxonomy of networks that so many people are looking for. I present four facets from which a network can be described: purpose (Chapter 3), structure (Chapter 4), style (Chapter 5), and its value-producing processes (Chapter 6).

- *Part II:* Practical guidance about designing, developing, and working with networks begins in Chapter 7, where I discuss how to create a network from the perspective of how its facets come into play through its life cycle. Subsequently I describe methods for examining and diagnosing the structure and health of a network (Chapter 8) and guiding a network through transitions in response to internal and external stimuli, planned or otherwise (Chapter 9).

- *Part III:* Chapter 10 summarizes the imperatives of "Net Work" for leaders today: the "work" required to create and sustain purposeful and thriving "nets" inside their organizations and outside.

As an organizational form, networks will never replace hierarchical structures or markets, but it is now clear that network forms (and they are varied) offer a range of choices for managing people, ideas, and work that were not previously available. I hope that by bringing all these aspects of networks into one place, we can start on the road to a common language of networks and an understanding of the "net work" required in making them successful.

The individual cases and stories about networks are threaded throughout the book. Each story may be referenced multiple times in different contexts. Think of the chapters as hubs, the stories as nodes, and you may see the logic of this network of stories. As you may not read the book in sequence, nor all in one sitting, I've keyed the stories using a ⊕ *.*

ACKNOWLEDGMENTS

It takes a network to write a book, and a book creates a network.

You will see much of my experience of Gennova in this book and also the experiences of many of the networks I've personally been part of. But part of the experience of Gennova is an attention to understanding what's already been studied and written. So, I hope that readers will find scholarship here as well as "networkship." I'm particularly grateful for the guidance of Mark Bonchek, Jan Twombly, and Jane Wei-Skillern for pointing me to some of the brilliant research and case development that has laid the foundation for an academic science of network management and, of course, for their encouragement throughout this process.

I am humbly thankful to my guides and mentors in the practice and methods of making sense of networks. Rob Cross, Dave Snowden, Valdis Krebs, and Verna Allee have all inspired and supported me in this effort, as have the entire Gennova group.

The stories that are woven throughout the book come from a variety of sources; the richest were enlightened by conversations with those who created or sustained them. The following are all due thanks:

Bob Wolf, Christopher Meyers, Colin Strutt, David Gurteen, David Introcaso, Eric Lesser, Eric Stein, Jack Vinson, Jay Vogt, Jenny Ambrozek, John Barrett, John Smith, Judith Herman, Ken Fagut, Larry Chait, Larry Prusak, Laura Spear, Laurie Lock Lee, Lisa Dennis, Madeleine Taylor, Mark Vasu, Mindy Gewirtz, Nick Salafsky, Peter Gloor, Roberto Cremonini, Ross Dawson, Sanjay Swarup, Stan Garfield, Star Dargin, Seth Earley, Steve Borgatti, Steve Waddell, Steve Weinecke, Terry Wilson-Malam, Tom Sadtler, Valerie Fleishman, Vik Muiznieks, and Zeke Wolfberg, as well as my always enlightening and supportive Gennovans Andy Snider, Art Hutchinson, Barbara Kivowitz, Bill Ives, Bruce Hoppe, Claire Reinelt, Dennis Smith, Gabriele Ganswindt, Jan Twombly, Kate Ehrlich, Mark

Bonchek, Mary Ruddy, Mindy Gewirtz, Nat Welch, Paul Trevithick, Peter Flentov, Rob Laubacher, Rob Peagler, Samantha Tan, and Tim Andrews.

Finally, to my personal network of support for producing this book: Mary Utt for editing, Sue Gault for photos and photographic inspiration, and my husband, Joe Hutchinson, for all the figures, his many patient reviews of chapter upon chapter, and giving up his summer so I could write this book.

Chapter 1

THE NATURE OF
NET WORK

What does it take to make a network work? If you are asking that question, then I hope that you will find that you have come to the right place—this book. If you haven't asked the question? Well, I hope you find a network perspective that you've not seen elsewhere—insights, tools, and practical examples of how thinking in network terms can enhance your ability to manage relationships. Why? Because we live in a networked world and a networked economy and the path to success—for ourselves and our world—requires that we understand networks. That's what this book is about: the work required to understand, sustain, and work effectively in networks, net work.

A spate of books on the science of networks appeared on the scene between the years 2002 and 2004; at the same time, our collective consciousness was trying to make sense of the terrible power of a seemingly loosely connected network of terrorists. Just a few years after the attacks of 9/11, the beneficent power of relief networks met the challenges of tsunami and hurricane: self-organizing relief networks flooded areas of disaster with medical and food supplies, helping hands, and support that surpassed the abilities of hierarchical government agencies. The science of networks brought analytic tools to the understanding of mapping the terrorist networks (to find and disrupt the bad guys)—and of connecting the relief networks (to help the good guys do better).

A dozen years earlier, management scientists started to see network forms of organization emerging in specialized economic sectors. They noted that hierarchical and vertically integrated companies were beginning to segment and distribute the work of the corporation among partnerships, alliances, coalitions, and consortia. They speculated on how leaders were adapting management styles to accommodate less control and more collaboration. At the same time, however, reengineering disrupted patterns of knowledge flow and eliminated many of the connectors, mavens, and salesmen who were in middle-management jobs in many of those same companies.

Later, the dot-com bust sent tens of thousands of knowledge workers into a free-agent nation, where, encouraged by placement agencies, many of them dutifully attended local "networking" events to make connections to find jobs. Others created and joined formal and informal business networks to connect as entrepreneurs to start new companies.

This imperative to network started to take hold at a time when broadband and wireless Internet access connected us to a real, live, worldwide network of hubs, switches, and routers. This "Internetwork" (as the Internet was first called) enabled us to make connections beyond the boundaries of home, business, community, nation, and geography.

We have always known that we had networks: families, clubs, groups of friends, coworkers, and former classmates. But in less complex, less globally inter-networked, times, we took these networks for granted. We now know that we have tools and methods to examine networks and that these tools and methods can help us make networks more valuable and more meaningful. Just as a photographer might use a wide angle lens to see a duck floating across a beautiful pond, that same photographer might use a telephoto lens to focus on the spot on the duck's head that identifies it as a Bufflehead. And just as the photographer's lenses let us see both context and detail in nature, tools from network science let us see—with the network lens—both context and detail in our networks.

This chapter summarizes a set of emerging principles about the nature of networks that come from my work and that of my own network in applying the network lens to organizations, businesses, communities, and groups. These principles lead to the mindful practice of net work, which is the theme of this book. Three of the networks I studied for this book provide useful starting points for illustrating these principles.

 In 2002, leaders from across the healthcare community in Boston, concerned about the increasing number and complexity of seemingly intractable problems in the U.S. healthcare industry began creating a network that represented all sectors of the healthcare community in New England—hospital, research, and physician associations; biotechnology and pharmaceutical companies; medical device manufacturers; insurers; and hospital and laboratory products suppliers. They believed that only a network so diversely constituted with a common commitment could create breakthroughs in research, problem analysis, and solution advocacy. The New England Healthcare Institute (NEHI) is entering its fifth year of identifying and tackling multi-dimensional problems in disease management and prevention, medical innovation, and systemic issues like healthcare waste and inefficiency and financing models for regional and national healthcare systems.

 In the urban centers of Boston, Philadelphia, and Chicago, groups of knowledge management (KM) practitioners formed communities to meet and share learning and experience in the nascent field of KM. Monthly meetings brought corporate workers, consultants, small business owners, and academic researchers together for topical discussions that stimulated conversation, business contacts, and a sense of identity. When leaders of these KM groups met each other (via teleconference) for the first time, they discovered similarities in the format, membership demographics, governance, and evolution of their groups. A discussion of differences prompted ideas and potential for augmenting their membership by reaching out to additional professional disciplines.

 The fifty-year-old Young Presidents' Organization is a 9,500-person global peer network of business leaders who leverage each other for personal and professional growth strategies and experiences. A professional staff manages the global board of directors and supports 175 local chapters that connect people face-to-face in learning experiences. Through these local chapters and a global website, "YPOers"

who travel worldwide know that they will find helping and welcoming peers wherever they are.

These three examples of groups of people who connect for a common purpose don't carry the term "network" in their name. But we can call them networks and we can use them to understand a few fundamental principles.

Principle #1. If it's a network, you can draw it.

If you can see potential relationships in any collection of two or more people, groups, or organizations, and if you can identify something that they have in common, then it's a network and you can represent it by drawing dots and lines.

Consider the two drawings in Figure 1.1. On the left-hand side are three groups of two or three dots. Consider that these dots (which we call *nodes*) represent people, groups, or organizations and that the lines between them represent a relationship of some kind (we call these lines *ties*). At this point it's not a well-connected network; but look what happens when A sees a potential common purpose with nodes B and C. If node A creates two ties, then the whole network looks more connected, right away.

Viewing our relationships with the network lens empowers us to seek and discover others like ourselves and to make connections. One person reaching out to two others enhances the potential of the whole network.

Principle #2. Every network has an underlying purpose, and every network creates value.

A collection of people and groups may be a potential network but will need a purpose to keep together. The purpose relates to the value

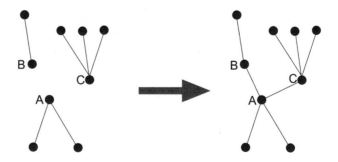

Figure 1.1
If it's a network, you can draw it

that the network creates, which may not always be articulated, but can always be discovered. The knowledge management groups that formed in different cities each discovered a shared interest in KM and continue to serve the network's purpose of shared learning, practice, and fellowship.

Principle #3. Once we learn to distinguish and identify the unique and individual characteristics of networks we can create, examine, and shape their properties, boundaries, and environment.

This book categorizes the facets of a network in terms of *purpose, structure, style,* and *value.* Within each facet are multiple elements and dimensions that illuminate choices in network design. The unique characteristics of any network determine how it creates value and just what that value is. For example, each of the three networks introduced in this chapter are structured differently; each has selected a structure that best meets the needs of the network and its constituents. Membership criteria provide boundaries. The leadership of NEHI selects members very carefully. YPO is open only to individuals who fulfill very strict membership criteria. Knowledge management meetings are open to any like-minded person who wants to show up. All three networks plan meetings and events carefully to fit the purpose and style so as to produce value consistently.

Principle #4. Because networks are systems of human relationships, we can best understand them using lessons from the study of complex adaptive systems.

A complex adaptive system is one that consists of elements, called *agents,* whose relationships may be changing all the time. Consider a flock of birds or a school of fish. The system (the flock, the school) itself has an identity, but the precise relationships among individuals at any given point in time cannot be completely known. Within the boundaries of a system, agents are capable of self-organizing, often following a simple set of rules. Even though its whole is not knowable, a complex system does exhibit patterns; from the patterns, we can sometimes understand the rules by which the system self-organizes and often can understand, after the fact, what particular patterns resulted in a given outcome. For example, the members of the knowledge management groups, attracted to a set of ideas, self-organized independently in three cities at different times, but the resulting group structures and styles have very similar patterns.

Principle #5. Everyone in a network influences the relationships in and the outcomes of the network.

Any change in a complex system, no matter how small, can have a far-reaching and potentially unexpected consequence. In any network, different people show up for any given meeting, thus altering the overall system of relationships in a way that cannot be predicted or controlled.

The development of personal relationships within the network—as when A in Figure 1.1 connects with B and C—may similarly alter the structure of the network as well as its style, purpose, or value.

Principle #6. A leader's work is to create and maintain the conditions that enable productive and innovative relationships.

Leaders may excel at traditional tasks of management, but they can never manage all the relationships in a network, nor direct all of its activities to predictable outcomes. Leaders can and must, however, provide an environment in which relationships produce innovative and productive outcomes for its members, stakeholders, shareholders, clients, and (in some cases) the network itself.

The network must be one that has clear norms for how people engage in interactions and acknowledge the contributions of others; it is the leadership that establishes and provides a role model for these norms.

Leadership in the knowledge management groups, for example, is typically shared among a core group; all members contribute ideas and topics for members to share and mutually explore, thus enhancing an environment that reinforces continuous innovation. NEHI and YPO network leaders design and structure events that provide continuous acknowledgment of individual and network accomplishment and foster the development of rich and trusting relationships.

Principle #7. Successful networks are reflective and generative.

Networks are complex, not chaotic. Chaos occurs when all the existing patterns and norms have broken down. When you live in or lead a network, and are grounded by these principles of net work, the network engages in both creative and reflective activities that maintain self-awareness and provide boundaries within which the unknown and unexpected can be welcomed and managed.

Successful personal business networks like YPO periodically survey their membership to ensure that they are meeting members' needs, using the results to generate positive change. Leaders of learning networks like the knowledge management groups welcome the opportunity to meet in a teleconference and talk easily with each other as they reflect on their past experiences and the possibilities for improving the value they bring to their members.

Net work is about balancing. As you'll see in Chapters 3 through 6, there are dynamic tensions across the facets of purpose, structure, style, and value. But we are in networks all the time and every day. Consciously choosing to put on the network lens gives us access to tools that let us better balance self-purpose vs. network purpose, open vs. closed, transparent vs. opaque, tangible vs. intangible, and perhaps most important of all, flexibility vs. accountability.

Principle #8 (The Paradox). All networks are alike, and all networks are unique.

The network lens requires us to look at how the structural components of networks—the nodes and the ties—and a fixed number of attributes enable us to characterize networks as all members of the same species. All networks have a purpose, a structure, a style, and value-producing mechanisms that are articulated or discoverable. But each network expresses those attributes in a unique and flexible combination.

The three networks introduced here each have a discernable purpose, structure, and leadership style; the insight from net work is that by providing a language to describe these attributes we can better see how networks are alike and therefore how any network can learn from the experiences of another.

The next chapter, Chapter 2, introduces the variety of contexts in which networks are currently present and available to us in their myriad forms.

Chapter 2

THE CONTEXT OF NET WORK

Networks matter. When individuals discover that they cannot complete a task by themselves, when a company knows that it cannot grow the talent, expertise, or means of production it needs to be successful in a new market, when a group of like-minded people with shared interests understand that their personal growth and development require learning with others, when an NGO mobilizes to protect a natural ecosystem, a network emerges. The reasons that individuals, businesses, and organizations create networks come down to the simple proposition that working together, in conscious collaboration, means that we can accomplish more than we ever could individually.

This chapter surveys the network landscape of the 21st century, beginning with the presence of networks at the top of the evening news, the economic shifts that presaged the need for networks, and the primary ways that organizations of all types are seeing the benefits of network organizational forms.

NETWORKS STATE OF MIND

If you've picked up this book, you already know something about networks. You are probably a member of at least one group or organization that calls itself a "network." And you've certainly seen and read many articles about networks. Since the dawn of the modern era called the "information age," and particularly since the beginning of this century, we've seen the word creep into our language and daily lives. We can—and must—thank the Internet and the network technologies that made it possible to actually be a networked world. In this networked world we conduct business globally 24/7, and we can learn instantly about and comment on events that touch us politically, economically, personally, and emotionally.

The Collaboration Imperative

"The world is flat," declared Thomas Friedman in his 2005 book of the same title, which remained on the business bestseller lists for over a year. Friedman is well-known for bringing insights about globalization to both the political and economic spheres. He distinguishes three eras: Globalization 1.0 (1492–1800), Globalization 2.0 (1800–2000), and the current era. The most exciting part of the current era, Globalization 3.0, he says, is about how individuals and small groups can connect: "the fact that we are now in the process of connecting all the knowledge pools in the world together."

He cites ten "flatteners" that created the platform for collaboration, including Windows 3.0 (near coincident with the tearing down of the Berlin Wall and all that it symbolized); the overbuilding of the telecommunications infrastructure that was triggered by Netscape's public offering and the dot-com bubble; and web-enabled workflow. "The last 20 years were about forging, sharpening and distributing all the new tools to collaborate and connect. Now the real information revolution is about to begin."[1]

Collaboration is the new corporate strategy. A March 2006 IBM study of over 750 CEOs found that collaboration—within the firm but more specifically with customers and partners—was a key priority for 76% of them. However, only 51% felt that they currently collaborate to a great extent.[2] Collaboration starts with an intention to collaborate—a purpose. From there, the network lens helps to identify relationships in which collaboration is already occurring and to see those relationships as a network in which collaborative interactions are directed toward a common purpose. What may be difficult for these CEOs to understand is that there is already a network of

relationships that exist outside the boundaries of the internal hierarchy and the formal alliances, and that this existing network is where
the collaboration must start.

eBusiness and Internet businesses

As soon as there was a web, there was the possibility of eBusiness,
that is, using digital technologies to improve business results.
eBusiness is about digitally linking the supply chain more quickly
and efficiently than had been possible with the cumbersome and
custom EDI (Electronic Data Interchange standard) solutions. Wal-
Mart and Cisco Systems provided leadership in linking suppliers to
customers through an Internet-enabled supply chain.

The first major successful web-based business was Amazon.com,
whose business model set a new standard for efficiency and market
reach. Launched in 1995 as an electronic bookstore linking publishers and buyers, Amazon leveraged the interactivity of the network to
enable visitors to the site to rate and write reviews of books; it maintains and connects purchase data to present "others who bought this
book also bought" recommendations to buyers. It has also created a
large business network by partnering with product vendors to extend
the range of its products and provide an online channel for retailers
like Toys 'R Us to market and sell.

eBay, also launched in 1995, is the poster child for creating an
economic community on the web, where ratings of buyers and sellers
provide a proxy for trust. A buyer's risk is reduced when she can
see how other buyers rated their interactions with a particular seller.
Through the end of the 1990s, dot-com startups emulated Amazon.
com and eBay while existing "brick-and-mortar" corporations
scrambled to figure out ways to reach their customers on the web.

From process to people: Social networks on the web

The World Wide Web is the physical face of the Internet, which since
its inception has brought continuously increasing content and band-
width into our businesses and homes. From the first page published
in 1991 until January 2005, the number of pages grew from one to
11.5 billion.[3] In 1993, when the web became public, you needed
technology savvy and access to an Internet connection to create a
page. Today, anyone with a couple of minutes of Internet access can

contribute to the web's store of content by creating a blog entry or posting an opinion on an interactive site. The mode of interaction expanded from one-to-many to many-to-many. IBM has developed "jam" technology that enables thousands of people to connect worldwide via the Internet over a span of days to focus on dialogue on key business issues. Taking the "jam" outside the company, IBM hosted a worldwide "HabitatJam," that brought together 39,000 participants from 158 countries to talk about pressing issues in the sustainability of urban areas.[4]

The possibility for connection afforded by the web led to Friendster.com and LinkedIn.com, the earliest of the social networking sites. These are today dwarfed by the popularity of MySpace.com and Facebook.com. Post your profile, look for people you'd like to meet, and—voilà—you could be connected. By July of 2006, over 140 different social networking sites were available on the web, with an estimated 200 million user profiles. Even considering that many people register on multiple sites or register on a single site with multiple personas, there remain tens of millions of people—mostly young people fixated on social networking sites—who are connecting daily with true acquaintances, "e-quaintances" (people known only electronically), and strangers.

The Economic Impetus

Much business news today reflects some urgency for businesses to think about getting better at both managing collaborative partnerships and managing collaborative networks in their own workforces. This is not really a new trend; the landscape has been shifting for some time. The shift is not only in the business models on which corporations were formed but also in the roles, expectations, and leverage of the people at work in those corporations.

Vertical disintegration

The availability and maturation of Internet technologies to connect businesses coincided with rethinking the model of a corporation as a vertically integrated unit that owned all of its resources, means of production, people, and knowledge, as well as sales, marketing, and delivery channels. The path to rethinking and disintegrating was outlined in the classic *Harvard Business Review* article of 1990, "The Core Competency of the Corporation" by G. K. Prahalad and Gary Hamel, that pointed out that companies would do best to focus on those areas of deep proficiency that enable them to produce unique value to customers. The outcome of strategies based on the core competency model was an increase in the occurrence of outsourcing, divestiture, and partnerships to fill those needs not considered "core."[5]

Given the increased ability to connect, and this mandate to strip to the core, the number of partnerships and alliances grew dramatically. Between 1996 and 2001, 57,000 alliances were announced by U.S. companies alone.[6] The business model shifted toward a model wherein partnering for innovation, competencies, access to markets, faster production and delivery of products, and resources was a key part of strategic planning.

But all the planning in the world didn't foresee or account for a failure rate that is variously estimated between 40% and 55% (and sometimes higher) among all partnerships. Partnering, business has learned, is risky, especially if you haven't developed the knowledge, skills, and experience to partner successfully. Partnerships, alliances, consortia, joint ventures, federations, coalitions—whatever you might call them—are all networks that can be examined on three levels:

1. The network of interactions among the business entities and organizational units that connected to meet a specific business objective;
2. The industry or sector ecosystem in which the partners, their suppliers and other partners, competitors, and markets are mutually intertwined and connected;
3. The network of human relationships that form at multiple touch points around a partnership, from executive-level agreements to the workers tasked at specific jobs.

The vertical disintegration and shift to networks of businesses has occurred during a time of great technology change and a shift to the knowledge economy. For many, this has altered the very nature of work.

Shift in the nature of work

A January 2006 *Economist* article highlighted this changing nature of the workforce by hearkening back to the "organization man," first described by William Whyte. The article declared the emergence of a new generation of worker: the "networked person." What distinguishes the networked person is that she works by choice, makes decisions based on interactions that occur any place, any time, anywhere, and is happiest when managing her own work on complex interdependent tasks.[7]

The increasing complexity of work and hence the requirement for people to be able to access a broad range of expertise and deep experience is highlighted in a McKinsey report (2006) that studied the nature of work and the shift from "transformational" and "transactional" interactions to "tacit" interactions. Tacit interactions require workers to synthesize and articulate what they know from experience; such interactions are more likely to involve decision making and problem solving rather than moving or transforming raw materials (the transformational) or performing coordinating, recording, and clerical work (transactional). Their research indicates that of 6.4 million new jobs created between 1998 and 2004, 70% of them required primarily tacit interactions. Even people in jobs not classified as tacit may be called upon to perform tacit knowledge work by virtue of union membership, employee programs, or tangential work activities.

Intellectual and social capital

Peter Drucker first alerted the business world to the idea of the knowledge economy in 1949,[8] but, as with many of his macro business insights, it wasn't until a few decades later that this idea created a conversation about measuring the value of knowledge in a corporation. Following the lead of Karl-Erik Sveiby, who first published a book on knowledge companies in 1986, Skandia AFS in Stockholm began practicing the concept. By 1997, the term *intellectual capital* was on firm enough ground to be used as the title of two books that came out that year, "capital" being a business-friendly term intended to denote the real market value of a company's intangible assets, including:

- *Human capital:* the knowledge, skills, and experience of the individuals required to provide solutions to customers; for example, its core competency;

- *Structural capital:* the internal procedures, processes, and internal organizational structures that have evolved to enable the organization to function as it does; for example, standard methods or heuristics passed from person to person;

- *Relational capital:* the value of an organization's relationships with its customers, suppliers, and others it engages with to accomplish its business; for example, its access to specific markets or resources.

But how do these three forms of capital, especially the latter, actually produce financial value? The common model of intellectual capital shown on the left in Figure 2.1 suggests that financial value accrues from planned interactions (the dotted line) among the three forms of intellectual capital, guided by diligent management.

My alteration of this model is on the right-hand side of Figure 2.1. Value—financial and otherwise—results from the interaction of human, structural, and relational capital; but it is the social capital that supports interactions. Social capital, write Don Cohen and Larry Prusak in their book *In Good Company*, consists of "the stock of active connections among people; the trust, mutual understanding,

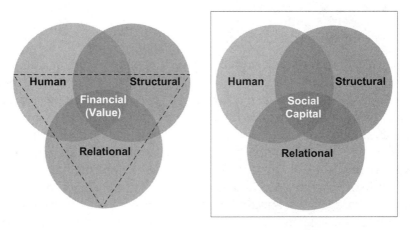

Figure 2.1
Intellectual and social capital

and shared values and behaviors that bind the members of human networks and communities and make cooperative action possible."[9]

Intuitively, we believe that every time a network grows in an organization in a way that creates bonds among members and spreads goodwill, the stock of social capital goes up. We also know that the value of that social capital can be incalculable in times of stress.

 A $500M global manufacturing company hired Mindy Gewirtz to help them develop an on-site early childhood education center. The CEO initiated the potential $500K project because he felt strongly about corporate social responsibility and was committed to providing a workplace where it was possible for workers to achieve work/life balance. Gewirtz created a network, linking management, human resources, the union, and employees on the inside with local community resources, including potential suppliers and providers. Just as the project was ready to launch, a fire wiped out nearly $500K in the company's profits, which was just the amount needed for the education center. The plans, as Gewirtz says, "literally went up in smoke."

Several months later, seeking competitive advantage, the management team proposed shifting the company into a 24/7 production schedule from the existing five-days-plus-overtime schedule. The union was so concerned about the impact on workers, especially on the issue of work/life balance, they began talking strike. The CEO again called Gewirtz. Because of the understanding of the personal issues of union workers on work/life balance that had been part of the childhood education project, she was able, first, to talk to the CEO as the "voice of the network," enabling him to see the implications of the proposed change. The implementation plan for the production shift was augmented with the addition of a Social Hardship Committee to be facilitated by Gewirtz. Many of the executives, supervisors, and union members and leaders were part of the network that she had created months earlier.

The committee tapped into and increased its social capital in the next few months, as Gewirtz and committee members "walked the floors" to talk with workers and identify those whose lives and families could not sustain the new work schedule. In this 3,000-person company, there was not one hardship issue left unaddressed

in the implementation. The social capital built in the failed child-
hood education center was better than gold in averting a strike;
tapped to develop greater understanding of work/life balance in the
mill, the capital store increased.[10]

Lessons from Knowledge Management

The work disciplines that emerged from the ideas behind knowledge management—which came close on the heels of the work in intellectual capital—are in their second decade. Multidisciplinary from its start, KM as a collected set of concepts, practices, and communities has consistently been engaged in the question of how an organization can best leverage its intellectual assets.

Complex, tacit knowledge transfer requires some basis for connection, some shared language, purpose, or physical model with which to interact. It helps to be physically or geographically co-located, as this closeness, or propinquity, creates an easier path to forming a relationship. Relationship is a prerequisite to quality knowledge transfer.

Learning on the Leading Edge

Organizations that have made the adjustment to the age of the knowledge worker and the primacy of networks continue to find new ways to use and leverage networks (and to join associations—networks—where they can exchange their learning with others).

Companies and organizations are rapidly acquiring the skills needed to work in a world of partnerships. With the rise of professional associations to support this competency development, companies are learning to manage the risks of partnering and look for the opportunities that come from collaboration; a few are adding "corporate alliances managers" to their executive committees.

Names for these networks include partnerships, alliances, consortia, and joint ventures. The language we use to denote business-to-business relationships is so rich that every specific relationship requires careful attention to its name as well as an agreement. Sometimes a letter of intent is all that is required; more often, formal contracts are put in place. The number of relationships builds, agreement upon agreement, until there is a complex web of relationships that needs to be managed. In 1980, 2% of corporate revenues came from alliances; by 2002, that percentage had reached 35%.

It's difficult enough to manage a partnership that is based on manufacturing or bringing goods or services to market, but when it comes to the realm of ideas—research, innovation, and problem solving—even more learning will be coming from the edge.

Research and Development

R&D lab managers are increasingly looking at the impact of global economic and demographic shifts on the ability of their labs to connect with and reach out to potential partners. In June 2006, Lucent announced the closing of the original Bell Labs Holmdel facility, which had been built in 1962 to house its research laboratory. That lab was founded on the model common to corporate research at the time: The central lab would be the place where new technologies were researched and applied to create innovative new products. The closing prompted many to think about how that model has changed. Between 1975 and 2005, the percentage of R&D sites geographically distant from their corporate headquarters rose to 45%–66%. This trend is likely to continue.[11]

The advantages of managing a network of local research labs were emphasized in a study by Booz Allen Hamilton and INSEAD. They found that the shift to a distributed, networked structure helped companies achieve 37% faster time-to-market and lowered costs by 24%. They defined the success factors as:

- Knowing when and where to create a new network node based on availability of talent and access to markets;
- Institutionalizing the use of collaboration technologies;
- Paying attention to developing the necessary networking and knowledge-sharing behaviors in the research staff.[12]

Even when companies are not reaching out to establish or join partnerships, they are carefully looking at how well their staff members are connected to scientists and researchers both inside and outside the company.

At Aventis Pharmaceuticals, the knowledge management team examined the connectivity among researchers doing related work on immunology and their connections to outside research (for example, in academia) to determine whether there were sufficient communications with external researchers and whether knowledge from those communications was transferred within the internal research groups. The team surveyed individuals in different communities and asked them about the internal interactions and outside contacts. What they discovered was that interactions were primarily one-on-one, among a few key individuals. Using data collected to create a map of the relationships, they did a "what if?" scenario, in which they removed the top ten communicators. They discovered that removing these people would reduce the overall connectivity by 60%.[13]

From Communities of Practice to Knowledge Networks

One of the most significant accomplishments of the knowledge management community has been the institutionalization of communities of practice (COPs). First so-named by Etienne Wenger and Jean Lave in 1991, a community of practice is a group of people who participate in joint activities to create and share knowledge to enhance their ability to succeed in a particular knowledge domain.

The ideas behind creating and sustaining such communities took hold quickly in the knowledge management community, particularly within professional services firms that have traditionally been organized as "practices." Ernst & Young, Accenture, McKinsey, CSC, IBM Global Services, and others have used their experiences to provide insight into methods for managing these new organization forms that co-reside, virtually, inside large, hierarchical companies. As the model has moved beyond the defined focus of a single domain of knowledge and has extended to cross-organizational knowledge-sharing on any possible topics, these COPs are increasingly being called, instead, "knowledge networks."

 Caterpillar Inc.'s Technical Center created its proprietary web-based Knowledge Network in 1998 to support its technical community. When the Knowledge Network (KN) was transferred to Caterpillar University in 2001, the system was redesigned with a focus on usability so that the KN would extend across all types of users in

*Caterpillar and (more significantly) to their value chain. Within the
KN, communities of practice form around either a specific project
with a limited life or a business function area for which knowledge
is continually being refreshed. Workers use the KN to store and
share information, capture lessons learned, solve problems, and
locate and identify experts. By 2006, the KN was supporting 4,300
defined communities of practice consisting of over 40,000 users,
over 11,000 of whom are Caterpillar dealers, agency employees, and
suppliers.*[14]

Global Action Networks

The knowledge network concept has also taken hold in the world of
nongovernmental organizations and nonprofits. As these organizations feel pressured by lower levels of funding and an increasingly
complex set of regional, national, and global governance bodies, they
are finding that knowledge networks are an important response to
achieving more value in difficult times. For example, the Forest
Stewardship Council coordinates forest management standards to
discourage bad forestry practices and promote good forest management. It certifies forestry operations in over 82 countries through
a network of national affiliates, providing a trademark for products
produced in those certified areas. Through a collective commitment
to responsible forestry, the individual member organizations, including businesses, environmentalists, and social activists, are working
collaboratively to achieve the NGO's goals.

Networks in Government

A number of trends are leading to an increase in networked approaches
within governmental and military departments and agencies. These
range from partnering with third parties (profit and nonprofit)
to projects and programs that "join up" multiple agencies to offer
one-stop shopping services for citizens. For example, the state of
Wisconsin's Welfare to Work program, designed to help welfare
recipients move into the workforce, has created a successful network
of local service providers who offer job training, transportation
assistance, and other services. By leveraging the skills and expertise

of organizations like the YWCA, counties in Wisconsin are able to use the networked services model to reach more people with better quality services.[15]

Innovation and Problem Solving

Innovation is no longer the sole purview of R&D. The most vital question for many companies is how to organize to support innovation. This question leads companies not only to look for better ways to leverage the ideas and knowledge of the entire workforce but to look to their customers and partners as well.

The key to promoting innovation from within the organization is to create the conditions that support a free flow of ideas and interactions. A traditional networked structure to bring a group of people together to solve a multi-functional and multi-dimensional problem is the task force. In setting up a task force, it's the collective work that is important—the whole being greater than the parts. A good task force selection process identifies members who have:

- The collective (diverse) knowledge, experience, and external connections to represent the key stakeholders;
- The personal motivation and drive to work for the good of the whole organization;
- The ability to engage in honest, open dialogue.

Communities of practice are another network organizational form that provides the kind of environment for people to work in collaboration comfortably with others and expand their personal networks. Knowledge networks, like those at Caterpillar, provide the infrastructure for idea exchange, as do expertise location systems, intranet directories, and so on.

For many, it's real-time exchange that generates cross-linkages. MITRE Corporation uses Technical Exchange Meetings to bring together experts from across its three major divisions who are working in the same areas of technology; these TEMs not only help create shared understanding of a new problem space but also help to further the growth of networks inside the company.

For real-time virtual exchange, "jams" bring thousands of people into a network for a period of three days to generate ideas. IBM's

WorldJam in 2004 was designed to identify the values that employees felt most important to the company and the ways in which the company could live up to those values. Over 32,000 ideas were generated in 72 hours; these were later analyzed and distilled to create 191 proposals. After employees voted on their choices, senior management committed to action on 35 of the top-rated recommendations.

Technology can be very powerful for surfacing divergent ideas, but collaborative problem solving of complex, industrywide challenges needs face-to-face dialogue. Face-to-face settings are particularly important when gathering senior executives to probe and develop responses to difficult challenges.

 In the wake of the Enron/Andersen Consulting audit scandal in 2002, audit firms, their clients, and corporate audit committees realized that the issues raised by that event and the resulting Sarbanes-Oxley Act would be complex. Ernst & Young sponsored an Audit Committee Leadership Network in 2003. Members included senior audit committee chairs from companies representing telecommunications, manufacturing, consumer products, banking, oil and gas, and large retailers. At their first meeting, they decided on the topics that they wanted to bring to the combined knowledge and expertise of the network. Their initial set of work reviewed best practices in setting up audit committees and managing the relationships between company employees and auditing firms.

We—a large collective "we"—are examining our relationships with the companies we work for, the organizations we belong to, and the impact of their structures, environment, and core values on the work we do and the way we live in the workplace and in the world. We are learning to understand networks.

THE NETWORK ORGANIZATION AND THE NETWORKED ORGANIZATION

At a lecture to the American Academy of Psychoanalysis in 1999, Michael Maccoby summarized the impact of the forces at work during the 1990s: "Changes in the economic environment—the business models on which companies were formed—coupled with the growth of technology have resulted in an increasing emphasis on innovation, interactive networks, customer responsiveness, teamwork, and flexibility in management practices."[16] Where does this understanding lead?

What's Different about Networks

It's tempting to look at the benefits of networks in organizations and decide that networks should be *the* organizational form of the 21st century. If networks have such benefits as increased innovation, decreased costs, and quality tacit interactions, why would companies tie themselves to the rigid hierarchical structures of an outmoded management form? But hierarchies are not outmoded, nor are networks particularly new. Network forms of organization have successfully coexisted with hierarchical forms for many years, and will continue to do so. What's different is that we are now able to use our new knowledge about networks to choose one organizational form over another.

During the 1900s, economists typically distinguished two economic forms of organization: markets and hierarchies. Hierarchies are based on authority and a division of labor. In markets, buyers and sellers coordinate exchanges based on price.

As a network form of organization emerged, some thought the network form was a hybrid of the two types, but now most people agree that the network form is a distinct type. This transition from hierarchical forms and the overlay of network forms is one we need to focus on to understand net work. Table 2.1 summarizes some of the ways that scholars and writers distinguish networks and hierarchies.

A 1998 paper, later a book, by Eric Raymond titled "The Cathedral and the Bazaar"[17] describes the environment in which the open-source software community creates large, complex software programs collaboratively. I believe this metaphor also applies to the choice of an organizational structure: to create an elaborate, complicated edifice whose interfaces, relationships, roles, and responsibilities are all carefully designed and constructed, or to provide the initial relationships and an environment in which interactions can occur.

Table 2.1

Contrasting Network and Hierarchical Organization Forms

Dimension	Hierarchical Form	Network Form
Differences in Structure and Governance		
Authority	CEO, directors, managers	Expertise
Accountability	To shareholders, owners, funders	Mutual
Where decisions are made	From the chain of command	Close to the point of action
Mechanisms	Bylaws, procedure manuals	Constitutions, norms
Membership	Contractual	Voluntary
Differences in Operational and Relational Style		
Role of management	Sets direction, manages implementation	Creates enabling environment; sets tone
Type of decision-making	Rational and formal	Intuitive, synthesizing
Reputation (identity)	Status dependent	Interdependent
Means of communication	Routinized through channels	Relational
Task orientation	Function	Project
Roles	Formal, fixed	Informal, organic
Climate	Formal, bureaucratic	Open-ended, reciprocal
Degree of flexibility	Low	High
Basis of trust	Loyalty, duty, status	Contribution, honesty, concern
Differences in Approach to Value Creation		
Basis of competition	Price, manufacturing intensity	Ability to innovate
Source of value	Tangible, status or rule-based	Intangible, expertise and reputation-based
Relationships	Competitive	Cooperative
Work	Transactional	Knowledge-based
Metaphor		
	Cathedral	Bazaar

Table 2.1 polarizes the distinctions between hierarchical and network organization forms, but only to illustrate choices and to describe their outer boundaries. The network is not the right form for all purposes and all types of work.

Repeat: The network is not the right form for all purposes and all types of work.

Consider, first, what a networked organization or industry looks like. Structurally, it doesn't map cleanly to an ordered chart, as different roles are needed for different projects; projects are staffed according to expertise, prior relationship, and availability. Think of the business of making a film. The hierarchical studio system model of the early days of the industry has evolved to the networked form that exists today. From concept to screening, a film is the product of multiple networks at work—people leveraging relationships, talking with people they've worked with in the past, requesting introductions to people they don't know but would like to work with, obtaining financing from a variety of sources, and constantly managing the network of relationships required to bring a successful film to market.

Craft industries, such as the film industry described here, are particularly well-suited to the network form. The construction industry, likewise, relies on the relationships of a general contractor with project subcontractors. Large trade publishing houses provide editors the freedom to create networked "boutique" operations within the corporate boundaries; the editors nourish a network of authors who more easily retain loyalty to an editor than to a large corporate entity.

But next consider that in each of these industries in which networks prevail, when it comes time to get into production, only a hierarchical project management model will get the work done in time and within budget. Well, sometimes! There will be a mix of forms, but once people have experienced the flexibility of the network style, they will expect that some or most of their work relationships will be governed by a network form.

When you look at the organization chart of a global company, you may notice only the hierarchy at first (who's at the top, who's at the next level, and so on), but as you examine it further, you start to see that there are really a number of different organizational principles at work. You can see the differences among lines of business, geographies, and functional units. Further differentiation occurs when you add in roles for distribution channels, industry segments, and knowledge areas, or manufacturing, production processes, and R&D. Jay Galbraith[18] suggests that companies need to have a network for each of seven strategic business dimensions: functions; business units; geography; business processes; customers, systems, or solutions; distribution channels; and knowledge areas. But not all of these networks need to be structured or managed in the same way.

For example, in a professional services organization, the sales and delivery responsibility for services—the company's products—rests with the local geographies. They are measured on revenue. Within the geographical structures, hierarchical control is important to ensure that the order and delivery pipeline is managed. However, the product development and support comes from practice areas. Each practice area focuses on providing solutions in different core knowledge areas. As knowledge-based networks, the practices need to include individuals from across the organization—including product development, marketing, and other global functions—who contribute to the overall understanding of the customer requirements, market opportunities, alliances, and technologies that feed the development of solutions.

Network Benefits

I have provided data for some of the examples in this chapter that illustrate the potential financial returns for adopting network organization forms, but the benefits of working in networks, while tangible in many cases, may also be qualitative and self-evident. The network lens enables us to look at networks:

- As the organizational form itself;
- As informal learning and activist units within large organizations;
- As a means by which organizations can view partnering arrangements.

In any of these cases, a network approach provides benefits beyond those available in most hierarchical forms.

Access to information, knowledge, and experience. Hierarchical forms equate a person's role with their knowledge and expertise. The goal in a network is to make all the experience, skills, and knowledge—tacit or explicit—available to anyone at the point of need.

Resiliency. Resiliency is the ability to survive and thrive in the face of change, whether internally generated or externally forced. Social capital, access to alternate suppliers, having a rich set of relationships to draw on during catastrophe all represent ways that networks enhance an organization's resiliency.

Credibility. Participation in a network, and connections within and across networks, enhance an individual's status, and also that of the organization's reputation among its peers, suppliers, customers, and funders.

Reach. For nonprofit organizations working toward social good, the ability to reach more people more quickly or more effectively is a primary motivator to work in networks. For companies looking to enter new markets, the networked partnership provides entrée into more geographic areas with more diversified products.

Diffusion of knowledge and innovation. Networks—especially aided by electronic communications—provide the most reliable way to transmit learning and ideas from one source to another.

Collective intelligence. Working collaboratively in networks, and using the participative technologies of Web 2.0, it is possible for anyone in a technology-advantaged network to have fingertip access to everything that the network knows (and has shared). Even without technology, a well-connected, trusting, and fluid network has access to the generative and creative abilities that make the sum ever so much more than its parts.

Individual and network performance. The networks and network forms that are the subject of this book are all dependent on the contributions and commitments of individuals. The performance of a network comes down to the way that human, social, and relationship capital support its goals. Being connected to others is vital to our physical and mental well-being and, it turns out, is a key indicator of individual performance.[19] Being and working in networks produces the virtuous cycle shown in Figure 2.2.

The context is shifting to an understanding of this virtuous cycle, at all levels in and across organizations. We are creating and working in networks. The more we work in networks, the more we learn from others and are motivated to contribute more and to make bolder commitments. The network lens and the language of net work will help us become more effective as we understand more about networks and how we work in them.

Figure 2.2

Impact of connectivity on individuals

NOTES

1. Thomas L. Friedman, *The World is Flat* (New York: Farrar, Straus and Giroux, 2005).
2. IBM, "Global Innovation Outlook 2.0" (New York: IBM, 2006).
3. A. Gulli and A. Signorini, "The Indexable Web is More Than 11.5 Billion Pages" (paper presented at the 14th International Conference on the World Wide Web, Chiba, Japan, May 10–14, 2005).
4. www.habitatjam.com/
5. Gary Hamel and C.K. Prahalad, "The Core Competence of the Corporation," *Harvard Business Review* 68, no. 3 (1990): 79–93.
6. Jeffrey H. Dyer, Prashant Kale, and Harbir Singh, "When to Ally and When to Acquire," *Harvard Business Review* 82, nos. 7 and 8 (2004): 108–115.
7. Tim Hindle, "The New Organization," *The Economist*, January 19, 2006.
8. Peter Drucker, *The Age of Discontinuity: Guidelines to Our Changing Society* (New York: Harper and Row, 1969).
9. Laurence Prusak and Don Cohen, *In Good Company* (Cambridge, MA: Harvard Business School Press, 2001).
10. Mindy Fried and Mindy Gewirtz, "Network Weaving: Using Organizational Strategies for Work-Life Integration," *Work & Family Connection* June (2006).
11. Eric Mankin, "R&D is Dis-Integrating," January 30, 2006, www.biz-architect.com/r_and_d_dis-integrating.htm

12. Thomas Goldbrunner, Yves Doz, Keeley Wilson, and Steven Veldhoen, "The Well-Designed Global R&D Network," *strategy+business*, May 15, 2006.

13. Doug Rush, "Measuring Connectivity at Aventis Pharmaceuticals: Assessing Networking's Value Qualitatively and Quantitatively," *Knowledge Management Review* 5, no. 2 (2002): 10–13.

14. Reed Stuedemann, Web presentation to SI Knowledge Management Community, May 2005.

15. Stephen Goldsmith and William D. Eggers, *Governing by Network: The New Shape of the Public Sector* (Washington, DC: Brookings Institution Press, 2004).

16. Michael Maccoby, "The Self in Transition: From Bureaucratic to Interactive Social Character" (lecture given at American Academy of Psychoanalysis 43rd Annual Meeting, May 14, 1999).

17. Eric S. Raymond, "The Cathedral and the Bazaar," *FirstMonday*, February 16, www.firstmonday.org 1998.

18. Jay R. Galbraith, "Mastering the Law of Requisite Variety with Differentiated Networks," in *The Firm as Collaborative Community*.

19. Thomas H. Davenport, *Thinking for a Living* (Cambridge, MA: Harvard Business School Press, 2005).

Chapter 3

Purpose

As humans, we need to make distinctions. It's part of our ongoing process of making sense of the world around us. Distinctions are based on worldview and context. A classic way to describe the concept of distinctions is to consider how fish describe "water." The fact (we believe) is that fish are unaware that what they swim in is "water." Similarly, we don't think, or haven't thought until now, about our existence itself as being embedded in networks.

What would fish do differently if they knew that they were in water? They might put on their "water lens" and start to examine the qualities and aspects of the water and how it affects them: the temperature, current, presence of food, or predators. Then they might work to change the environment. They might even ask the larger question, "Is this the right water at all?" If the pond, river, bay, or ocean they are in is not meeting their purpose, they might decide that they are not in the right water and look for something larger, smaller, more or less briny, richer in nutrients, with more or less sunshine.

What fish need, and what we need, with our network lens, is a set of terms that lets us categorize what we perceive so that we can know when we are talking about the same thing. One problem with creating such a set of terms—which in this case is a limited taxonomy—is that it implies categorically clean lines of demarcation; another problem is that it implies that we actually share the worldview and the perspective that enabled us to choose the terms.

As a starting point for creating a shared language of networks and coherence within these pages, I'm going to describe networks using the following four aspects, or facets:

- Purpose
- Structure
- Style
- Value

The *purpose* of a network is that which animates it and causes its members to care about it. This chapter summarizes types of networks based on the *purpose* the network serves.

A network's *structure* reflects its form, the possible patterns and arrangement of the relationships; the assignment of roles and responsibilities within the network; and the network's texture in terms of the flexibility, strength, and density of social bonds. The elements of *style* include the network's visible manifestation; the nature of the interactions in the network; its social climate, which includes culture, core values, and norms; the manner of interactions; the balance of its orientation toward results or discovery; and its leadership style. Every network produces *value*, tangible and/or intangible, in direct alignment with its purpose or tangentially. Structure, style, and value are further discussed in Chapters 4, 5, and 6.

The Range of Purpose

There are many ways of looking at the purpose of a network, particularly because I've defined "network" broadly so as to include almost any set of relationships. For example, if you think about the networks you participate in, you'll see that many of them fulfill multiple purposes. A service organization or club, for example, can fulfill an individual's personal or business needs at the same time that it has a mission to contribute to a greater good. Rotary Clubs International, for instance, is a worldwide network that avails members access to business contacts. At the same time, it is a network that supports individual growth, and people join it to enhance their personal reputation. But it is first and foremost a mission-oriented, civic service organization. Similarly, less structured "green" business

Type	Design Center/motivation
Mission	Social good or environmental improvement at the local, national, regional, or global level
Business	Creation of tangible value – business development, production of goods and services, financial wealth, or any project or any operationally output-focused endeavor
Idea	Generative thinking for innovation, problem-solving, or advocacy
Learning	Continuous improvement and enhancement of personal or collective knowledge
Personal	Individual support, growth, and knowledge

Figure 3.1

Network purposes

networks exist to serve a particular business-oriented goal, but the businesses may be dedicated to or based in a social purpose; for instance, to produce products based solely on recycled materials.

That said, it is still useful to provide a taxonomy of purposes for which networks exist, as shown in Figure 3.1.

I need to make two important points with respect to what is missing from this taxonomy:

- *A place for the definition of "community."* I believe that a community is an aspect of a network that is aware of its common purpose. It exists as a community because it says it is a community, but it is always a network, just as are partnerships, alliances, consortia, and other names that people attach to specific sets of relationships.
- *Subdivisions within the purpose type of "business"* to allow for various forms of networks within for-profit, nonprofit, educational, and governmental enterprises. The identification of sub- and combination forms and their individual purposes may be interesting, but would detract from the main thrust of this book, which is to help network creators and contributors understand the nature of networks.

There are always networks within networks and networks of networks. The goal of the model, however simple, is to provide a starting point for the examples of each type of network that I introduce in the sections that follow.

PERSONAL GROWTH AND SUPPORT NETWORKS

Our personal networks have many dimensions—our families, school friends, coworkers, neighbors, people we know through religious, civic, or wellness activities—all of which tend to be informal. We leverage these networks when we need assistance looking for a job, a new car, or a good book to read. These networks grow organically and randomly as we meet people in our daily comings, goings, and stayings. The sum of the people we know through our networks constitute our personal network, those we are most likely to turn to when we have an idea, need advice, or desire fellowship.

Clubs are the traditional mechanism for meeting people, sharing ideas or activities, and learning new skills for recreational, social, health, or business purposes. Alumni clubs, garden clubs, scouting, rock climbing, skiing, mushrooming—if you have an interest, you can usually find a club for it. Are clubs different from networks? Within organizations or groups of various sizes, the terms "network," "club," "cell," and so on tend to have distinct meanings. Since I have reduced the definition of *network* to its simplest form, namely a collection of people linked by some common interest or attribute, then of course we can say that a club is a network.

When you develop a new interest or are wrestling with a new problem, and there's no one in your personal network who can help nor are there clubs that meet your needs, what can you do? Create a network. This is what a number of people across the United States did between 2000 and 2002 as the continuing impacts of corporate downsizing left many professionals out of work and hoping to "network" to find jobs.

Marie had worked at a large U.S. corporation for ten years before she followed her dream to work in Europe. For three years she worked in Amsterdam and then decided in 1994 to return to the Boston area to be near her family. She realized that the decline of that corporation's fortunes and the extensive downsizing since she had been overseas would make it difficult for her to "plug back in" and easily find a job. With just an idea about what a network would look like, Marie and Celeste, a close friend and colleague, decided to invite women they knew to join in a conversation around dinner at a local Italian restaurant. The initial focus at these meetings was on jobs: spreading information about job openings, letting others know you were looking, hearing speakers talk about job search and career changing strategies, and starting your own business. The network did not shut down when, as the job crisis in Massachusetts abated, the topics changed to address personal change and development. Women kept coming. The Women in Networking (WIN) group continues to meet regularly, evolving to meet the needs of its members.

What are the individual, personal needs of the members that WIN and networks like it meet? For people who are on leave from their careers or have just moved to new geographical areas, meetings like WIN's provide an opportunity to meet new people, be introduced to new ideas, and form, yes, a good job network. Networks focused on career growth give people a chance to share what they know about possible job openings or to talk about their own work. After listening to a woman who had recently become a career coach, one WIN member changed her own career—and became a career coach!

WIN exhibits many good practices for building and sustaining a personal growth network:

- It has a self-selecting leadership model. Members who contribute to the planning and infrastructure activities naturally reach a point at which they are ready to take on leadership roles.

- It has a lightweight infrastructure. Each year, members sign up for the necessary tasks of managing meeting attendance, coordinating dates with the restaurant, managing e-mail announcements, and so on.

- It sustains itself through a consistent, regular meeting schedule punctuated with annual planning meetings.

- It periodically surveys its members to make sure that the meeting content is relevant and meaningful.

- Its membership is completely open (to women). Anyone who shows up and pays the meeting fee is welcomed.

In the age of broadband access, geography no longer constrains membership in personal growth, support, and information networks. In fact, the term *network* has become so familiar to us and easy to use because this great, global communications infrastructure has enabled us to join, create, and manage networks that are constrained neither by geography nor time. The histories of networked communications software designed for research or business (the Arpanet, Usenet, e-mail discussion groups, Lotus Notes, VAX NOTES) usually include a footnote about how users almost immediately began using the tools to form special interest groups about personal topics.

One of the longest-running personal networks supported by an e-mail discussion group is the Systers list. The Systers network, for women in computer science (systems), started when the 12 women attending a 1987 academic computer science conference met for dinner and decided to make the connection formal. Anita Borg then shifted the private e-mail community to a computer-based infrastructure, Mecca, and went on to create—with her "systers" support and that of the companies they worked in—the Institute for Women and Technology (IWT).

Systers is an example of a network founded for one purpose that evolved over time into a formal organization with a superordinate purpose. IWT today provides a platform for finding innovative ways to engage and retain female computer science and engineering students. Working with partner universities and corporate sponsors, IWT develops workshops and programs to encourage young women to enter the field of computer science and to enhance the work life and work/life balance of women in computing. Anita Borg died of brain cancer in 2003, at which time the network was renamed the Anita Borg Institute for Women and Technology; it has reshaped its mission to increase the impact of women on all aspects of technology and to increase the positive impact of technology on the world's women.

Idea Networks

From the philosophers of ancient Greece to the New England transcendentalists to the bloggers of the 21st century, people have always conversed in networks to share and develop ideas. Idea networks are based on a creative exchange that lets ideas build on each other. The results or outcomes of idea networks are emergent: When you enter an idea network's virtual space or enter a room where it is meeting, you do so knowing that you will not know where the conversation will lead.

 Boston-based Gennova, begun in 2002, is an idea network. In the early stages of its evolution, its conversation focused on generating ideas about what Gennova could actually be: It was an examination of its own purpose, which was yet to emerge. Members would complain that meetings "never went anywhere." But a core group kept showing up, not because the specific ideas about what Gennova could be were compelling, but because the conversational tangents and personal connections were so stimulating. Over time, Gennova ceased to worry about what "it" was and became a network to which people brought ideas—about networks, complexity, technology, the art of dialogue, organizational resilience—for the shared relish of participating in generative conversations.

Innovation

IBM's 2005 Global Innovation Outlook survey found that 75% of top managers around the world agreed that collaboration was essential to innovation. The consensus was: "The greater the level of collaborative innovation, the greater the financial performance. Regardless of the metric—revenue growth, operating margin growth, or average profitability over time—strong collaborators consistently come out on top."[1] The study also found that companies are continuing to use existing approaches to solve new problems, creating R&D departments that are hierarchically set up and managed. If you recall the examples in Chapter 1, some companies now are using a network approach to distributing their R&D labs. This is only one aspect of creating an innovation network that supports business growth: The challenge is to create a "culture" of innovation that includes a wide range of sources, including all company employees, partners and suppliers, and even customers.

 One of the largest consumer products corporations in the world, The Procter & Gamble Company, has developed its innovation

*strategy based on the concept of "connect and develop." P&G
works with several proprietary and open innovation networks to
identify good ideas that it can then bring into P&G for
development.*[2]

Advocacy

An advocacy network takes the power of an idea and gives it legs;
political and spiritual networks attract people of specific attitudes,
opinions, and values who are passionate about a viewpoint and want
to educate and persuade others to that viewpoint. Grassroots political campaigns and social movements have always used a network
model to diffuse ideas, enroll membership, and lobby for change or
reform. Today, bloggers of all stripes connect and interconnect using
the power of the World Wide Web to meet, exchange, and build on
each other's ideas.

LEARNING NETWORKS

Learning networks focus on augmenting the personal capacity of an
individual or a group in a particular area of skill, expertise, vocation,
avocation, or knowledge. The regulars at the pickup games at the
city basketball courts are learning networks, as are Bible-study
groups, wine-tasting clubs, and breeders' associations. Vocational
learning networks range from the informal and ad hoc to the
rigorous, such as the Program Management Institute (PMI), which
is a central clearinghouse and certification agency for over 200,000
program managers worldwide who are continually honing their
skills, meeting at conferences to learn from each other, and sharing
their own new work and practices.

Interest and Information Networks

We all have many interests and activities. We pursue those most
important to us through participation in learning networks. For
business and civic topics, we rely on either formal structures (corporate communications, phone trees, newsletters), or word of mouth.

If you need to know something, you need to trust that it will be made known to you by virtue of your membership in these groups. Interest networks, often called "communities of interest," went mainstream with the availability of free services from Yahoo! and Google Groups. The vast majority of e-mail that I receive everyday comes from subscription to such distribution lists, which make it possible to stay abreast of news, events, and ponderings on the topics other members and I jointly care about.

With the advent of blogs, wikis, social networking sites, and the participatory technologies of Web 2.0, it's now possible to be better in control of how we manage these interest networks. Blogs, in particular, provide a powerful way to build an interest network and perhaps transform it to a practice network through focused, thoughtful sharing beyond the level of "interested."

Communities and Networks of Practice

The most formally studied of the various types of learning network is the *community of practice*, a term that was first coined by Jean Lave and Etienne Wenger in 1991. Formal communities of practice are distinguished by three intentional characteristics:

- A shared domain of interest and a desire to develop competency in that domain;
- Community activities through which one shares one's own learning experiences with others;
- The development of a shared repertoire of practice that includes resources, stories, techniques, and methods.

This concept has been widely adopted in the corporate sphere—profit and nonprofit alike—and has become a key lever in developing and retaining expertise and bringing people from across different groups to learn together and to create that repertoire of practice.

John Seely Brown and Paul Duguid chose the term *networks of practice* to emphasize that people in a network of practice do not necessarily have to share the same occupation, nor be physically co-located. Such networks are about learning. Social ties and relationships emerge from people's interactions relating to their practice.

Professional Associations

Professional associations exist to enhance the integrity of the practices on which they are based and to provide educational and reputation-building opportunities for members. Many associations are formal, incorporated organizations that provide learning and networking opportunities through newsletters, publications, and annual meetings. Within an association, special interest groups provide focus on individual topics. For example, the Association of Computer Manufacturers lists 34 "SIGs" that cover topics as diverse as microcomputer architecture and computer-human interaction.

Some professional associations provide both a learning network and a certification function. For example, the PMI, as mentioned above, has developed a rigorous certification program that has become the standard for professional project management.

Research Networks

Research laboratories, both those dedicated to pure research and those doing applied research for product development, are looking for more and better ways to not only collaborate across internal boundaries but also be more active in bringing ideas from academic and professional networks into their companies. As more and more companies look for product innovation or understanding from outside their own boundaries, they are becoming more, not less, inclined to formalize connections with academic institutions and to form research consortia on topics that touch an industry broadly.

Antitrust laws prohibited research consortia until the 1984 Congressional passage of the National Cooperative Research Act. One of the first consortia formed in the wake of the passage was Microelectronics and Computer Technology Consortium (MCC). MCC was funded as a joint venture of the key computer manufacturers in the United States, as a direct response to the threat of a similar consortium in Japan. Such consortia today are a common network organizational response to the need for multidisciplinary research that benefits member companies, enhances the reputation of universities, and creates economic opportunity for local economies.

Mission Networks

Mission networks are directed to the social good. Arts and culture, education, environment, health, human services, religion, and social justice are the primary categories of service to which nonprofit organizations (NPOs) devote themselves. Legally, NPOs are not distinguishable from nongovernmental organizations (NGOs), but the work of NGOs carries a connotation of global efforts, or at least the assemblage of international expertise, resources, and leadership to support humanitarian or environmental activities in nations that cannot afford to sustain such services themselves. The governments of richer nations, individually, in partnership, or through the United Nations, also develop programs for humanitarian services.

The networking strategy for these organizations is often dual:

- Creating a network of organizations to develop and maintain the program;
- Creating networks in the target population.

This model of "getting the network right" and then "moving the network model out" is not unique to nonprofits; it is, in fact, one of the patterns of network evolution that we will revisit in this book.

Local Service-Oriented Nonprofit Organizations

A local service organization begins with a person or small group who sees injustice in the distribution of wealth, the wrongful use of environmental resources, or an opportunity to enrich the personal lives of others through education, music, or the arts. These local networks produce value for their neighborhoods' present and future.

 The idea for City Year was launched in a dorm room at Harvard University by two law students, Michael Brown and Alan Khazei. They started with the idea of a service corps that could provide a year-long volunteer experience for youths between the ages of 17 and 24. City Year would broker the needs of local schools, youth centers, and parks in Boston by attracting and training young people

to work in those schools and organizations. Brown and Khazei set to work refining the idea and building a network, attracting corporate donations and identifying schools in need of mentors and tutors, youth centers in need of staff for after-school programs, and park directors who needed hands for building, creating, and restoration. In 1988, they put the first 50 members of the Youth Service Corps to work in Boston. In 1992, presidential candidate Bill Clinton visited their offices to see firsthand how national service could be a force for building a strong democracy. After Americorps was founded in 1994, City Year joined the ranks of member networks in that organization as it continued to grow. By 2005, City Year had founded programs in 15 other cities in the United States and had launched its first program in South Africa.

Global Networks

Since its inception, the United Nations has founded and funded global networks for human services, including disaster relief and healthcare, education, economic development, human rights, and the development and application of international law. Alongside the U.N. are multitudinous NGOs and a growing number of global action networks (GANs) that through public and private funding tackle specific problems and programs using a networked approach.

Another set of prominent global networks are those devoted to environmental causes. Groups like Greenpeace and the World Wildlife Fund have embraced the network form of organization to enable local action in the face of threats to species and habitats (including human ones).

Regional Economic Networks

Silicon Valley in California and Route 128 in Massachusetts are often cited as regional ecosystems that sustained healthy economies in their respective geographic areas. The flow of ideas, startup creation, and partnering activities produced value for the companies and individuals involved, and also for the regions as a whole. These networks grew organically as a result of the conditions of available technical talent and experience: a combination of existing high-tech companies and a supply of graduates from nearby universities like Stanford and MIT.

But regional economic vitality does not have to be a serendipitous occurrence.

ACEnet, the Appalachian Center for Economic Networks, was founded in Athens, Ohio, in 1985 to provide assistance to food, wood, and technology entrepreneurs in the southern Appalachian counties of Ohio, which have some of the highest poverty and unemployment rates in the country. Early on, ACEnet identified a number of uncoordinated small clusters of food businesses: a farmer's market, a natural bakery, a worker-owned Mexican restaurant, and entrepreneurs making unique food products. To stimulate interconnections, ACEnet built a "kitchen incubator," a licensed processing facility where the entrepreneurs could rent the use of ovens, stoves, and a processing line to produce their products. This incubator attracted many small businesses, which received both training in food production safety and access to a growing network of potential partners and collaborators.

While ACEnet manages the network in a specific local region, the Business Alliance for Local Living Economies (BALLE) was founded in 2001 as an alliance of networks that shared a common goal of combating the effects of corporate globalization on increasing wealth inequalities and worsening environmental conditions. This network has grown to connect 30 business networks with more than 5,000 small-business members in the United States and Canada. Membership is open to locally owned businesses, individuals, and local business networks such as Chambers of Commerce.

Another type of regional economic development network, the New York City Investment Fund, was created for investors and entrepreneurs to create new businesses to diversify the economy of New York City. After 9/11, the network shifted its energies toward the rebuilding of lower Manhattan. Five years later, it began to focus on the city's overall economy.

This purpose-shifting in a network is not uncommon, nor is the overlap of purposes. The members of the New York City Investment Fund anticipate that they will receive financial gain from their investments at the same time that their work as part of the network contributes to the overall mission of improving the city.

BUSINESS NETWORKS

The goal of a for-profit business network is production and growth—growth of revenue, profit, and returns to shareholders through growth of market reach, product breadth, and expertise and knowledge. In this category of business networks are nonprofit organizations (including public and educational institutions) whose stakeholders demand accountability for financial and operational functions. All these types of business-based institutions are seeing the benefits of the network approach to growth—to partner rather than acquire, to work through alliances, to bring customers into the planning and assessment processes, and to reach out and reach within to leverage networks for strategic change.

Supplier Networks

The traditional view of the supply chain as a linear flow of transformation, movement, and storage of goods has shifted with the growth in understanding of the important role of relationships in managing risk. When competitive advantage comes from delivering a quality product to a customer at the time it's needed, companies must focus not just on the ties to their suppliers but also on the strength of those ties. The company–supplier relationships are taking on a network approach to linking suppliers with one another through knowledge-sharing, both online and face-to-face, involving employees and senior executives in their supplier companies through everything from planning and forecasting to improved quality and work methods. This shift is illustrated in Figure 3.2.

Figure 3.2
Networking the supply chain

🕸 *Toyota proved the wisdom of open knowledge-sharing and connection across its supplier network when the supplier of 99% of its
brake fluid-proportioning valves experienced a fire that destroyed
its plant and virtually all of its specialized machinery. Because
almost all vehicles that Toyota builds use this valve, the potential
loss from a shutdown was enormous. However, within hours, Toyota
met with all its tier-one suppliers, who rapidly spread the news
throughout their own tier-two networks. Suppliers who stepped
forward were able to jury rig production lines in 62 locations using
blueprints provided for the machinery and some salvageable parts.
Eighty-five hours after the fire, Toyota received its first valve and
went back into production.*[3]

Alliances, Partnerships, and Trade Associations

As anyone who has worked to set up alliances or partnerships knows,
the creation and maintenance of such alliances is a delicate task of
managing relationships between and among individuals at all levels
of an organization.

The healthcare industry is one that has embraced the shift toward
networks. The shift has been a response to the cost pressures of
providing medical care as well as the need to provide a broader range
of services. The nonprofit Catholic Health Initiatives, Inc. (CHI) was
founded in 1996, when the leaders of three independent Catholic
healthcare systems agreed to consolidate. In addition to improving
the operational excellence of the more than 60 hospitals and over 40
long-term care facilities, the CHI network has been able to deliver
on its mission to bring ministry to the communities in the 19 states
where its hospitals provide services. Working in a network has
improved the business operations of the hospitals but, more importantly, has enabled CHI to take on a local mission: It provides grants
and low-interest loans to organizations that promote "healthy communities," particularly in support of the disadvantaged.

Independent Business and Consulting Networks
and Alliances

The economic and demographic shift that prompted the startup of
WIN, described earlier in this chapter, also created a large pool of

professionals joining the ranks of independent consultants. These consultants quickly understood the importance of networking, joining networks and being attached to connections within their geographical or topical areas of interest. These networks begin with a goal of tangible outcome: generating business. To survive and be successful, however, these networks must also offer opportunities for practice development and shared learning.

Customer User Groups

User groups have been a mainstay of technology companies since a group of computer enthusiasts started the Share organization in 1955 to create educational programs, provide an opportunity for professional networking, and influence the direction of the industry, which was at that time IBM. IBM now interacts with its users in a variety of communities, including Share. The model has worked well, and not just for IBM: Software companies of all sizes either host annual user group meetings or support member-led user groups. LivelinkUp, for example, is OpenText's annual user conference; OpenText provides the agenda, logistics, and venue for this event, at which their partners provide technology demonstrations and workshops. Attendees are encouraged to network and learn from each other.

Novell Users International (NUI), on the other hand, is an independent organization focused on helping its members build their technical expertise, reputation, and careers on the use of Novell technology. Novell supports NUI by providing speakers for events, training and certification programs for NUI members, and more direct access to Novell developers. Both types of organizations fulfill several purposes:

- Sustain a practice community among users;
- Provide a platform for the company to divulge future product plans or shifts in corporate strategy;
- Create social capital by having users come into direct contact with the employees and executives of the companies whose products they use;
- Create a channel for obtaining valuable customer feedback on current products and future plans.

Many companies also encourage the establishment of smaller special-interest groups on topical areas or local geography groups that provide more frequent face-to-face opportunities for networking and learning.

Online customer communities

Since the introduction of the World Wide Web, it's became far easier for technology companies to support user groups using web portals that include discussion groups for specific topics or users. But the Web has also enabled consumer product companies to interact with their customers to get product ideas and feedback. Online customer communities are typically branded, password-protected sites where up to 400 invited customers spend an average of 30 minutes a week over a period of months.

Communispace, a leader in this business, has helped clients set up over 225 of these communities. What Communispace has learned is that an online customer community can generate breakthrough product ideas while building relationship capital. Its research shows that customers who participate in conversations in these communities are much more likely to be repeat customers and that they will give negative as well as positive feedback on products while maintaining brand loyalty—and spreading the word to friends, family, and colleagues about the products.

The conversations in these communities have several dimensions:

- *Company to customer:* Sharing ideas about new products, packaging or design concepts, or market trends can produce both gut reactions and suggestions for refinement; customers can use advance information for their own planning and preparation;

- *Customer to company:* Unsolicited feedback and suggestions provide ideas and brainstorming opportunities that would not be possible outside the bounds of such an intimate network community;

- *Customer to customer:* The rapport among customers generates spontaneous customer-generated conversations that often lead to revealing insights into their needs and wants.

Online customer communities provide a space for the development of new norms through which customers can interact with the company; customers build trust in the company not just through their interactions with the company but also through their interactions among themselves. The company reciprocates their customers' honesty by providing feedback on how it has taken decisions based on the ideas and suggestions emerging from the community and by continuing to share its product plans.

Leadership Networks

The value of developing personal networks has been on the leadership agenda since the first *Harvard Business Review* article on the topic appeared in 1991. Ram Charan described networking practices in ten large corporations in which network building was a top priority for senior managers. In his article, "How Networks Reshape Organizations for Results," he described how networks change the frequency, intensity, and honesty of the dialogue among managers on priority tasks.[4] He noted some common characteristics of these networks:

- Unlike task forces, these are not temporary, but are long-standing networks that sustain change in the organization;
- Members identify with the network and with each other; the frequency and honesty of their dialogues reshape personal relationships;
- Continuous interaction over time builds a shared understanding of the business;
- Managers' performance and potential for promotion is evaluated against their contributions to the network and sometimes by the network itself;
- Networks are dynamic and take initiative, becoming the vehicle for redirecting the flows of information and decisions, the uses of power, and the sources of feedback within the hierarchy.

Two additional articles that appeared in HBR's July-August issue in 1993 also helped shape thinking and research for the next ten years. In "How Bell Labs Creates Star Performers,"[5] Robert Kelley and

Janet Caplan listed networking as one of the nine work strategies that enables star engineers to succeed. The second, "Informal Networks" by David Krackhardt and Jeffrey Hansen,[6] first introduced the concept of mapping networks of advice and trust in the organization. It also examined how insight into networks can be used as a management tool.

External networks

Internal networks are vital for managers, but their external networks can provide the diversity of ideas that come from connections to people in other companies, regardless of industry. The global Young Presidents' Organization (YPO) ⊛ provides these connections in forums where members can share experiences and ideas relevant to how they run their businesses. Another example is Company-commander.com, a network (and a community of practice) of military leaders who are responsible for commanding Army companies. Using a private internet space and face-to-face interaction, these commanders are able to support and exchange ideas with their peers.

Many executives build their personal external networks through industry associations or through participation in consortia-sponsored research. For example, the sponsors of the Media Lab at the Massachusetts Institute of Technology include senior leaders from a wide variety of industries. They are united by a common interest in the future of multimedia, with an increasing number curious about social software. They want to understand how new technologies will impact their businesses and how they, as early adopters, might harness these technologies for business advantage. In the presence of their peers in these settings, they are able to exchange information, ask questions, and engage in dialogue that might not be possible otherwise. These outside networks are vital channels of access to new and diverse ideas.

Advisory networks

Leaders who wish to remain competitive and agile in the changing landscape of industry use networks to create intimacy or to engage in joint problem solving with their customers and/or partners. For many years, marketing organizations have developed customer-advisory boards that bring in senior executives from their largest clients to present new product ideas and give customers a chance to build relationships. Such networks enable senior executives to learn from their customers and engage them in the co-design of products and processes. Monitor Networks has researched this specific type of cross-boundary, executive-level network and dubbed them "Worknets." Among the benefits that they see are[7]:

- Ideas for product and service innovation;
- New business opportunities;
- Stay abreast or ahead of regulatory changes;
- Internal visibility and brand exposure.

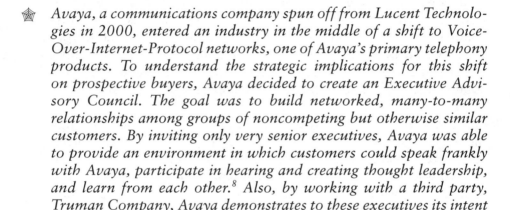

Avaya, a communications company spun off from Lucent Technologies in 2000, entered an industry in the middle of a shift to Voice-Over-Internet-Protocol networks, one of Avaya's primary telephony products. To understand the strategic implications for this shift on prospective buyers, Avaya decided to create an Executive Advisory Council. The goal was to build networked, many-to-many relationships among groups of noncompeting but otherwise similar customers. By inviting only very senior executives, Avaya was able to provide an environment in which customers could speak frankly with Avaya, participate in hearing and creating thought leadership, and learn from each other.[8] Also, by working with a third party, Truman Company, Avaya demonstrates to these executives its intent to create "reciprocal value" so that members receive as much benefit as Avaya.

Strategic Change

Social capital, as discussed in Chapter 2, represents the bonds, norms, and trust that exist among people in an organization. A corporation that is high in social capital is a fertile breeding ground for networks: The more people know others and are comfortable connecting to them, the easier it is to form and work in networks.

Informal networks have always operated in the spaces between business processes, in small teams or at the water cooler, baseball leagues, training courses, and cafeterias. Ties between and among people strengthen as people work together on projects and are drawn together by a common purpose.

In 1994, a midlevel IBM employee had an idea about the Internet and what it meant for IBM, which at that point had resisted working on a strategy for the Internet and in fact had accumulated $5 billion in losses over the previous three years. David Grossman, working on a supercomputer at Cornell University's Theory Center, saw potential as soon as he downloaded Mosaic, the first Web browser. When he realized that IBM might lose a major market opportunity at the 1994 Olympics, Grossman met with a top marketing executive at IBM and showed her the Internet. Another senior marketing executive, John Patrick, attended that meeting and immediately saw the implications for the limitless possibilities of the Web. Grossman and Patrick went on to become the hub of a large virtual "Web-heads" network that grew rapidly after they published a nine-page manifesto, "Get Connected." With support from key IBM executives, Patrick created a small Internet group separate from the rest of the software engineering group; he and Grossman built support for embedded Internet thinking in all aspects of IBM engineering and culture, while creating strong demonstrations of the Web's ability to support real-time sports events. For the 1996 Summer Olympics, they were ready; IBM had a website capable of supporting 17 million hits a day.

The small Internet business group never grew into a large division of IBM; by shifting resources (trading and transferring) from their group to other groups in IBM, Patrick and Grossman succeeded in creating a boundaryless network within the corporation that made a pivotal contribution to IBM's turnaround.[9]

This example illustrates the power of an idea network within a large corporation that took on a mission of transformation. Over time, the work of this network went into real project and work networks within various business units of IBM. So it is with networks: They emerge, self-organize around a purpose, and develop a unique structure and style that enable them to create value, often beyond their members' wildest dreams. The next chapter looks at the first of these facets: structure.

NOTES

1. IBM, "Global Innovation Outlook 2.0" (New York: IBM, 2006).
2. Larry Huston and Nabil Sakkab, "Connect and Develop: Inside Procter & Gamble's New Model for Innovation," *Harvard Business Review*, 84, no. 3 (2006).
3. Philip Evans and Bob Wolf, "Collaboration Rules," *Harvard Business Review* 83, no. 7 (2005); and Duncan Watts, *Six Degrees* (New York: W.W. Norton & Company, 2003).
4. R. Charan, "How Networks Reshape Organizations—for Results," *Harvard Business Review* 69, no. 5 (1991).
5. R. Kelley and J. Caplan, "How Bell Labs Creates Star Performers," *Harvard Business Review* 71, no. 1 (1993).
6. D. Krackhardt and J.R. Hanson, "Informal Networks: The Company Behind the Chart," *Harvard Business Review* 71, no. 4 (1993).
7. Chris Meyers, internal presentation at Monitor Networks (2006).
8. Rob Leavitt and John DeWitt, "High Impact Customer Councils: Executive Relationships Reshape the Way Avaya Goes to Market" (Information Technology Services Marketing Organization Case Study, August 2006).
9. Gary Hamel, "Waking Up IBM: How a Gang of Unlikely Rebels Transformed Big Blue," *Harvard Business Review* 78, no. 4 (2000).

Chapter 4

STRUCTURE

The underlying structural pattern of a network is the most tangible of a network's properties: It is the aspect of the network that you can draw or visualize. You can examine how the parts relate to the whole and how the structure of the network reflects and supports its purpose. This chapter introduces the structural patterns of networks and two key elements that keep a network's structure together: governance and texture.

PATTERNS

Network theory reflects the isomorphism in the patterns of network formation, growth, and evolution across natural, manmade, and human networks. Telephone networks, railroad and airplane routes, computer networks, the swarming patterns of bees, the structure of ant colonies, the starbursts of nova and dandelion seeds, the metabolic structure of *e. coli*, and social groups all exhibit many of the same properties. In nature, commerce, and society, we can't help but repeat ourselves. Figure 4.1 illustrates some of nature's patterns that remind us how closely our human-constructed networks mirror those in nature.

As you read this section, you'll see how these patterns are reflected in the structures of networks, both as they are built and as they emerge. But even though the fundamental patterns are the same,

51

However they are arranged, hierarchies are networks within this book's definition of a network as any collection of nodes that are connected by a relationship. As we shift into a network-oriented world, it's important to remember that networks don't replace hierarchies; the two organizational forms can coexist and complement each other. Within the hierarchical networks are multiple "subnetworks" of various shapes.

Mesh

As people in a network collaborate over time, they form new relationships or strengthen existing individual relationships among the members. A mesh (often called a *heterarchy*) is a network in which all members are equally connected to everyone else. This structure, shown in Figure 4.3, is common within highly focused, close-knit teams in organizations.

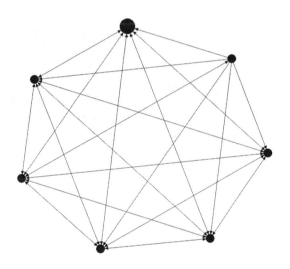

Figure 4.3
Mesh

Hub-and-Spoke

The right-hand side of Figure 4.2 shows several *hub-and-spoke* patterns that reflect the star or starburst pattern. Typically, the hub holds the purpose of the network and sets the style.

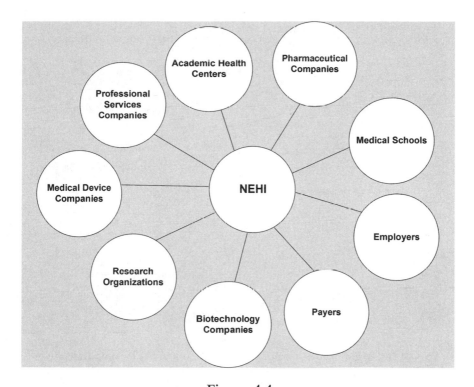

Figure 4.4
Connecting healthcare sectors to make a network

Hubs can be intentionally created or can emerge from the interactions of people within a network. When the founders of NEHI 🏵 saw the possibility for connecting leaders across the sectors of the healthcare community, the first thing that they did was to draw a network map of the sectors from which members of this network would come. This map is shown in Figure 4.4.

NEHI's effectiveness today is evidenced by its results, which are the outcome of the research and methods guided and sponsored by the members, who were drawn into the network because of its compelling purpose.

A driving motivation of network analysis is to find the interaction patterns that show how an organization "really" works. These analyses frequently identify the informal hubs: the people whom others go to for information or who are best at communicating across boundaries in an organization. Figure 4.5 shows a classic example that

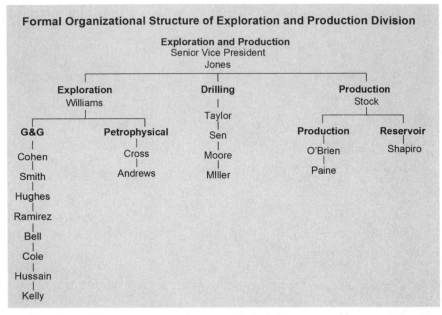

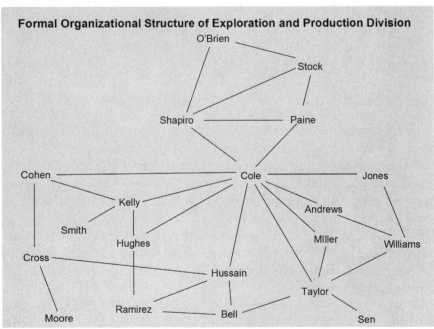

Figure 4.5
The hidden organizational network
Reprinted by permission of the *California Management Review*.

contrasts the organizational structure and the informal network structure in an organization.

Cole (all names in this map have been changed), at the third level down in the organization, is clearly the hub of this network. Note that Senior Vice President Jones shows only two ties, one of which is to Cole. You can also see that Cole apparently fills a hole between two distinct subgroups within this division.

Clusters

As we look at larger and larger networks, we see patterns of either connected or isolated groupings, or *clusters*, of nodes. These might reflect either an intentional organization structure, or else the emergence of small groups of people who work together, live and work in the same geographic area, or share some other common demographic, knowledge, or task property. Figure 4.6 shows a network map that shows a number of patterns. There are clusters not connected to what appears to be a backbone; these clusters themselves show different patterns of connectedness: Most are hub-and-spoke, and one of them is almost a mesh.

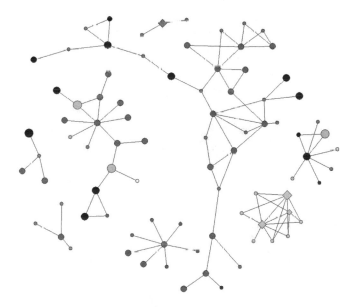

Figure 4.6
Organizational clusters

You might say that the illustration in Figure 4.6 isn't a map of a network but of multiple networks, but in fact this is a network view of the actual connectivity (who gets information from whom) among people in the same organization, with some outside connections. The clusters represent different geographic regions that are operating more or less independently. When a network shows this structure, it's time to ask questions about which nodes need to be connected and how to connect them.

Core/Periphery

Network diagrams help identify the network "core," which is often a small number of people well-known to each other, usually surrounded by a larger set of people on the periphery. In this *core/periphery* pattern, a core set of people form a hub, from which they connect to others.

Figure 4.7 shows a small network with an emergent core/periphery structure. This map, like most of those you'll see in this book, is

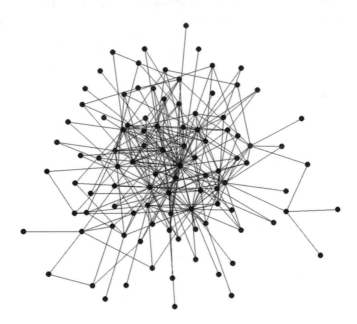

Figure 4.7
Core/Periphery pattern

based on networks that have clear boundaries: names fixed to an organization chart, people on the membership list of an organization, and so on. Very large networks that continue to grow and have no discernable boundaries are often characterized as *scale-free*. The World Wide Web is an example; there are a small number of very large hubs (think of Google and Yahoo!) in this network, and a vast and ever-expanding number of sites and pages on the periphery that initially link to other sites but may not be linked *to*.

How a network is formally instantiated is the topic of the next section here, governance.

GOVERNANCE

All networks have some form of governance, explicit or assumed, embodied in a matriarch or patriarch, hub, convener, guru, director, committee, or officers who use a variety of levers to keep the organization in balance and relationships intact. Governance is the fine art and delicate practice of guiding and steering an organization in a steady operational state. Governance is not static (unless an organization is dysfunctionally rigid) but flexible, attuned to the environment, and capable of change; it is also sensitive to the need for accountability and decision making.

Stages of Coherence

Financially chartered companies and nonprofits set out organization charts that describe the operational and function models and lines of authority. Informal networks rarely leap into being thinking about organizing roles and responsibilities and especially don't think about chains of command. It's important, therefore, not to think of a governance model as an end state but as an expression of increasing levels of coherence. The more conscious a network is of its need for governance, the deeper the conversations will be about how to achieve coherence and the greater the formality required to maintain it.

Figure 4.8 shows one way to think about how the governance models themselves evolve and change, regardless of the structural pattern of the network.

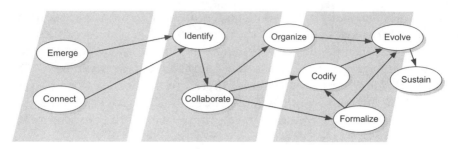

Figure 4.8
Governance stages

Emerge and connect

As the examples earlier in this chapter suggest, the formation of networks can be a matter of making a series of connections, intentionally or by discovery, or emergence. An intentional network may be the idea of a founder who creates a business or a nonprofit organization because of a personal motivation to bring people together. This person is the hub, the main connector. Networks can also emerge from swarms; when a sufficient number of people are gathering around a common notion of how they can be connected in a common purpose, the network emerges.

 The Knowledge Management Group (KMG) of Philadelphia began with a small group of people who met in a Philadelphia suburb in March of 1999 to talk about KM strategies and practices at Hewlett-Packard. A month later, the Philadelphia Area Chamber of Commerce sponsored a meeting to explore the possibility of a KM learning community. Among the 50 people who attended this meeting, eight signed up to host future meetings; five of these became members of a steering committee to coordinate and host meetings and to formalize the direction of the group. The group has held monthly meetings ever since.

These first two conversations, represented as "Collaborate" in Figure 4.8, represented a transition of the KMG from an emergent network to an actual network.

Figure 4.9
One network's logo

Identify and collaborate

Collaboration begins at the point that the network is aware of itself: It makes itself distinct by giving itself a name. The minimum a network needs in order to exist is a name. That sounds simple (or existential), but so is Principle #1 of Net Work: If you can represent the relationships, you can draw it as a network. It follows that if you have a reason to draw it, it probably should have a name. This is certainly true if you create a network using any online tool; an e-mail list needs a name, as does an online community. If it meets face to face, it's easier to name it so you can talk about it, even if it is a generic-sounding name, like the Knowledge Management Group or "the network of support for branding Product X."

A network edges further into legitimacy when it creates a logo for itself, which is important as a business or mission focus pushes the network out into the world. If the network uses a web presence to market, advertise, or maintain information about itself, then a logo or graphic is an essential part of the generative process. The Gennova Group's logo is shown here as an example.

A logo is a symbol of the network's identity, useful for more than stationery and web page design: It gives members a sense of what it is that they belong to and validates that the network is more than the sum of its members.

The emergence of identity is also the point at which the members of a network begin to collaborate on establishing coordination processes, roles, and responsibilities—that is, the point at which it begins to organize itself.

Organize and formalize

A self-organizing network begins the work of making itself sustainable when it starts the conversation about what operational processes and infrastructure are required to maintain it. In the case of the

KMG, the five people who self-selected to be on the steering committee (later renamed the executive committee) began the conversation about how to organize. In most networks, a steering committee consists of the people who will take up the task of writing a mission statement and putting the infrastructure in place to manage the network's operational processes. For example, if a network collects money, either as annual dues or as individual meeting fees, the steering committee will assign a single person to fulfill the role of treasurer, managing the network's bank account. Another common network task is communication, which includes managing a mailing list, sending out announcements, and so on. The steering committee will assign someone to be responsible for that task. If meetings require speakers, someone else may take responsibility for engaging a speaker for every meeting, and so on. Emergent networks self-organize around the work that needs to be done.

Online networks self-organize around the technologies they use, which range from simple e-mail lists to highly structured community spaces. These networks still require at least one person in the "organizing" role of facilitator or moderator. The more complex the technology, the more roles may be needed to support and maintain the community.

Codify

A key task of the leader, steering committee, or moderator is to make the network's existence and governance model public by codifying it: writing it down and putting it into a reproducible form accessible by others. The simplest and most common document is a simple mission statement or charter that is posted on the website for the network. The site may also summarize the governing principles, as in "who is responsible for what tasks," along with the membership criteria, how to join, and so on.

These emergent, self-connected networks have a flexibility and informality that enables them to shift their structures as they grow and change in purpose or scope. Many networks, especially those that reach strategic transition points, engage in activities that require tax reporting, or grow outside local geographic boundaries, require something structurally stronger.

Evolve and sustain

Sustaining a network at its full capacity to accomplish its purpose and to produce value for its stakeholders is the result of intentional activities during its development and growth. Part II of this book is devoted to the work of designing, examining, and managing networks through the transitions that occur during the life cycle and ongoing work of the network.

Managing Accountability and Decision Making

In the domain of incorporated businesses and nonprofits—that is, networks that require investment from partners, investors, or donors—the stakes are higher and require more formality than mission statements and procedural documents. There are good reasons for thinking about institutionalizing a network structure using a regulated form of governance, either a business or not-for-profit organization:

- When the size and scope of the network is such that non-volunteer staff are required to operate it;
- When the network needs legal authority to negotiate with other corporations or governmental institutions;
- When members put their personal financial or intellectual capital at risk.

Each country has its own laws regarding the establishment and management of private or public corporations or companies, both for-profit and nonprofit. Regional, national, and global nonprofit organizations are networks most likely to be concerned with issues related to a corporate structure of some kind: These organizations are responsible for receiving monies from a variety of sources and distributing them according to the network's purpose.

Some networks codify their decision-making rules. For example the Massachusetts Smart Growth Alliance, a coalition of seven organizations that came together to encourage policy reform in community development, articulated its decision-making process as part of its governance:[1]

- An alliance-published policy requires unanimous consent;
- Individual groups can take their own policy decisions but can't use the name of the alliance;
- The alliance will attempt unanimity on all non-policy decisions (workplans, staffing, fund drives, or budget allocations) but a simple vote will serve to enable action if there is not unanimous consent.

There are few legal resources for networks to establish governance models outside the extensive formality and commitment of contractual and corporate agreements. But we do have practice fields: Corporate strategic alliances, cooperatives, and NGO networks are responding to the network imperative by experimenting and taking risks with new organizational governance models.

Leadership

Some networks are directed or guided by a single leader. This person is the hub who defines the purpose of the conversation, the network decides whom to bring into the conversation, and assigns or allocates resources to tasks. The visionary who creates the network may be the de facto leader of the network or may choose (as many do) to move into the background after getting the network started.

Typically, rules are encoded in bylaws that (among other things) identify the officers of the company. These officers are required to provide annual financial and operating reports on the work of the organization. They hold the trust of the people in the network, and they are accountable both to the governmental authorities that sanction them and to the members of the network (employees, volunteer staff, and so on). With this accountability comes the authority to make decisions on behalf of the network. In successful and sustainable networks, those vested with decision-making authority are skilled consensus builders. Rarely (if ever) do they make unilateral decisions; they are always guided by the wisdom of the network itself.

From acquisition to alliance

In industries with strong vertical integration, an entry into a new product area or geography historically has led to acquisition, with an attendant growth in size and (often) increasing inflexibility. More recently, many companies began to look at the joint venture model, which entailed the creation of a new corporate entity combining individual groups from within participating companies. This enabled companies to share the risk of the venture but at some arm's length and with some financial protection. But since the late 1980s, the trend toward "strategic alliances" has become a more prevalent model, as it provides for more creativity in outcome and flexibility in management.

Businesses are realizing that formalizing a partnership into a set of legal agreements is not always the best thing to do. In fact, Benjamin Gomes-Casseres, an expert in international alliances, says contracts in alliances are always incomplete: "a contract is incomplete when, despite the fine print, it does not specify fully what each party must do under every conceivable circumstance."[2] Unfortunately, it is difficult for legal staff, particularly in large organizations, to make the transition to the operational rhythm of networks, which is very much one of continuous change.

A flexible approach to creating consortia-type alliances typically entails establishing a governing body and crafting a set of documents that provide principles that members of the consortia must agree to. The World Wide Web Consortium (W^{3}C) 🏛 uses a document called a member agreement that spells out purpose of the consortium, the obligations of membership (and of W^{3}C to the members), and the principles for assigning copyrights to materials developed during the work of the consortium.

Other typical documents that support the establishment of an alliance include:

- Charter or letter of intent;
- Confidentiality and nondisclosure agreements;
- Guiding principles;
- Operational plan.

The minimal governing body for a large-scale, multicompany alliance is often an executive committee or steering group of some type. Members of the steering group need to have sufficient seniority in their companies to be able to assign and allocate resources to the alliance, and must also be champions for the alliance within their own companies.

Cooperatives

One type of legal structure that is gaining wide interest is the cooperative. Cooperatives as a formal governance model date from the 1800s in Europe, have been recognized as legal business entities in the United States for almost a hundred years, and have recently seen a growth spurt in Europe.[3] Cooperatives, which exist solely to serve their members, range in size from small storefronts to Fortune 500 companies. They may be local, regional, national, or global, but they share the essential characteristics of co-ownership by members, who share in surpluses or profits according to their contributions.

For example, YaYa! Bike is a cooperative business owned and controlled by specialty bicycle retailers. Its 268 independent bike dealers have access to shared services (insurance, debt collection, computer purchase) through the negotiating power of the cooperative, as well as to rebates and special offers from the 35 vendors who are part of the cooperative. Ken Fagut, Director of Supplier Programs, emphasizes the benefits of a network that includes retailers and suppliers. He says there is a "greater intimacy" between the suppliers, vendors, and members. The suppliers and vendors especially are able to get direct feedback much more rapidly, allowing them to improve quickly.

NGO networks

Increasingly, nongovernmental organizations are using networks as an important element in their strategies, particularly in building and extending organizational capacity and the reach of services that they can provide.[4] For example, Foundations of Success (FOS) works with conservation practitioners to enhance their knowledge and skills in the area of adaptive management. To be successful, FOS has created a network of donor agencies, NGOs like The Nature Conservancy, the World Wildlife Fund, international and multilateral organizations, other networks, and academic institutions.

Managing Growth

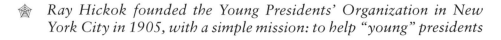

Ray Hickok founded the Young Presidents' Organization in New York City in 1905, with a simple mission: to help "young" presidents

(those under 45 years of age) to become better presidents by learning from each other. The basic operating unit design, a chapter, was a group of 10 to 12 young presidents who would meet on a regular basis to share their challenges and ideas with each other, developing trustful relationships in the process. As the network grew, so did the desire for more formal structures to manage events that would bring members from each of the different chapters together; a regional structure was established to oversee regional and chapter activities. The idea quickly spread to surrounding regions, and by 1961 the first European chapter opened; today there are over 175 chapters. The overall organization is staffed and managed by volunteers.

The most common structure that has developed for networks that are spread geographically is the federated model. In a federation, the core network serves as the hub of multiple, relatively autonomous hubs. This is the classic model for alumni associations, civic groups like the Rotary or Chambers of Commerce, and professional associations, as well as business groups like YPO. This model is shown in Figure 4.10.

YPO is typical of the organizations that use this governance structure:

- Its board of directors (which can be called a steering committee, council, an executive board, advisory board, and so on)

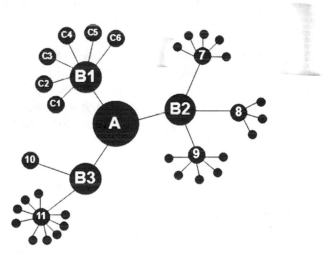

Figure 4.10
Federated network

maintains the long-term vision and strategy for the network. The members of this committee populate node A in Figure 4.10.

- The regional officers who monitor the health of the chapters within the region and coordinate educational opportunities populate nodes B1, B2, and B3. Chapters are represented as nodes C1 through C6 and 7 through 11.
- An international professional staff who manages the daily business, finances, and so on also resides in the core, node A.

This degree of structure supports the needs of chapters to share learning and the needs of members to connect locally. It also provides the infrastructure needed to maintain a communications hub and to plan and convene annual conferences. In the case of YPO, the annual conferences, called "Universities," have been a primary feature of the organization since early in its founding. These two-day events provide networking, learning, and social experiences that enhance intellectual, relational, and social capital.

The federal model is a common governmental form (as in the United States), but is also a typical model for a global corporation that provides a good deal of autonomy to specific regions or countries. This enables those countries to develop business that is appropriate and relevant to the business conditions and ecosystem in those areas.

Online networks correspond to the core/periphery model (Figure 4.7) pattern. There are usually a number of people at the core, those who moderate online discussions, set up and facilitate teleconferences or face-to-face meetings, and engage and invite the members. CPsquare ⬡, the community of practice for people engaged in working with or studying communities of practice, began with this pattern, and continually welcomes people into the core.

Managing Membership

An emergent network comes by its initial membership through conversations based on common interests, pursuits, and aspirations. Once established, a network, like other living things, has an impetus to grow. Sometimes a network grows because it has defined a purpose or mission that requires additional expertise and resources; sometimes it grows because people are drawn to it and want to be a part of it. A critical task of network governance is the mechanism by which the network identifies and accepts new members. There are three basic membership structures: open, criteria-based, and invitation-only.

Open

Networks that promote personal growth and affiliation, learning, and ideas tend to be completely open to anyone to join, but with different levels of personal cost. When you create an online group in Yahoo! Groups, the network's name and description may be published so anyone can join. Similarly, small associations and groups that have monthly local meetings will publish meeting agendas and announce special speakers on their websites, inviting anyone interested in the topic to attend, as long as they pay a meeting fee slightly higher than that paid by registered, dues-paying members.

Networks establishing a norm for open membership trust that only people who have a serious intent on sharing the network's purpose will become participating members, and they welcome visitors with the idea that those who are truly interested will join. Membership dues are important for two reasons. They provide the network with operating funds (for room rentals, web space, and so on), and the payment of dues signifies that an individual who is joining the network believes participation is valuable. Dues or annual fees are a common component of all three membership structures.

Criteria-based

We are familiar with standard criteria for many of the networks we participate in: Professional associations require degrees or certifications in a discipline; alumni associations require that you hold a degree from a specific institution; cities and towns require residents to work on committees; and so on. Some networks require members to sign an agreement that specifies their rights and obligations; the World Wide Web Consortium 🏛 mentioned earlier uses the member agreement as the criterion for admission.

Formalized networks that focus on enabling meaningful learning experiences for a particular demographic often set strict criteria. YPO ⚙, for example, requires that members hold significant leadership roles in a corporation; that they be under 45 when they join YPO; that their business employs a minimum number of workers (approximately 50); and that the business has a minimum annual dollar revenue (in 2005, $8 million/year for sales, services, and manufacturing companies).

Nonprofit networks, which are answerable to funders, must also carefully delineate criteria. For example, to become an affiliate of the Women's World Banking (WWB) ⚙ network, a nonprofit organization that links microlending institutions globally, a member organization must provide direct microfinance and/or business development services to low-income women. A written application must include a letter indicating why the organization wants to become a WWB affiliate and the contribution that the organization can make to WWB. The letter must be accompanied by organizational documents, including:

- Mission, vision, and principles;
- Organization strategy and business plan;
- Legal structure;
- Governance structure.

A WWB Regional Manager can provide provisional acceptance into the network after she has visited the local organization, but the full approval process for entry into the network normally takes about a year.

In the 21st century, all businesses are attuned to the need to partner throughout their value network, including suppliers, research, customers, and channels. The management of strategic alliances begins with understanding whether the alliance provides access to natural resources, trusted suppliers, knowledge, skills or expertise, or sales or delivery channels; but the most important step after that is identifying the right partners. Certainly, legal and financial due diligence remain important when a complicated contract is required, but it has become very common to use a company's social capital as an indicator as well. The more a company is already embedded in an existing network of relationships in an industry sector, the more likely it is to have had repeated interactions and transactions with other companies in that network. Senior executives leverage this embeddedness and their own social capital within these networks for referrals and recommendations.[5]

Invitation-only

An invitation-only membership structure might suggest the closed exclusionary bias of a country club. However, it can be a useful model for an idea network that bases its value on the nature of the member interactions that occur in it. A colleague of mine who was organizing an "unconference" of thought leaders invited me and said I could invite anyone else, as long as they passed the "bus test": *If you can sit on a bus with this person for six hours without getting bored, impatient, or frustrated, then they're probably going to fit in.* This kind of subjective evaluation is difficult to put into specific criteria and is not 100% effective, but it has worked for many leadership and idea networks, including Gennova 🕸.

Rotary International combines the models of criteria-based, invitation-only, and open membership. One of Rotary International's principles in membership is maintaining a diversity of professions within a local club, so this imposes a "criteria" structure. Most new members are brought in and recommended by existing members. However, a person who aspires to join the Rotary but doesn't know any of the current members can apply to the local club president, who will provide introductions to members.

TEXTURE

The people in a network are connected through ties that describe the nature of their relationships. Some relationships are based on the type of the interactions, which can range from simple information exchange to problem-solving collaborations to rich dialogues that surface ideas and insights. In some relationships, there is an emotional component to the interactions, an interpersonal trust that allows for sharing about family, hobbies, and political views. The exact nature of these interactions reflects one of the elements of what I call the style of the network (the topic of Chapter 5). From a structural standpoint, the sums of the ties—of any type—in a network give it texture.

If you think about a network as a woven cloth that contains strands of many types of thread, yarn, and string, you can start to see what I mean by texture. If you were to examine a fabric you might notice how tight or loose the weave is, or how fragile. How many types of thread are used? How thick are they? Does the fabric look finished and self-contained, or does it appear open to the addition of new colors and materials? And then—possibly—you might ask if the piece is holding together well and look for rips, moth holes, pulls in the fabric, and so on. Finally, you'd be curious about whether this fabric was built to last, structurally, and how it accommodates new materials, withstands losses, and adjusts its governing mechanisms to maintain equilibrium among the sum of the ties. Depending on its purpose (a dress, coat, hat, or wall hanging), you'd think about adding colored thread, fur, feathers, and other fabrics to enrich the texture.

This flexibility and craft apply to networks as well.

The Sum of the Ties: Structural Metrics

The figures in the first part of this chapter illustrated a variety of patterns that recur in networks. Social network researchers and practitioners have become familiar with these patterns over the past twenty or more years as they have developed methodologies for examining networks closely. But researchers also knew that when they looked at very large networks, they needed mathematical analysis to develop rigorous models for understanding the network structure.

There are now hundreds of metrics that can be calculated from the ways that the ties in a network connect the nodes. In Chapter 8, I'll go into more detail about the metrics that provide insight in an organizational network analysis; four in particular relate specifically to the texture of a network:

- Density;
- Distance;
- Centrality;
- Open or closed.

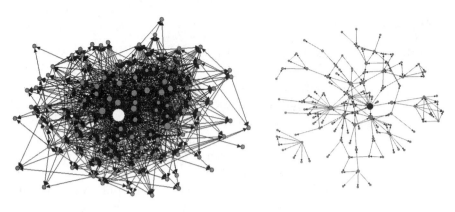

Figure 4.11
Contrasting network relationships

Density

Density is the tightness of the weave. Start with a fixed number of people in a network and calculate the total number of connections that would exist if everyone was connected to everyone else. This would be a density of 100%. All nodes have equal connections to all the others. Denser networks are likely to have a greater resilience. Density is also correlated with the effectiveness of networks: The more people know each other, the more likely they are to collaborate and be more productive.

Figure 4.11 illustrates two different relationships for the same network. On the left is the network showing which people say that they are very familiar with the knowledge and skills of the others. The density for this network relationship is 46%. On the right, the ties between the nodes indicate that the people have frequent and regular interactions with one another. The density of this network relationship is 8%. This network has a great potential for collaboration, in that even though people do not interact on a frequent basis, they do know whom to seek for information or advice on specific topics.

The highlighted, enlarged nodes in these maps are not the same person in each network; the most central person in the network of awareness is different from the person most central in the flow of information.

Distance

Distance is a measure of how many people a piece of information needs to go through to get to everyone in the network. This is the "degrees of separation" concept, which is an important factor in a network's agility in responding to external conditions; it can indicate how quickly information can spread out across a network to reach all members. It can also indicate how easy it is for any individual to reach—through the shortest number of degrees—the person who may be able to solve a specific problem.

A large potential network may include many people on the periphery who have not yet met or interacted with others, or people who come into the network through emerging hubs. Such networks would have very high average distance. A high average distance among members can also be an indication that there are not enough hubs or connectors.

Centrality

Centrality is a measure of how dependent a network is on one or two people. Imagine what happens to a hub-and-spoke network when the hub drops out or moves on. If the network relies on the hub to set the agenda, start conversations, bring in new members, and coordinate activities with outsiders, then the network will go into crisis if the hub disappears.

Open or closed

The metric that reflects the extent to which the network is open to the outside is officially called the internal/external (E/I) ratio, or E/I index: This is the balance in the network between external ties (those ties that people in the network go to for interactions relative to the work of the network) and internal ties (those ties among people within the network).

Let's go back to the structure of a heterarchy, or mesh (see Figure 4.3). Not only does it have a density of 100%, it also has an E/I index of −1. It is closed to outside disturbances, irrelevant interruptions, and the meddling of outsiders. Open networks, on the other hand, are those in which members of the network actively use their connections with people outside the organization, company, or

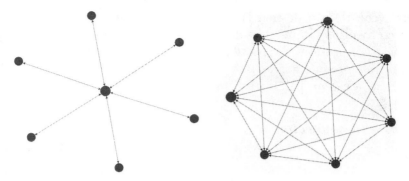

Figure 4.12
Open and closed networks

culture to leverage and bring ideas, insights, and environmental changes to the network. Consider the pair of networks in Figure 4.12.

Sources of Tensile Strength

Tensile strength is a term borrowed from the physical sciences: It is the ability of a material to withstand stress and change without breaking down. The texture of a network can also demonstrate tensile strength akin to that of spiderwebs. Spiders create webs by first laying down a sticky substance, a glue, that anchors the web to the ground, a fence post, or a doorknob, and then throwing out threads that have a tensile strength that is five times that of steel. Likewise, the texture of the networks we create depends largely on how easily ties are created, the steadfastness of the ground points, and the strength of the connections.

Strong and weak ties

A network's texture is also evidenced by the mixture of strong and weak ties. Strong ties are those between people who have known each other for some time, worked together on projects, or are affiliated through family or community ties. Within a densely knit project team, the strength of the ties is enhanced by the fact that people share the same connections.

A weak tie is a tie that is not active, not used very much, or not shared by others in the network. It may reflect a casual acquaintance or past connection. External ties may be weak, but very powerful. Weak ties provide access into other networks, where there may be different ideas or access to different resources.

Hubs and connectors

People who have closely examined organizational networks frequently observe that organizations are often held together by people who do the invisible work of creating connections and relationships, paying attention to and mediating conflicts, or generating energy when the network needs it. These people are often not measured by or valued for these tasks, which are critical to organizational viability. Network analysis uses network maps and metrics to identify these people. Often, they are very easy to see in diagrams, as in Figure 4.13.

Hubs, as you've already seen in this chapter, are the center of the network or of a subnetwork within a network. People are sometimes in hub positions because their jobs put them there. Often, though,

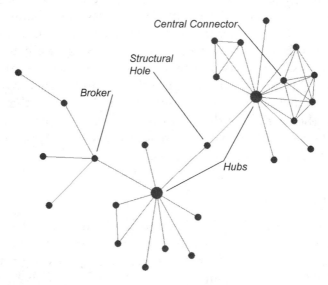

Figure 4.13
Hubs and connectors

they become hubs because people are attracted to them for their expertise, energy, effort, or connections to other hubs. One of the principles of scale-free networks is "the rich get richer," that is, the popular hubs tend to grow more connections (think of eBay and Amazon). Thus, hubs that serve as the sticky ground points of a network continue to attract more hubs.

There are different types of connectors that play important roles in maintaining a network's tensile strength:

- A central connector is a person who makes connections among people within a cluster or subgroup;
- A broker is a person who makes connections across groups (a person who maintains weak ties between two otherwise disconnected groups is often said to fill, or to be, a "structural hole").

Recall the distinction between open and closed networks. Open networks require a number of people who can broker information from the outside (or from other clusters in the same network) and bring it inside. This is often called bridging. A network or cluster that is not well connected internally may need more work to create stronger ties; this may be called bonding.

Whether bridging or bonding, those who play hub and connecting roles have always existed in organizations. Our network lens has provided us with insight into these roles and is now teaching us how to design and launch networks with an understanding of the importance of these roles to the strength of the network.

The "Right" Structure

So which of these patterns is best? If there is a Holy Grail in the field of organizational network analysis, it's an absolute metric for telling whether a particular network is "good." One researcher I know has been asked by a military agency to tell it the optimal number of people for a heterarchical analysis team. He's still shaking his head about what they don't understand about networks: Values for such metrics will vary based on the purpose, style, and value-creating characteristics of a network.

Table 4.1
Structural Patterns for Different Network Functions[6,7]

Functional Need	Network "Need"
Complex knowledge transfer	Strong ties People aware of each other's knowledge
Simple knowledge transfer	Weak ties
Simple coordination	Hub-and-spoke network
Transformation, change management	Strong ties from the hub to central connectors in subnetworks
Complex coordination	Dense, decentralized network
Innovation	Extensive weak ties to diverse groups
Public good	Strong ties External embeddedness
External information needs	Diverse external ties

While we do not have all the answers, studies are showing that different structures are more or less suitable for different categories of work. It has become conventional wisdom among researchers and practitioners that the open, core/periphery model (Figure 4.7) appears to be best for vibrant innovation or learning networks and that closed, highly connected teams are required for focused detail work (Figure 4.3).

Another way to look at the structural design of a network is based on its needs, as shown in Table 4.1.

 Procter and Gamble's "connect and develop" innovation strategy includes working with internal and external networks in a variety of ways and with a variety of structures. Its internal technology entrepreneurs are based in geographic hubs around the world; these senior P&G people are responsible for finding innovations from regional products and innovators. This top-down, multihub approach is complemented by focused technology and idea sharing with their top fifteen suppliers. It taps into open networks created by P&G or others that broker new ideas and technical solutions. For example, NineSigma is a firm that takes a technology problem from P&G (and other companies) and publishes it to an array of research labs, consultants and universities to solicit solutions. Yet2.com is a two-way network that enables companies to market

ideas as well as to look for technology solutions. Meanwhile, P&G maintains its own close-knit, proprietary research networks as well.

Weavers and pulse-takers: Intentional net work

In their work with ACEnet, 🕸 Valdis Krebs and June Holley refined the role of the network *weaver* in creating regional economic networks. Such networks rely on the ability of small independent businesses to be able to use each other as resources; for that, they need to know about each other. Using their principle of "know the net, knit the net," Krebs and Holley have identified the following process that weavers follow:

- Discern patterns;
- Make connections;
- Build trust and skills while organizing collaborative projects.

Often during the formation of a network and its building stages, the network weaver is the hub as well; this is the person who has the greatest access to resources, knowledge, and connections. The critical transition in the development of a network is when the network has achieved sufficient social capital that the weaver can remove himself from the hub, allowing the network to grow organically to a robust core/periphery form.[8]

Weavers also often act as the pulse-takers in networks during their growth, but must cede this role to a network member when the network is on its own. Pulse-takers are indirectly connected to people who know the right people; they cultivate relationships that help them to see a very wide view of the network. From this vantage point they can monitor the health of the network, and take actions to change the dynamics.

As we've seen, the dynamics of a network can be altered by how its purpose is declared and by how it is structured—the pattern of connections, governance, texture. You can also alter a network's dynamics by changing its style. The next chapter introduces the elements of style.

Notes

1. Mary Wissemann and Kristina Egan, "Building a Multi-Interest Movement for Smart Growth," Massachusetts Smart Growth Alliance, May 2006.
2. B. Gomes-Casseres, *The Alliance Revolution* (Cambridge: Harvard University Press, 1996).
3. Ricardo Lotti, Peter Mensing, and David Valenti, "A Cooperative Solution," *strategy+business*, July 17, 2006.
4. Claudia Liebler and Marisa Ferri, "NGO Networks: Building Capacity in a Changing World," November 2004.
5. R. Gulati, N. Nohria, and A. Zaheer, "Strategic Networks," *Strategic Management Journal* 21 (2000): 203–215.
6. Nancy Katz and David Lazer, "Building Effective Intra-Organizational Networks: The Role of Teams" (working paper, Center for Public Leadership, John F. Kennedy School of Government, Harvard University, 2003).
7. Daniel Brass and David Krackhardt, "Social Capital of Twenty-First Century Leaders," in *Out-of-the-Box Leadership*, ed. J.G. Hunt, G.E. Dodge, and L. Wong (Boston: Elsevier Limited, 2001).
8. Valdis Krebs and June Holley, "Building Smart Communities through Network Weaving" (white paper, www.orgnet.com, 2002).

Chapter 5

STYLE

All networks have a "feel" that derives from the complementary interplay of the people who participate in its conversations and the places and spaces they occupy. To characterize a network by its style means looking at five key factors that contribute to its uniqueness—locus, culture, interactions, orientation, and leadership—and breaking those down further into characteristic elements. As I discuss these elements in this chapter (summarized in Figure 5.1), you will begin to see themes common to creating successful networks. These style elements have a key role to play in the design of networks, which is the topic of Chapter 7.

LOCUS

A network must both "live" somewhere and have a repository for its history. I call this element the locus of the network; its dimensions are place, space, and pace—a real place, information space, and interaction pace, or rhythm. For networks that meet and interact face-to-face, the locus is a real physical place: the office, a conference center, a club house, meeting hall, a restaurant. With the Internet, we have become used to calling organizations, groups, teams, and networks "virtual" whose primary mode of interaction is in information space. For such virtual networks, the live interaction "place" is a teleconference phone line.

Figure 5.1
The elements of style

Networks in any culture create and collect information artifacts: business records, reports, meeting minutes, photographs, banners, marketing brochures, and so forth. This second dimension of locus represents the need for real and virtual information spaces, a library or repository, perhaps, or the equivalent of an old store room or file folder (somewhere). The third dimension of locus represents the pace of the network—the intensity, frequency, and speed of interactions and activities that are the dynamic heartbeat of that network's life.

Real Place

Ownership of a specific physical place is the norm for businesses, large national and global mission networks, and for many benevolent/fraternal mission networks as well. Strong social capital comes from the association with a physical structure that has on its walls the artifacts related to the identity of the network—flags, mottos, photographs of past presidents and sports teams, trophies and ceremonial objects.

Owned place

Over the past ten years, businesses have come to an understanding of the need of knowledge workers for spontaneous (or even more serendipitous) encounters, for places to have ad hoc meetings and dialogues, and for physical surroundings that inspire and reflect the style of the organization.

Office design is always a trade-off between closed offices for "heads-down" work on tasks requiring deep concentration (like writing code or analyzing data) and open spaces that promote informal communications and chance encounters. Architectural design firms and office furniture manufacturers are passionate about the impact of workplace design on organizational change. They emphasize the need for the design of atria, offices, and conference rooms to reflect the open, transparent relationships that enhance knowledge flow.

Fraternal and benevolent societies often construct their own edifices, which serve as permanent meeting places, community centers, and spaces to hold events. Apart from the practical purposes these buildings serve, they are also expressions of the identity of the society, from logos carved in granite on the outside to flags and banners inside. Architect Frank Duffy says that there should be a critical mixture of:

- *Efficiency:* How well the space inside is structured to meet a variety of needs;
- *Effectiveness:* How well the space enables the productivity and imaginative work of the people using it;
- *Expression:* The messages that the space conveys.[1]

Headquarters for the NGO Greenpeace in Washington, D.C., for example, was designed with the principle that Greenpeace's physical place would reflect the messages central to Greenpeace's environmental mission. The construction renovated rather than demolished existing buildings, was finished using recycled materials, and eliminated the use of polyvinyl chloride. The headquarters is located close to public transportation and bicycle-accessible pathways. The prominent use of open space harnesses sun power for lighting.

Borrowed place

Leasing space is the natural option for smaller networks that support staff for leadership and administration purposes. A single room or a storefront can serve to position the network in physical place, and this is often sufficient to make the work of the network visible when physical presence is required. In such spaces, there is still opportunity to design the space so that it reflects the style of the network.

   Most informal networks have no permanently owned space, and
rely on public spaces or conference rooms provided by local companies. The Knowledge Management networks 🕸 that have emerged
around the globe reflect the various options available to small learning networks. In Philadelphia, each monthly meeting of the KM
Group is held in a conference room offered by a network member
from a different company. The Boston KM Forum uses a different
model for each of their three types of meetings:

- For monthly practice meetings, they use a conference room at
  the offices of one of the members;
- For monthly dialogues on hot topics, they meet in the cafeteria
  atrium of an office park on Route 128;
- For quarterly conferences, they rent a large meeting room from
  Bentley College.

Hotels are the venue of choice for the Gurteen Knowledge Networks
in the United Kingdom; it happens that hotels are often happy to
provide a meeting room with the proviso that those attending a
meeting will spend time in the hotel bar afterward. Both hotels and
restaurants will provide space as long as the meeting includes the
price of a meal. Bars and coffee shops offer regular meeting places
for informal, ad hoc networks; office networks are often successfully
maintained on the basis of drinks on Friday nights or Monday
morning coffee.
   The "right" space can enhance a network's generative capacity.
When the Boston Company of Friends (CoF) 🕸 formed, it held its
first meetings at the local Boston office of the global consulting firm
CapGemini; but not just in the office. Capgemini had designed a
physical environment purposefully based on the belief that environment influences outcome; it created six of these Accelerated Solutions
Environments around the world, one of which was in Boston. As
Lisa Dennis, leader of the Boston cell, puts it, "This environment
had a large part in the growth of the CoF—providing a very unusual
environment that was creative, suited the mindset of our members,
and allowed for more collaborative and creative meetings." This was
a mutually enhancing relationship, as the *Fast Company* magazine's
learning network was bringing out new and innovative ideas for
doing business, and these ideas were important for Capgemini's own

learning agenda; the CoF was the right fit for the kind of events and discussions they wanted to bring about. Later, as the network expanded, the CoF rotated its meetings, looking for other companies that had created innovative workspaces that the members could tour as part of the meeting experience.

Networks in Information Space

It would be rare to find a nonpersonal network that does not have a virtual presence of some kind in an information system somewhere. The minimal footprint in information space can consist of a single web page, a private e-mail distribution list, or both. There is a great variation in the extent to which a network is visible (publicly, or only to itself) in the electronic world. On one end of the spectrum are the networks that exist wholly online and are fully open to the Internet-browsing public. On the other end are virtual communities inside companies that use a protected space inside the corporate firewalls to share proprietary or carefully held information.

Just as physical places support meaningful interaction in an expressive context, so too can a website that is designed to reflect the purpose, structure, and style of the network. This is the role of information architecture and design: creating useful navigation for purposeful online work. Much of the work in an online community exists in the conversations recorded in e-mail or on bulletin boards, unaccompanied by the comfort of a friendly logo or a careful color scheme. In these latter cases, color must come from the conversation.

Online discussion group networks exist in words and are not aided (or obscured) by body language, vocal inflection, or kinetic energy. Because the people who join these networks come with a wide range of cultural backgrounds, experience and knowledge in a subject area, levels of computer literacy, and personal communication styles, online groups require careful facilitation. The tasks of virtual facilitators (moderators) resemble those of physical-place meeting facilitators: keeping the conversation on topic, trying to keep the conversation from being dominated by one or two people, admonishing or removing members who use inappropriate language, and so on.

There is, as you might expect, an online network of practitioners of online facilitation. This community, founded by Nancy White in

1999, is a vibrant network that lives within the public online infrastructure called Yahoo! Groups. (Yahoo! Groups, when I counted in July 2006, listed 3,357,914 groups.)

Online networks

Advertising-funded online groups like Yahoo! are free to anyone who wants to create a network. Their precursors, server-based listservs and usenet groups, require that the network be affiliated with a larger (usually academic) network that runs such a server. All of these provide an archive of conversational posts that make it possible to search and examine the content of those conversations. A major advantage of Yahoo! Groups, Google Groups, and other such mechanisms is that they provide space for artifacts (folders to share files and web links) and capabilities to construct simple polls of the membership, keep a calendar of announcements, and display the list of members.

As members of these groups interact over time, they develop their own norms and behaviors that promote trust and reciprocity. The writing style and tone of members and the even hand of facilitators enforcing norms and stimulating conversation are the expression of the community's life.

Sometimes begun with a single e-mail to a distribution list that extends out to and beyond the personal networks of those on the original list, such groups can be incubators for communities of practice development or seeds for larger movements. Think about moveon.org, which began as an effort to use the Internet to collect signatures and is today a multifaceted nonprofit civic and political action network.

Virtual workspaces

Publicly available tools for online e-mail communities and document sharing are not free (they are supported by advertising), nor are they robust, secure, or flexible enough for the needs of communities and networks both inside and outside corporations. Since the advent of Lotus Notes in the early 1990s, many software vendors have created specialized applications for networks. Products like IBM QuickPlace, EMC's eRoom, and Microsoft's SharePoint and Groove are designed specifically to provide an information, display, and community space for knowledge workers—even those who work in adjacent offices.

Information space is easily rented over the Web, so emerging networks do not have to purchase equipment or rely on a corporate infrastructure. Groove, in fact, was designed just so that people could connect and share files, even across secure boundaries.

Integrating place and space

Online networks often lack the intimacy of place that is often crucial to developing a purposeful network, despite the best facilitative methods. But, given that these networks are almost always geographically dispersed, what are the alternatives? This is where telephony (and its digital counterpart VoIP) come in: the teleconference place. In virtual meetings around the globe, businesses have long been linking remote teams with home offices; project managers have successfully kept projects on track; and any two or more people can interact in dimensions that provide more tools for discourse than the simple arrangement of keyboard characters called emoticons.

The introduction of videoconferencing began with great expectations. In 1995, Andy Grove, then CEO of Intel, gave a demo of ProShare, Intel's early entry into the desktop videoconferencing market. I was at a small conference at Lotus headquarters in Cambridge, Massachusetts, when Grove demonstrated the product by speaking to us via ProShare from his home in California. But he wasn't just a talking head; ProShare was designed to include the ability to look at a file together or share an application. He made a prophetic point about how such technology would actually be used: Collaboration doesn't occur because you can see each other; collaboration occurs as people work on something together. The video in this case was an adjunct to the real point, which was to examine his presentation slides.

Sure enough, the ability to collaborate in real-time over artifacts is what we use in the current generation of web-based conferencing. Tools like Webex and others merge the teleconference with a web-based presentation of PowerPoint slides, software demonstrations, or video, putting the attention of the community's collective eyes on shared work products.

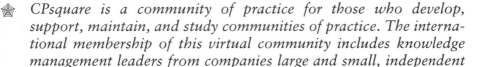

CPsquare is a community of practice for those who develop, support, maintain, and study communities of practice. The international membership of this virtual community includes knowledge management leaders from companies large and small, independent

consultants who help companies create a strategy for leveraging COPs for sustained knowledge advantage, and academic researchers who are motivated to understand how people learn in socially constructed networks. CPsquare was launched by John Smith and Amy Keill with support from Etienne Wenger and Bill Snyder in January 2003. While the small staff funded from membership fees worked to set up an interactive website, the initial startup of the community was managed through a series of phone calls. The goal of the website was to hold a space for deep conversations about the nature of work in and for COPs; to collect stories, methods, and analyses of emerging technologies and social practices; and to be an incubator for small, focused "practice groups" that would mingle their online conversations with frequent voice-based teleconferences.

There is wide discrepancy in the technological capabilities available in different parts of the world, and even inside different parts of the same company. (A 2005 survey inside Intel Corporation found that 49% of employees who work with collaboration technologies and tools routinely work with people who are using different collaboration technologies and tools.)[2]

Pace

The pace of a network comprises both rhythm and momentum, balancing connections in both place and space. Consider the rhythm of interactions in networks. We adjust to a specific rhythm in a network, and we synchronize and modulate our participation based on that rhythm. It has both intensity and frequency. What the network actually does and where depend on the network's context in place and space, but rhythm is what enables members to synchronize. A network's context influences its synchronizing:

- Face-to-face networks require a regular schedule of meetings; i.e., the same day each week or month, or specific intervals with dates specified well in advance.
- The virtual networks of professional associations thrive on annual conferences where people can meet face to face.
- Online, e-mail–based communities set expectations based on the frequency of the postings; significant downturns in activity

may signal moderators that it's time to inject a stimulating question or set up a teleconference to jumpstart thinking on a new topic.

- Web-based communities expect to find new items on a regular, daily basis; members committed to the community will integrate checking these websites into their daily routines or set "alerts" so they receive e-mail when something is added.

Consistency in pace is best supported by using a consistent format for sending out meeting notices and by publishing minutes. Notices provide more than just the vital reminder that there is a meeting; they also set the stage for what will happen in the meeting: what's on the agenda, who the invited speakers will be, the issues or main topics to be discussed, and administrative tasks.

The partner of rhythm is momentum. Momentum is not just the gathering of speed to accomplish outcome-based tasks (though it is very important for that); it is also the way that a meeting connects itself to previous and future meetings or that a conversation connects itself to the previous or next conversations. *Robert's Rules of Order* (which goes back to 1876) reflects this by including the following items in the standard order of business:

- Reading the minutes from the last meeting;
- Dealing with unfinished business from previous meetings;
- Introducing new business;
- Adjourning.

In today's meeting environment, we are more likely to substitute "status of tasks" with "unfinished business" and to add a meeting review into the adjournment process, but otherwise we would do well to recall momentum's need for continuity and consistency. This momentum is aided by using a consistent format for the design of meetings, including management of the time provided for specific agenda items and developing a reputation for managing the agenda and sticking to the timing of it.

 Home Depot's success during its growth phase was founded on aversion to bureaucracy, autonomy of individual stores, and freedom of managers to respond to local market conditions. However, by the

late 1990s, it was plain to senior managers (in the bureaucracy) that this model prevented Home Depot from economizing on value discounts from vendors, for example, because individual store managers could choose whether or not to put goods in their stores. It was impossible to use a consistent set of metrics for profitability or to manage the distrusting relationship among merchandising, operations, and the stores themselves. The individualism was also starting to cost Home Depot in leadership—there were no leadership programs that created a collective social architecture that reflected the way that people work together across an organization, interact socially, and make decisions.

When Robert Nardelli become CEO in 2000, he and his head of human resources, Dennis Donovan, began a large-scale program to change the way that the company worked. One of their style innovations was to hold a two-hour call every Monday morning in which the top executives reported on the previous week. Initially, the meetings helped Nardelli to learn about Home Depot and its operations, but as the weeks passed, it became clear that these meetings were also about accountability and being responsible to follow through on feedback from week to week. Today, that Monday call is videocast (called "Same Page") on Monday afternoons to all the Home Depot stores in the United States. Same Page includes a focus on the week ahead and gives the individual stores a sense of the bigger picture in which they operate.[3]

Agenda-based meetings and a consistent structure of agendas help maintain the rhythm of a community, but it's also important to stay flexible. In fact, says Mark Bonchek of Truman Company, what is most important is to promote the flow of the conversation in the meeting, to build trust among members, and to advance the overall purpose of the network. The content and agenda are instrumental to these goals. Content, in the form of agenda topics, broadcast, or sharing of information needs to be designed to enhance trust in the relationships in the network. "Content is scaffolding," he says. The work is the conversation and what emerges from it.[4]

Events

All types of networks are refreshed and rejuvenated by successful events—be these ad hoc dinner meetings, highly structured conferences, or something in between. For networks that meet regularly face-to-face, an event is an opportunity to spend an extended amount of time engaged in dialogue. Ideally, events offer the opportunity to bring in people from outside the core group of the network, or outside of the network itself.

Online communities can develop face-to-face opportunities for members, for example, by creating practice working sessions or sponsoring dinner gatherings at wider conferences that members are likely to attend. Many view this as a survival factor. CPsquare 🕸 developed an "ecology of interactions" that it believed would be necessary to sustain the relationships within the network and, thereby, "survivability." A "CPweek" in June of 2003 brought members (other than the founders) together for the first time. Since then, different members have hosted workshops and learning events on core themes that bring a dozen or more people together. Cofounder John Smith, when asked about the importance of these face-to-face meetings in the development of the network, said, "I think CPsquare would not exist had there not been some face-to-face sessions at key points in time. Flat out. Of course it may be only that face-to-face [meetings] *accelerate* development. But as every community seems fragile and half-formed as well as beneficial, acceleration is a big deal."[5] Smith's comments are significant given that he, along with many of the core group in CPsquare, are experts in online facilitation.

Online communities within large corporations also mix meeting opportunities, like inviting speakers for brown-bag lunches or holding teleconferences. These opportunities for personal interaction are very important to maintain and develop social capital and the climate it needs to thrive.

Communications

When a network is not actively engaged in a project, it needs to have some regular pace of communication so that its membership continues to identify with it. Communications can range from formal, published, hardcopy monthly newsletters to ad hoc e-mails about potential topics of interest. Formal, regularly scheduled communications require resources for collecting articles and items, writing, production, and distribution. Absent such resources, networks maintain relatedness with the members by ensuring that some form of communication occurs without significant time lapses.

CULTURE

The locus of a network (with its components of place, space, and pace) provides grounding and infrastructure. Within the context of these environmental conditions, people interact with one another. While locus is important, the vitality of the network comes from the overall tone, the "what-it-is-about-this-group-that-keeps-me-coming-back." Cultural factors that set the tone for how the network is experienced include identity, core values, and norms. These all lead to and enhance the social capital of the network.

Identity

A network has an identity that it lends to all its members. A corporation's divisions, business units, departments, and groups all provide common identity to employees and expect them to adopt the "culture" of these network(s). Orientation (often called on-boarding) programs provide as much access as possible to the stories of the corporation, its heros, battles fought and won, and prevailing norms of work.

Many associations and networks are based on a common cultural identity that is the basis for membership—an Italian social club or the Hibernians, for example. For such networks, the culture is derived from existing social capital, and continues to grow based on family ties and common memories or experiences of the "tribe."

A local chapter in a federated network will adopt the external elements of identity of the larger network, that is, the brand, policies and procedures, and governance structures. But it may evolve locally based on social bonds, values, and expectations of the local community. When a person joins a "knowledge management group," this is an expression of identification with the concept and a desire to associate with people who share common interests.

In an emergent community, the identity is formed when the network is identified as a network per se and given a name. The name may be known colloquially only to members (the biking network, the book club) but when a network gets to the point of collaborating on governance, names like the Women's Business Network, the Houston Breakfast Club emerge. Inside organizations, the name provides a clue to the purpose of the network in language that is appropriate to the larger organization (the Brake Linings Tech Club or the Talent Management Community of Practice, for example).

Mark Bonchek, when founding Gennova 🏛, gave it an identity in the invitation for its barn-raising. He had a founding purpose for the network, and he declared its existence by naming it and even developing the logo. You can see part of this invitation in Figure 5.2.

Routines, rituals, and signs

Strong networks create and adhere to routines and rituals. A round of opening introductions ("check-in") is the lifeblood of network gatherings, whether face-to-face or voice-to-voice. There is comfort in knowing what to expect when a network convenes or when a member opens the network's page in its information space. When you open the home page on a website, you expect the calendar in a certain position, news items to be offered, and announcements of any and all events that affect you. If you work in a consulting environment where the staff all work offsite or from home, it's good to know that everyone comes into the office on Fridays, because then you can plan meetings and also look forward to unexpected encounters.

Meetings with refreshments, award ceremonies, annual dinners, holiday parties, summer picnics, post-product-release rafting or skiing expeditions, and Friday beer busts are all rituals that create shared experiences, one of the most important bonding elements of social capital. (Food helps.)

Core Values

The purpose statement of any network implies specific values—social good, shareholder profits, enhancing the use of nanotechnology, whatever—that reflect the common beliefs of people committed to the purpose. Within the network, the core values are articulated broadly, are visibly enacted, and are in harmony with the network's purpose.

There are a key set of values that are common to successful networks: openness, diversity, and transparency.

Dear Friend and Colleague,

I would like to invite you to a community barn-raising.

You won't need a hammer or saw. You won't even need suspenders or a straw hat.
All you need is a passion for helping individuals and organizations fulfill their potential.

You see, we are not actually raising a barn.
We are raising a different kind of structure: **a professional community**.

As you know, I have been working for some time on a new model of professional services.
One that honors the trust placed in us by our clients.
One that inspires passion and purpose for our entire careers.
And one that creates ample wealth for ourselves and our clients.

I believe this new model is a "professional community." In such a community, a select group of professionals from diverse organizations and disciplines join together around shared values for a common purpose. Members benefit from fellowship and a greater flow of ideas and opportunities. Clients benefit from having the specialty and focus of a small firm combined with the breadth and resources of a large firm.

My vision for Gennova Group is that of a professional community for the world's foremost executive advisors and organizational catalysts. Our common purpose will be to help individuals and organizations fulfill their purpose and potential. We will do so through innovative solutions that address people as human beings, organizations as complex systems, and the planet as a vital stakeholder. Community members will retain their autonomy while acquiring a richer environment in which to build their business and practice their craft. Clients will achieve breakthrough gains in performance that are sustainable and meaningful.

If you are inspired by this vision, I invite you to join in the

Gennova Group Barn-Raising

Wednesday, July 10
12–4:30 pm

Bentley College, Waltham, MA.

There will be no charge for attending the event and you will not be required to make any formal commitment.

Like any good barn-raising, we will start the afternoon with a healthy lunch…

Figure 5.2
Invitation to a network "barn-raising"

Openness

In Chapter 4, I used the word "open" in the context of the texture of the network. That is, a network is closed if there is little or no interaction with members outside the network. A cloistered monastery is a closed network, as is a focused work team concentrating on a specific deliverable under a tight time frame. A network that is open is one that has bridges to many other networks and access to outside expertise and *actively* uses the connections made possible by those bridges. A research network with a strong core and large periphery is an example of a structure that is open.

Open-source software networks use the distributed talent of hundreds of people worldwide to contribute to the development of complex software platforms and applications. The software is owned by no one and by everyone who uses it.

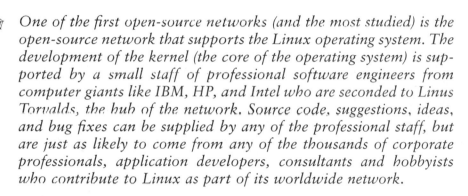

One of the first open-source networks (and the most studied) is the open-source network that supports the Linux operating system. The development of the kernel (the core of the operating system) is supported by a small staff of professional software engineers from computer giants like IBM, HP, and Intel who are seconded to Linus Torvalds, the hub of the network. Source code, suggestions, ideas, and bug fixes can be supplied by any of the professional staff, but are just as likely to come from any of the thousands of corporate professionals, application developers, consultants and hobbyists who contribute to Linux as part of its worldwide network.

An open network has broad criteria for membership. Open-source software networks, like the Linux community, don't bar anyone from peripheral learning or from contributing, but do have a peer approval process that validates the quality of code that is submitted.

A network with a core value of openness will apply the criteria for membership evenly, and will also actively encourage its members to develop connections outside the network. In a large corporation, the extent to which employees are encouraged to work across corporate business lines and functional boundaries provides insights into its openness to collaboration. Similarly, an open company provides support for employees and staff to attend conferences and symposiums to learn about and bring back new ideas and connections with people from academia and other companies (even competitors).

Diversity

Diversity is the extent to which the network welcomes, acknowledges, or leverages people of diverse ethnic groups, genders, political and religious views, levels of experience and expertise in a given subject matter, and personal affective style. "The more diverse a network, the greater its ability to respond to change," says the Law of Requisite Variety[6] as it has developed as part of the theory of complex adaptive systems. In an environment where numerous social, political, economic, and geographic disturbances can interrupt the routine, value-producing activities of a network, the network is more likely to succeed if, within it, there is a diversity of talents, experience, perspectives, resources, and tools.

Diversity is not just a matter of the inventory of the intellectual and social assets inside a network—it's also a matter of the diversity of outside networks to which individuals in *this* network are connected. Mark Granovetter's research on "the strength of weak ties" demonstrated the importance of external networks. He looked at the success with which people who were looking for jobs were able to find opportunities. People who circulated their resumes or talked to people in their own personal networks were less successful at finding jobs than people who reached outside of their personal networks and called people that they knew less well (the "weak ties").[7]

Recent (2005) research at Northwestern's Kellogg School of Management looked at the importance of just two aspects of diversity in the success of teams. Brian Uzzi from the School of Management teamed with Luis Amaral from the Department of Chemical and Biological Engineering. They looked at coauthored publications in four fields of the sciences and at the teams that produced Broadway musicals. They found that the most successful teams (measured by publication in prestigious journals and box office receipts, respectively) were those that included people experienced in their discipline who had not previously worked together.[8] This research partnership occurred through the Northwestern Institute on Complex Systems (NICO), which was created to bring scientists together for collaborative path-breaking research in the area of complexity science using an interdisciplinary perspective.

Diversity is not just a matter of individuals' aptitudes, skills, and expertise; it's also the cross-connection among businesses, and academic and public institutions. For instance, government-funded research in the United States and in the European Union increasingly requires that grant proposals reflect diversity among researchers. A study by the National Academies of sciences, engineering and medicine established a set of recommendations urging policy changes to promote interdisciplinary research.[9] For universities like Northwestern, as mentioned above, and Stanford, which established its Bio-X program of interdisciplinary research in 1998, this has become common practice.

Local, national, and business development agencies also leverage a diversity approach in creating new collaborations to spur regional growth. The Scottish Enterprise, responsible for the economic growth of Scotland, is an agency that is using networks in a variety of ways. One of its largest development projects includes a collaboration with one of the world's largest pharmaceutical companies, Wyeth, in a deal worth almost £50 million to create the world's first Translational Medicine Research Collaboration. The network includes partners in each of Scotland's leading universities (Aberdeen, Dundee, Edinburgh, and Glasgow) and four of Scotland's regional National Health Services groups. A collaborative effort of research, drug development, and practitioners will provide diverse resources and perspectives necessary to create innovative results in the field of personalized medicine.[10]

Transparency

Innovation and discovery across disciplines are not possible without the property of transparency. A fully transparent network is visible to all: Its artifacts are public, its decisions (including those on the topics of purpose and value) are taken in plain sight of and with the participation of the whole network, and the boundary between leadership and membership is permeable. In a transparent environment, communications are widely distributed, and designations of secrecy are confined to those areas of personnel sensitivity, legal transactions in process, and national or corporate security.

The three properties of openness, diversity, and transparency complement each other, as shown in Figure 5.3.

Innovation and problem solving across disciplines, functional lines, or research centers don't happen in closed networks where the same people work together all the time. The more diverse the network, the more potential it has for being open to other, outside networks. If problems under research are not publicized, it's not possible to field a diverse team to solve it. And so on.

There is no "right" formula for the mixture of these properties. Networks sometimes must be closed, for example, to accomplish

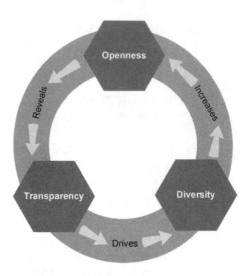

Figure 5.3
Core values of a network

critical tasks that require the combined deep collaborative concentration of a group of people. Certainly, an executive team that is committed to transparent communications across the company will need to hold close its legal transactions in case of mergers, acquisitions, or lawsuits. But in these cases, the criteria by which information is restricted are clear: You know that you can't know some things, and you know and accept why you can't know them.

Norms

Cultural norms consist of expectations about how people will behave in various situations. One set of norms is based on how well the members of a network enact and live up to their core values. For example, given a core value of transparency, one expects that leaders will communicate broadly and freely; given a core value of openness, one expects that new potential members will be welcome to join the network; and so on. There are also specific norms that are foundational: commitment to the collective, reciprocity, and trust.

Commitment to the collective

In all types of networks, there is tension between what's good for the network, that is, what supports both its purpose and its existence, and what's good for the individual members.

In a mission network, for example, those who join will be very clear in themselves about their commitment to the shared purpose of the network, whether it is to provide basic needs of food, shelter, and medical care in regions suffering drought or political upheaval; to influence policy to protect the environment; or to sustain democracy through a youth services corps. Participating, serving, and contributing to the social good provides the individual with a sense of well-being. This commitment shows up in other types of network as well. For example, Linux 🕸 open-source network programmers share an intense commitment to a network that does not pay except in reputation; over half the respondents in an 800-user survey said that their open-source work is the most valuable and creative endeavor in their professional lives.[11]

The commitment is qualified in business networks: Networks produce sustainable value only when all members of the network are committed to a higher purpose—as long as that higher purpose returns benefits to each of the participants. The idea embodied here was the heart of the good intentions of the early 1990s activities in concurrent engineering, the task forces of total quality management, and reengineering. Properly chartered and managed, such cross-organizational work in a large corporation can elicit selfless and nonparochial behavior on the part of members.

Commitment to the collective sometimes requires subsuming a parochial goal, but most importantly, it is also a commitment to building and sustaining relationships as a core obligation of the work.[12] NEHI 🕸, the New England Healthcare Institute, vets its membership carefully to ensure that members "leave their corporate hats at the door." Members joined the network in the belief that as a network they could accomplish more for the benefit of patients in the healthcare system than they could accomplish individually.

Reciprocity

Reciprocity is a person-to-person norm: If I share something with you, I expect you to share something of equivalent value with me (now or in the future). Reciprocity is an expectation that underlies many of the transactions between individuals. Reciprocity may be a specific norm about how two people support each other by providing time and or resources back and forth, but it may be a "generalized" reciprocity in which everyone in the network gives freely to others, knowing they will be recipients as often as givers.

Especially important in the domain of generalized reciprocity is the practice of acknowledgement. Online reputation systems, such as those on eBay, rely on the accumulation of acknowledgment for having provided a service well. Some knowledge management systems also provide a rating capability so that people who have had a positive experience can acknowledge the people who helped them. But technology can only track so much, and it can be gamed. Nothing substitutes for personal "thank you's" and public acknowledgments when members of a network go out of their way and beyond the call of service to help others.

Trust

The extent to which members of a network are able to freely seek and share information, ideas, and insights is based on the level of their trust. In a network with high social capital, there is a generalized potential for "trust by proxy." That is, by trusting that the network is organized to reinforce the core values, members tend to trust without evidence all those in the network. Of course it doesn't always work this way, and additional person-by-person trust building must occur.

It's important to distinguish between two different types of trust:

- *Competence-based trust*: "I trust you know what you are talking about."
- *Benevolence-based trust*: "I trust you will act without malice and help me the best you can."

Research in social networks has shown that the key attributes that impact a knowledge seeker's trust of a potential knowledge source are having a common language and common vision, as well as the perceived integrity of the source. For interactions in which the knowledge seeker may be vulnerable in some way (e.g., having to admit to not knowing something), two additional attributes are required: The knowledge source must be perceived to be a good listener, and there must be a strong existing tie based on affiliation, frequency of contact, or other relational factor.[13]

In the development of a network, trust is the factor that takes perhaps the longest to build and is the one that can be destroyed with a single act. Violation of trust—or any of the network's norms— can be managed well only in an environment rich in social capital.

Social Capital: The Sum of the Bonds

Social capital is the sum of the bonds among people in a network and the behaviors that are expected, allowed, and enabled by how people meet, greet, interact with, and otherwise express their shared identity with others. Consider the social capital available to those of us who attended a meeting after receiving the invitation to Gennova's ✿ barn-raising (Figure 5.2). The invitation stated the principles of the network, it acknowledged the unique and individual talents of each person invited, and it held the promise that the design of the future of the network would be in the hands of the network, not in a single person or persons. In short, it outlined the cultural values Bonchek wanted the network to have, and provided an identity that can be shared and leveraged both inside and outside the network.

Culture is enacted in the hallways of buildings, in the conference centers, hotels, and restaurants where networks meet, and in the words, phrases, and symbols that show up in online communities. These reflect both the culture on which a network was built and the culture it has personalized over time. Some enterprises use site visits as a way to either assess or present culture, letting visitors experience the way that members treat each other, the flow of conversation, the focus toward purpose. City Year ✿, for example, hosts site visits to groups from cities who are interested in setting up local City Year organizations. During the visit, they see the work in action and are able to observe the tasks and interactions, the culture of City Year at work.

In personal networks, the sociological notion of *affect*—whether or not people like each other—is one of the most important elements in social capital. That is why we stay in networks of people who are most like us in terms of personal support. The WIN 🏵 network offered many women the opportunity to meet others who shared similar work and family situations. One woman joined WIN shortly after moving to Massachusetts (the locus for WIN meetings). Today, she says that her personal network of friends is almost entirely composed of women she met at WIN.

Good social capital implies the bonds of shared interests that have been strengthened through shared experience, as well as making connecting more natural. Many people think that they have to be born or raised with a specific set of traits to be a "good networker," but this is definitely not the case. Being in a network nurtures people's own networking skills. Another woman who joined WIN and later became its president said, "I really didn't think of myself as a 'networker.' I didn't think I could do it." What helped her, of course, was WIN's top-of-the-agenda check-in at every meeting, the opportunity for a member (any woman who shows up is a member) to introduce herself, her current work/life situation, and request or offer support to the network.

INTERACTIONS

Conversations are the main work of the knowledge economy; speaking and listening, writing and reading are the primary tools we have. Our brains are amazing analytic engines, but what we understand and learn decreases in value if we keep it to ourselves. The change in the nature of work over the past four decades has interested a number of scholars. Recently, research at McKinsey & Company[14] examined three types of economic activity—transformational, transactional, and tacit—to develop models showing the shift in work across industries from the production and exchange of goods and services to more complex forms of knowledge work. Monitor Networks included the social component described above as one of their three interaction types: economic, informational, and emotional.[15]

Both of these models make a primary distinction that is familiar to anyone who has read about or practiced knowledge management: the distinction between "explicit" and "tacit." The explicit exchanges are all those that we can observe, touch, count, map, reproduce, write down as repeatable instructions, broadcast, distribute, archive, and use for tangible transactions in any number of other ways. Tacit exchanges are those that occur between individuals and groups in the conversations that elicit interpretations, syntheses, relationship, hunches, and ideas that have not been or cannot be articulated except through experience, dialogue, and reflection.

I differentiate three primary modes of interaction: transactional, knowledge-based, and personal, or relational.

Transactional Interactions

Task-based work can be measured in terms of transactions. In our shopping lives, we make transactions every day by exchanging money for goods and services. If we make a phone call, we've completed a transaction for a resource but we've also accomplished a task. We create and manage our own tasks daily, with or without "to do" lists, criteria for prioritization, and a map of the supply chain needed to accomplish it.

When we work with others in any form of network, we perform tasks in service of the network's purpose (our business, our mission, our practice), and we also perform tasks in service of the survival of the network.

Task management at either level can be managed mechanistically. We can make a clear and unambiguous request for any type of resource—information exchange, the use of someone's time, or the use of someone's brain to produce an analysis, document, or database. The person we ask can respond by accepting, declining, or renegotiating. The person either completes or does not complete the task, and (we hope) notifies us of when and whether the task is complete and its result. Between two people, it's pretty easy, but as networks grow larger and larger, the coordination of tasks and transactions requires infrastructure in terms of people, processes, and technologies.

We understand this task-based aspect of work. It led to the 19th- and 20th-century model of scientific management that is now being called into question, especially as it's been found that knowledge workers do not respond well to command and control. As we have shifted into the 21st century, it is this knowledge-based aspect of work that is up-ending so many models of management and organization design and leading us to networked, relational organizational forms.

Transactional interactions are not necessarily confined to hierarchical processes. One of the largest networks in the world consists of the 10 million-plus people who participate monthly in craigslist.org, the Internet marketplace that provides job listings, classified ads, housing rentals, and other services for urban centers around the globe. The community of craigslist users expanded beyond the transactional postings to discussion forums that encouraged reaching out for personal knowledge networking.

Knowledge-Based Interactions

Knowledge-based interactions occur only in the context of the moment, the point at which someone with a particular mix of expertise, skills, and experience generates a thought, a question, a response to a question, or the solution to a problem. These tacit interactions require the skills of language and conversation, for it is through knowledge-based interactions that breakthroughs—innovations—occur.

As mentioned in Chapter 4, the network form of organization is generally considered the best-suited for knowledge work, particularly given a positive mixture of openness, diversity, and transparency. The more open the pattern of connections and the more receptive the individuals in the network are to using those connections and creating new ones, the more serendipitous encounters are likely to occur along with the daily transactions.

Personal Interactions

People choose to join networks because of the emotional satisfaction that comes from affiliation with others and a passion to make a difference. In personal and mission-oriented networks, heart—the personal emotional attachment to the work of the network—comes from the shared passion. Similarly, in idea and learning networks, where membership is self-selected, the work can be deeply personal.

Even in an online setting, networks work best when there is an emotional commitment to a shared purpose. The Linux 🐧 open-source network, for example, is sustained by the recognition that programmers receive for contributing to the code base and by the exhilaration of collaborative problem solving.

Many networks extend specifically to members' spouses and families in a way that provides an additional bonding element to the network. For example, the Young Presidents' Association ✦ sponsors large member events ("YPO Universities") that provide intellectual stimulation and an opportunity to connect and develop personal networks. These events always include spouses.

Other networks let the emotional side grow as a natural function of the interactions among people and the revelations of personal life. Dialogue in particular is one method of interaction in networks that enables people to be fully themselves and to bring their personal context into a check-in or round of introductions.

Developing emotional ties in online networks is not easy, but it's not impossible, either. Over time, people display different parts of themselves through their use of language and humor, their readiness to acknowledge the contributions of others and their own faults, and in the spirit of helpfulness they display to others' requests for help solving problems.

Integrating Interaction Styles

We are all a mix of task, knowledge, and emotion. Over time, networks evolve a style or mode of interaction that sometimes may appear casual, other times rigorous, sometimes personal, and at other times formal. The style of a network—and its ability to accomplish its purpose—is shown not just in the extent to which interactions of one kind or another predominate, but in the ability of its members to know which style of interaction to use at what time.

Balancing knowledge work with task-based work requires that one be able to distinguish between the two and manage the network's activities appropriately. For example, a meeting may require both task-based and knowledge-based conversations. Knowledge work—brainstorming, problem solving, responding to complex external events—requires a different kind of pace, space, and place than task-oriented activities. It can be very important to understand an organization's overall style with respect to its bias for one type of interaction over another.

I once worked on an HR community of practice project in a financial services firm; my client was an organizational excellence leader who was charged with implementing communities of practice. The culture of the firm was strongly action-oriented with a high focus on transactions, task coordination, and measurement. In fact, the communities of practice received executive support only when the COP leader assured management that the communities would actually produce companywide guidelines and other artifacts that would be continuously maintained and updated as part of the "practice" activity.

A meeting schedule was set to establish relatedness among the HR staff selected to participate and to allow them time for reflective inquiry into how specific HR processes—succession planning, performance appraisals, workforce planning—could be improved if they worked in the context of a community of practice. The first meetings of these COPs, I later heard, were very painful. Spending time "in dialogue" was not in the culture! They wanted to know exactly what they were to do (tasks and transactions) and didn't expect to be put in a situation where they might have to admit that they didn't know something. It took over a year before these networks started to become productive; their eventual success was thanks to the cultural savvy of the COP program director, who quickly shifted the balance of work in these COPs to a blend of transaction and knowledge.

Emergence comes from spending some time at the edge of chaos, where there is always some discomfort. Becoming a network is often about learning to think in a new way, to expand beyond one's comfort zone so as to connect with people at all levels—the transactional, knowledge-based, and even the emotional. Gennova spent over a year grappling with its core purpose as conversations spilled from transactional to knowledge-based and personal. Coming through the discomfort of this time provided a shared experience and shared history, which created strong social capital. It also enabled Gennova members to understand that a criteria for inviting new members was to be sure that they were people who could be comfortable with ambiguity!

A network that designs for such occurrences— time for random, divergent interactions to allow its next stage to appear—is a network whose style is innovative and entrepreneurial, capable of responding rapidly to changes in its environment. This leads us to the discussion of the fourth element of style, orientation.

ORIENTATION

A network focused on outcome designs its infrastructure, place, space, and pace toward production. Habitat for Humanity is focused on building homes; a car manufacturer builds quality vehicles for families; a community of practice enhances the knowledge in its field and the reputations of practitioners; research partners bring successful innovative and attractive products to the marketplace.

A network focused on discovery and learning might look very different than one focused on outcome. Drug discovery requires scientists to open multiple channels of research and follow reams of data until a match occurs. A diner waitress attending an AA meeting listens to a corporate attorney talk about his addiction and discovers a truth about herself; a researcher messes up a batch of glue and discovers Post-It Notes. That is to say, discovery is about being open to the unexpected even while driving to specific outcomes.

While the interactions in a network are a blend of the transactional, knowledge-based, and relational, the orientation of these interactions should also be a balance of outcome and discovery. It's not a matter of a "right" orientation, but a matter of making that orientation visible so the network can decide if it's balanced appropriately for the purpose of the network. Who decides? What is the role of network leadership in balancing this matter of orientation, or any of the other elements of style?

LEADERSHIP

Leadership is both top-down and bottom-up in a network, no matter how small or informal. Figure 5.1, at the beginning of this chapter, illustrates the leadership element of style as an integrating, hovering unit that works up and down and across the elements of interaction, orientation, locus, and culture to ensure that the members of the network can work in harmony.

Expectations of Leaders

The capabilities required for network leaders vary, depending on the size and type of the network. In traditional business networks and large nonprofits, the CEOs and presidents perform traditional managerial tasks to coordinate the work of the organization. But network leaders place a greater emphasis on capabilities for sustaining networks:

- Holding the collective vision;
- Creating and managing relationships;
- Managing collaborative processes.

The style—the look and feel, rhythm, purposefulness, social capital—in a network reflect the personal qualities and style of its leadership. We want our leaders to be smart and confident (without being arrogant). We expect them to exercise their intelligence in the mutually generative processes of listening and learning. These processes both require and instill the qualities of flexibility and a tolerance for ambiguity; the knowledge that emerges from them enhances the leader's key roles of communicator, connector, conversation creator, and coach. The skills of listening, networking, facilitation, and empowerment of others can, and must, lead to a style of shared leadership.

Holding the vision

Most networks begin with an idea in the mind of one person or a small number of people. This vision is an attractor that can draw diverse members who share that vision or some particular theme within it that resonates with them. To shape this vision into a shared articulated purpose requires leadership that is not invested in ownership. Traditional management texts provide leaders with advice about how to share "their" vision, but network leaders provide the environment in which the vision is created from the network itself. Paul Skidmore, in an insightful short article called "Leading Between," says that good network leaders start from the outside and provide the structure in which a vision can emerge:

Network leaders know that they cannot provide some definitive vision statement; but they can structure the right kind of conversation, create a language that enables people to cross boundaries that they otherwise would not.[16]

The network itself has a collective mind that can create and hold a vision, if the leader can create the space for it to be articulated.

Creating and managing relationships

Network building is an initial and ongoing activity throughout the life of a network. The initial "weaving" of the network as described in Chapter 4 must be supplemented by an ongoing commitment to sensing the network of relationships at many levels:

- The personal network of the leader(s), and the ways in which that personal network supports the cohesiveness and collaborative capacity of the network;
- The patterns of relationships among the members of the network that contribute to its texture;
- The relationship of the network itself to others in its eco-system.

Each relationship will have some combination of interaction styles, depending on the immediate and long-term needs of the network.

Inside businesses and in the world of nonprofits, there is a path in the network that leads to either the funders (in the case of the latter) or to the holder of the budget. At the end of the day, a network needs to be accountable to those who have invested corporate, foundational, or personal treasure in the network's purpose. Leaders in structures of all kinds manage these relationships, usually through transactional activities of reporting and being reviewed.

However, leaders must also communicate the value of discovery-based activities, and manage a funder's expectations. A study of NGO networks, for example, examined this issue to develop a set of emerging best practices. The authors noted that "donors need to let go of their customary results orientation when they support networks. . . . [and] rather trust that the network will do its job."[17] At the same time, they acknowledged the role of network leaders in managing all stakeholders' expectations using personal, relational skills to develop trust and rapport.

Creating and sustaining relationships are the heartbeats of the leader's work; they require attention to purpose, structure, value, as well as style, and lead to the "leader's net work," the topic of Chapter 10. For now, let's look at the role of the leader in setting the style for collaborative processes.

Managing collaborative processes

Network leaders are the hubs, brokers, gatekeepers, and pulse-takers of the organization. They need to be able to both generate and facilitate conversations that matter, conversations that involve the network constituencies, including its members and its network of stakeholders.

Networks are not entirely democratic, but participation in a network is largely voluntary. "In the knowledge economy," as Peter Drucker said, "everyone is a volunteer." He went on to say, "But we train our managers to manage conscripts."[18] This does not work in a society where we can (and often do) vote with our feet. As networks evolve and we learn to work in them, everything needs to be shared: it's more sensible for people to learn to "exercise voice rather than exit."[19]

Collaborative processes enable people to exercise their voices. These processes include visioning, strategy, design, and decision making in addition to the management of the network itself.

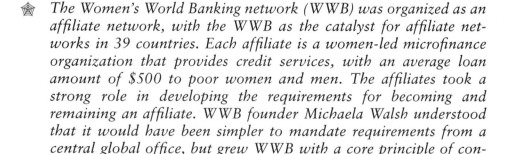

The Women's World Banking network (WWB) was organized as an affiliate network, with the WWB as the catalyst for affiliate networks in 39 countries. Each affiliate is a women-led microfinance organization that provides credit services, with an average loan amount of $500 to poor women and men. The affiliates took a strong role in developing the requirements for becoming and remaining an affiliate. WWB founder Michaela Walsh understood that it would have been simpler to mandate requirements from a central global office, but grew WWB with a core principle of consensus decision making.

Decisions that set the overall strategy for a large network may require more facilitated processes. Whole-system methods that enable large groups to build shared vision, design strategies, and get into action are becoming more and more common: Future search, open space, and the world café are but a few mature methodologies that have developed over the past twenty years. Chapter 9 describes these methods in more detail. The use of such collaborative methods is a vital clue to the leadership of a network, in particular to the ability of a leader to let the network self-organize.

Letting Go

The most difficult task for network leadership is to let the network manage itself. As Peter Block put it in his 1993 book: "Stewardship . . . is the willingness to be accountable for the well-being of the larger organization by operating in service, rather than in control, of those around us. Stated simply, it is accountability without control or compliance."[20] This sense of stewardship is the most important quality in a network leader. Good stewards of a network's purpose will put their personal goals and often the growth goals of a network aside to support the larger mission of the network as a whole.

 The British nonprofit Guide Dogs for the Blind Association (GDBA) was founded in 1931 to breed, train, and place guide dogs with visually impaired people. As the organization focused on growth, it added services that supported the visually impaired in other ways. This included purchasing and managing hotels and travel services that were specifically designed to accommodate this segment of the population, ultimately positioning GDBA as a provider of "mobility services." This extension of the nonprofit's initial mission had begun causing financial stress when the board hired Geraldine Peacock to join the organization in 1997. Peacock led the nonprofit through a series of partnerships that divested GDBA of the hotels and travel enterprises, and she began to pilot the idea of developing agreements with local authorities for GDBA to manage their budgets for support of the visually impaired. Meanwhile, Peacock and Stephen Remington, chief executive of Action for Blind People, started working with two umbrella groups that had begun to foster collaboration among the many organizations working with the

*blind in the United Kingdom. In 2001, their efforts culminated in a
seminar that led to the foundation of Vision 2020 UK, a network
of voluntary organizations providing services to the blind. Under
Peacock's leadership, GDBA traded growth for service: Through
Vision 2020 UK, a much wider range of services is available
throughout the United Kingdom. GDBA celebrated its 75th year in
2006.[21]*

Management training focuses on creating growth for an organization. Consider the courage needed to reduce a network's size so as
to better serve its purpose. In the business world, this comes about
through outsourcing, establishing networks of trading partners, go-
to-market solutions alliances, and so on.

Inside the organization, the goal of network leadership should be
to create more leaders. By providing employees with opportunities
to work with good network leaders in collaborative projects and
initiatives, the organization—network of any type—fosters the environment in which new leaders emerge, as illustrated in Figure 5.4.

"Leadership develops over time," suggests an article from MIT's
Sloan School of Management.[22] What I've seen over time is that
leaders are learning to share their role. As the same article says,
"[l]eadership is distributed," that is, "leadership is not solely the

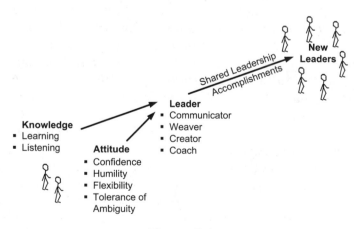

Figure 5.4
Leadership qualities create new leaders

purview of the CEO, but can and should permeate all levels of the firm."

In a network organization, it is possible and desirable to shift decision making as close as possible to the source of the problem or opportunity. For nonprofits, this represents the pressure to push the work to the point of delivery of services. In a business, it's called being customercentric. In military organizations, this is called net-workcentric warfare or network-enabled command and control. This is the essence of "net centricity." Strategic, large-scale decisions still are taken and direction is provided from a core command or leader-ship team; information technology—and good conversational prac-tices—make it possible to provide both information and context to the person at the decision point.

Shared leadership

 The governance structure for the Women's World Banking network included a core global team whose work included advising the affili-ate lending organizations that provided microloans to poor women in underdeveloped parts of the world. As the visibility of the WWB's work increased, its staff and especially its leader, Nancy Barry, became engaged in policy advocacy and network expansion. At a global meeting in 1996, the affiliate leaders recommended a shift in priorities for the work of the global staff because they felt the global team was not spending enough time serving the affiliates. A deep process of introspection with pro bono consulting from the Monitor Group led to the realization that Barry had become too much like a CEO of a large company "who [has] a mastery over many areas and [wants] to control everything."[23] From that process, Barry began to build a more cohesive and larger global team that could in fact meet the needs of the affiliates, while at the same time using the networks to mobilize knowledge being created in the affiliates them-selves. The participative process of redesigning WWB and the result-ing vibrant networks assured the continued success of the WWB.

The Orpheus Chamber Orchestra actually has no leader at all. Musicians in this network move freely in and out of leadership roles, taking responsibility for individual practices or performances, team leadership, or leading one of the orchestra's many different and informal teams. One of the core principles on which this small orchestra (approximately 28 people) operates is to "share and rotate leadership."[24] The result is an artistic collaboration that produces superb performances based on a shared passion and individual commitment to the whole. This model has been so successful, in fact, that the orchestra provides seminars to business, government, and nonprofit community networks on its shared leadership model.[25]

Executive councils, boards, and other structures have evolved to have a network leadership component, while providing a training ground for new leaders. The Women in Networking (WIN) ⬟ model illustrates this pattern. The network has always been led by a small core group. Each year, the president is selected from within this core group (some presidents serve for many years in that role). The annual planning meeting is open to anyone who wants to attend; those who attend and volunteer to take on network tasks become members of the core group. As new members come into the network and attend the monthly meetings, they feel the sense of collective leadership that permeates the network. When they are ready to take on a leadership role, when they see the possibility of shaping the experience, or when they have something they know they can contribute, they begin attending planning meetings. This is how WIN nurtures new leadership. The group of women who are current and past leaders strengthens the core group. The style of this small, personally motivated network remains inclusive, welcoming, and self-organizing, while providing a platform for new leadership and expanding the network's value.

NOTES

1. Frank Duffy, Author's notes from Multiples x 1 Conference, November 2003.
2. Brian Gorman, Author's notes from Systems Integrators and Knowledge Management Leader's teleconference, August 2006.
3. Ram Charan, "Home Depot's Blueprint for Culture Change," *Harvard Business Review* 84, no. 2 (2004): 60–70.
4. Mark Bonchek, Conversation with the author, June 2006.
5. John Smith, e-mail to the author, July 2006.
6. Attributed to W. Ross Ashby, a pioneer in the study of cybernetics and complex adaptive systems.
7. Mark Granovetter, "The Strength of Weak Ties," American Journal of Sociology, Volume 78, Issue 6 (May, 1973), 1360–1380.

8. Megan Fellman, "Dream Teams Thrive on Mix of Old and New Blood" (press release, Northwestern University, April 29, 2005).

9. Committee on Facilitating Interdisciplinary Research, National Academy of Sciences, National Academy of Engineering, and Institute of Medicine, *Facilitating Interdisciplinary Research* (Washington, DC: National Academies Press, 2005).

10. Stephen Sharp, "Scotland Leads Way in Pioneering Approach to Developing New Medicines," *Scottish Enterprise*, April 3, 2006, www .Scottish-enterprise.com.

11. Phillip Evans and Bob Wolf. "Collaboration Rules," *Harvard Business Review* 83, no. 7 (2005).

12. Charles Heckscher, and Paul S. Adler. *The Firm as a Collaborative Community: The Reconstruction of Trust in the Knowledge Economy* (New York: Oxford University Press, 2006).

13. D.Z. Levin, R. Cross, L.C. Abrams, and E.L. Lesser, "Trust and Knowledge Sharing: A Critical Combination," in *Creating Value with Knowledge: Insights from the IBM Institute for Business Value*, ed. L. Prusak and E.L. Lesser (Oxford: Oxford University Press, 2003).

14. Bradford C. Johnson, James M, Manyika, and Lareina A. Yee, "The Next Revolution in Interactions," *McKinsey Quarterly* 4 (2005), www .mckinseyquarterly.com.

15. Monitor Networks, www.themonitornetworks.com/.

16. Paul Skidmore, "Leading Between: Leadership and Trust in a Network Society," in *The Democratic Papers*, ed. P. Hilder (London: British Council, 2004).

17. Claudia Liebler and Marisa Ferri, "NGO Networks: Building Capacity in a Changing World," Study supported by Bureau for Democracy, Conflict and Humanitarian Assistance Office of Private and Voluntary Contribution (PVC), USAID.

18. Dave Snowden's notes from a talk by Peter Drucker at the 1st International Conference on Knowledge Management, 1998.

19. Walter W. Powell, "Neither Market nor Hierarchy: Network Forms of Organization," in *Research in Organizational Behavior*, vol. 12 (Greenwich, CT: JAI Press, 1990).

20. Peter Block, *Stewardship* (San Francisco, CA: Berret-Kochler, 1993).

21. Allen Grossman, Jane Wei-Skillern, and Kristin J. Lieb, "Guide Dogs for the Blind Association" (Harvard Business School case study 9-302-084, November 2002).

22. Deborah Ancona, "Leadership in an Age of Uncertainty," M.I.T., *Center for eBusiness Research Brief*, January 2005.

23. Susan Harmeling and James E. Austin, "Women's World Banking: Catalytic Change through Networks" (Harvard Business School case study 9-300-050, 1999).
24. Harvey Seifter, "The Conductor-less Orchestra," *Leader to Leader* 21 (Summer 2001): 38–44.
25. Orpheus Chamber Orchestra, www.orpheusnyc.com/process.html.

Chapter 6

NETWORKS AND VALUE CREATION

This book starts with a bias that networks are good. I've also worked from the principles that all networks have a purpose and that these purposes can be classified within five types: personal, idea, learning, business, and mission. The corollary principle "All networks produce value" raises the questions:

- What is the value?
- Who receives the value?
- How does the value flow?
- When does the value show up?

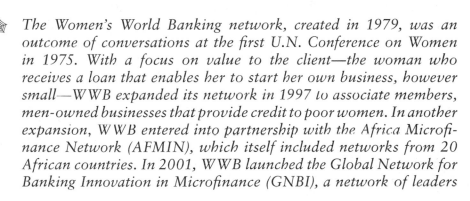 *The Women's World Banking network, created in 1979, was an outcome of conversations at the first U.N. Conference on Women in 1975. With a focus on value to the client—the woman who receives a loan that enables her to start her own business, however small—WWB expanded its network in 1997 to associate members, men-owned businesses that provide credit to poor women. In another expansion, WWB entered into partnership with the Africa Microfinance Network (AFMIN), which itself included networks from 20 African countries. In 2001, WWB launched the Global Network for Banking Innovation in Microfinance (GNBI), a network of leaders*

of mainstream financial institutions committed to microfinance as a profitable business opportunity. WWB remains at the hub of this network that has in sum provided loans to 18 million people worth a total of US$18 billion.

Beyond the tangible impact on the economic health of the regions into which WWB's network spreads, WWB has also generated knowledge about microfinance. The staff of WWB in 1999 consisted of 24 office staff in New York City and 10 talent bank consultants. The Ford Foundation estimated that this was the largest concentration of microfinance expertise on Earth. Team members from over 20 countries, mostly 30 to 40 years old, embodied about 300 collective years of relevant experience. WWB has had an influential impact on the paradigms, policies, and performance standards of the microfinance industry and movement, globally and locally.

In March 2006, WWB kicked off a leadership training program at Wharton Business School to preserve and enhance the role of female leaders in microfinance. The program not only provided essential skills and case experience but also created a personal, practice network for the women who attended the program. It began with 24 rising microfinance female executives from 11 countries, including Colombia, Brazil, Russia, Uganda, Philippines, and Jordan, who convened for the initial five-day training.

What Is the Value?

Chapter 2 introduced the concept of interlinking types of capital—financial, intellectual, and social—along with the distinction between tangible and intangible. So when it comes to defining the "what" of the Who-What-How-When-Where equation of value creation by a network, it is time to look more closely at this distinction. In the WWB network, there are tangible flows of money (funding for WWB itself, grants for the regional microfinance institutions, loans from the microfinance institutions to the clients); knowledge that is codified into training, policy, and standards; operational guidelines; and communications. Intangibles flow across the stakeholder groups of funders, MFIs, clients, the microfinance industry, leaders, and local economies.

Verna Allee was among the participants of an idea network whose dialogue about tangible and intangible value launched the worldwide conversation about intellectual capital. Her 1997 book, *The Knowledge Evolution*,[1] was among the first to put the notions of tangible and intangible value into the perspective of the knowledge economy. She articulates the three sources of intangible value as coming from the three forms of intellectual capital introduced in Chapter 2: human, structural, and relational.

- *Human capital* is about what people in the organization know: the knowledge, skills, experience, and problem-solving capabilities of the individuals who work in and for the organization;
- *Structural capital* is about how the organization accomplishes its work: the internal procedures, processes, and internal organizational systems and structures that have evolved to enable the organization to meet its goals;
- *Relational capital* is about how an organization connects, inside and outside: the value of an organization's relationships and reputation with its customers, suppliers, employees, partners, the cities and countries in which it does business, and so on.

Linux 🐧 and other open-source software communities have an interesting tangible/intangible proposition. Source code itself is a tangible product that the network delivers to the Linux "kernel." Companies that use the code in their own products are receiving tangible value in the form of that source code. The intangible benefits include the enhancement of knowledge about a particular software domain, as well as the considerable benefit that this network has provided about what it means to work this way (structural capital). Individuals who participate in these networks receive no monetary or organizational reward. All the reward for contributors comes from the intangible values of recognition, acknowledgment, and reputation (social capital), as well as from their own enhanced skills and expertise (human capital).

The stated purpose of a network provides an attractor; members and potential partners are drawn to it based on how it articulates that purpose and who and what it serves. Open-source frameworks and standards organizations attract the participation of both individuals and software companies. Individuals participate because of the opportunity to enhance their reputation; companies participate because these networks have a significant influence on the industry.

SocialPhysics is an open collaborative project sponsored by a small company called Parity, Inc. The founders of SocialPhysics, John Clippinger, Paul Trevithick, and Mary Ruddy, started with an idea for a software framework called "Higgins" (after a species of long-tailed Tasmanian mouse) that would give individuals more control over their digital identities, in particular the ability to manage different identities or personas online and the extent to which their personal and relationship information was accessible to others. Through a series of conversations, the ideas behind SocialPhysics attracted the attention of a number of diverse partners. It first gained an affiliation with the Harvard Law School's Berkman Center for Internet & Society. The Eclipse open-source community soon became interested in the framework and offered to host the Higgins project. IBM and Novell felt it was critical to their business to participate in the development of Higgins and announced that they would contribute code to it in February 2006. In addition to Higgins, SocialPhysics initiated the "Identity Gang," an online community of over 300 individuals (as of 2006) and more than 60 companies. Through its wiki and mailing list, it supports an "ongoing conversation about what is needed for a user-centric identity "metasystem" that supports the whole marketplace, especially individuals."[2]

Ultimately, the work on Higgins will benefit all the members of the Identity Gang and the stakeholders of Socialphysics, but it could not produce value without the clarity of purpose that has attracted the best minds in the computer industry to solve an important problem.

The concepts behind the organization of the open-source groups are spreading beyond the bounds of software engineering to content, as evidenced by the extraordinary growth of Wikipedia.org and the use of Creative Commons licensing for content. The concepts are spreading to other spheres as well. Cambia, an international research institute, has developed BIOS (Biological Open Source) to share technologies for research as well as biological materials. (Wikipedia reports that the concept is also being used in the formulation of cola and beer products.[3])

Organizations using the cooperative governance framework and legal structure design their organizations using seven internationally recognized principles; five are related to governance itself. Two more are related specifically to value-producing activities that are outside the bounds of the goods or services the cooperative supports:

- Education, training, and information that enables them to work effectively in the cooperative organizational model (structural capital);
- Cooperation among cooperatives[4] (relationship capital).

Many organizations define themselves through the intangible value that they produce. City Year 🕸 , for example, offers year-long, full-time service opportunities for young people from all backgrounds while providing resources to local educational and cultural institutions: good, tangible value to the community. But City Year's mission statement defines its real value proposition to the social good:

City Year's mission is to **build democracy** *through* **citizen service, civic leadership** *and* **social entrepreneurship.**[5]

City Year is clearly focused on the outcome of a more democratic society; it has structured its program in the belief that an educated citizenry is the absolute prerequisite to democracy, and it assigns volunteers to civic organizations that provide services like after-school programs and tutoring for inner-city kids. Its work has considerable outputs that can be measured in terms of number of volunteers who have contributed a year of service, the number of local service organizations that have been helped, kids who participated in those after-school and tutoring programs, and so on. It may have the very intangible outcome of democracy in mind, but it produces very tangible outputs.

The desire to balance civic responsibility with business outputs is not an alien concept to business. The idea of the corporation as a benevolent force for social good has been around for a long time. As companies work to achieve their tangible financial goals, they are also paying attention to their roles in the communities and nations in which they operate.

Increasing intellectual capital and social capital underlie the importance that companies are beginning to attach to intangibles. Think of the traction that can come from a host of strategic initiatives that acknowledge the value of intangibles: human capital management (also called talent management), strategic alliance management, process improvement, customer relationship management, corporate social responsibility, and knowledge management.

Who Receives the Value?

Table 6.1 summarizes the five basic types of network and suggests a value focus for each as well as the intended beneficiaries of the value.

The WWB 🏛 story illustrates how a mission-focused network has, through its evolution, created value for a number of stakeholders:

- The original clients, poor women, benefit from small loans to start a business;
- The microfinance institutions that are part of the network increase their business viability, either individually or through groups like AFMIN or GNBI;

Table 6.1

Mapping the Network's Purpose to Beneficiaries

Purpose Type	Value	Intended Beneficiaries
Personal	Emotional, health, vocational or avocation-based support, growth and information	Individuals who participate in the network
Idea	Generative thinking for innovation, problem solving, or advocacy	The network generally; the intentional network creator
Learning	Continuous improvement and enhancement of personal or community knowledge	Participants in a discipline of knowledge or field of endeavor and the discipline itself
Business	Creation of tangible value and intellectual capital	Owners and shareholders
Mission	Societal or environmental change or improvement on the local, national, regional, or global scale	A target population

- The WWB staff gain knowledge, social capital, and influence;
- The microfinance industry grows in competencies and reach;
- Women executives in emerging economies develop professional competency through communities of practice;
- WWB's funders are rewarded by seeing their funding well spent;
- The local town or region in which loans are being granted diminish in poverty.

The extension of benefits to such a range of stakeholders during the evolution of a network is not unusual. All networks meet the needs of their members in addition to the beneficiaries of their core purpose; in the case of a personal network, the additional beneficiary may be the network itself (as in the case of YPO ⬠).

How Does Value Flow?

In her more recent book, *The Future of Knowledge*,[6] and in talks at many leading business seminars and conferences, Allee expands our understanding of intangibles with her concept of a value network, which she defines as "any web of relationships that generates economic or social value through complex dynamic exchanges of both tangible and intangible benefits." She also introduced the technique of value network analysis (VNA) to a wide audience. Her specific methodology, ValueNet Works, is practiced in organizations and businesses worldwide and has recently moved to an open-source model for practitioners to codevelop and enhance the method.

A value network approach takes a whole-system view of processes and the exchanges that occur among a network's stakeholders. The mapping process starts with a sketch of the core business model and goes on to show the relationships between tangible and intangible exchanges. Basically, a value network map is a map drawn by members of a network who identify value, both tangible and intangible, exchanged through interactions among network participants. The map provides a baseline of current activity in a network; the map is used (in the methodology) as the starting point to identify key leverage points for change in the network. Value network analysis can be used for internal networks, for example, in a company or department to understand its operational processes, and for external networks where the company looks at its relationships with partners in its extended network.

The relationship between an organization's value network and its supply chain is very similar to the network map of the informal networks and the formal organization structure. A supply chain map will show the outputs of the tangible goods and services from supplier to customer, but the process of creating the value network map will uncover the intangibles. Figure 6.1 sketches the value network that a nonprofit organization like WWB might look like.

In this figure, you can see the relationships among the beneficiaries of a nonprofit's value network. The key tangible types of value exchanged (solid lines) are:

- Funding ($$);
- Reports on activities;
- Guidance documents, templates, policies, standards, and so on;
- Services.

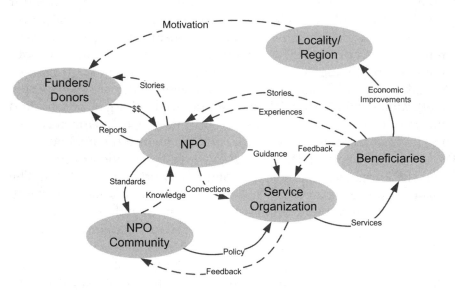

Figure 6.1
Value network for a nonprofit

Intangible value (dotted lines) include the goodwill provided to the donors, the feelings of self-confidence gained by learning about how to develop sustainable networks, and so on. In the WWB example, the individual beneficiaries receive loans that enable them to participate in their local economies. Along the way, WWB and its network of microfinance institutions continue to learn and share what they know about this emerging economic structure. Money flows from funders into WWB, which provides financial statements and summaries of activity in return. Funders are also encouraged by the success stories to continue to support work that improves the lives of poor women and also the local economies in which they live.

 Truman Company uses a similar approach in mapping how it helps clients develop executive-level networks. Truman Company specializes in executive-level marketing, strategy, and innovation. One of Truman Company's services is the creation and management of senior-level, executive networks for its clients. The starting point for the network is a need by the client to create executive-level relationships and market insight, then to leverage these insights and relationships internally to drive change and externally to establish thought leadership and enhance revenue growth.

As an example, Avaya, a $4 billion Fortune 500 telecommunications spin-off from Lucent Corporation, works with Truman Company to manage an Executive Advisory Council that comprises CIOs from some of the company's most important customers. Avaya's intent is to foster strategic relationships with these companies by sharing their thought leadership and innovation with this select network and in return to get advice and insight from "the voice of the customer."[7] Truman Company's model for structuring networks so that all stakeholders—the client sponsor, the executives from the participating companies, and the potential stakeholders in the marketplace—achieve desired value is shown in Figure 6.2.

Note that the tangible exchanges in Truman Company's model occur between the client sponsor and Truman. Truman Company's role in the network reveals the potential value of a third party to provide expertise as well as an external perspective in creating and managing the network.

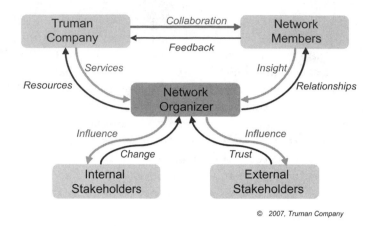

© 2007, Truman Company

Figure 6.2
Truman's value network approach
© Truman Company, Inc. Used by Permission.

When Does the Value Show Up?

A strong, transaction-oriented network looks to achieve value rapidly. For example, a network of fund raisers that generates a call to action in response to a natural disaster needs donations within days. A cross-functional task force may need to respond with recommendations to meet a market threat within a matter of weeks. A network of change agents committed to transforming an organization may know that it may be years before the work bears fruit. It's all a matter of perspective.

Networks also have a powerful latent value. An engineer who had retired from Hewlett-Packard recounted how he had wanted to reach back into the company for some advice when he came upon a potential product idea. When he called a former colleague, he was greeted warmly and able to tap into the expertise that he needed, quickly. We may leave personal networks behind when we go to new places, but that doesn't mean that they vanish.

Networks from service organizations can be very strong and accessible, particularly for those organizations that provided peak growth experiences for their members. City Year 🕸, for example, had been planning to launch a new site for its youth service organization in New Orleans, Louisiana when Hurricane Katrina hit in late summer of 2005. The City Year founders sent e-mail to the 3,000 registered alumni of their program asking if they would be "willing to put on their red jackets and rejoin the corps." Within a day, they had 100 responses and were able to start City Year New Orleans in January 2006, with 33 of those alumni building schools and running an after-school program for Katrina victims who had migrated to Baton Rouge.

Alumni offices from schools traditionally try to keep alumni networks active through fundraising campaigns, reunions, and alumni activities. Less-active alumni remain part of their latent pool of support to draw on in times of crisis. Similarly, businesses are beginning to see the value in their "alumni" corps of retirees as latent sources of intellectual capital. Some companies are initiating programs to bring in retirees as part-time consulting resources to fill the knowledge gaps not yet filled by a new generation of workers.

All networks appear to have some latent value, which may appear either directly or indirectly over time. We like our tangible investments returned quickly, but we must be patient for some of the intangibles to occur (like democracy).

MEASURING VALUE

Through these last three chapters, we have been building a language and set of models that enable us to characterize networks. Purpose, structure, and style all contribute to the "who, what, how, and when" of the value of the network. But how is value measured? In a business context, the return on investment (ROI) question always comes up, particularly when there is corporate investment involved (often in expensive collaboration software). It will take time before we see the shift from "How will we measure this network?" to "How will we leverage this network?" But in the meantime, I offer the simple answer: You measure the tangibles the old-fashioned way—counting, summing, collecting and analyzing data, and so on when accountability is required. Think about intangibles when you want to demonstrate the ability of a network to generate possibility and opportunity.

In a business or mission network, counting certain types of results is not difficult. City Year 🏛 knows how many projects have been staffed by its volunteers, how many cities it serves, and how many youths have participated as volunteers over its nearly 15-year history. City Year became the model for AmeriCorps, which by 2004 had had 330,000 volunteers: 75,000 people volunteer annually. A research project conducted that year showed that youths who had participated in AmeriCorps were significantly more likely to remain connected to their communities, participate in community-based activities, and fulfill neighborhood obligations.[8] The value to the students served in after-school programs and of the enhanced self-esteem of the volunteers? Intangible.

Similarly, the WWB knows exactly how many total credit clients it has reached through its affiliates, retail associates, and banks:

- Through the core affiliate network, loans have been provided to 847,027 people;
- Through AFMIN, WWB reaches 5.6 million people;
- Through retail GNBI, 9.5 million people.

For a total reach of over 18 million the majority of whom are women who benefit from a sense of independence and pride in becoming self-sufficient.

Measuring results using statistical measures like those shown in the AmeriCorps study and WWB's metrics helps a network sustain its momentum. But when goals are long-term and less distinctly measured, it may take time for results to appear. In networks formed by businesses to increase innovation (as in measures of new patents, new products brought to market, and so on), some results are only now beginning to show up.

Networks and partnerships have been very important to the growth of biotech and pharmaceutical companies. These partnerships provide young biotech companies with a proven drug testing and marketing infrastructure while the pharmaceutical firms get in early on new products. Wharton School of Business research in 2000 showed that such partnerships increased the probability that drugs would pass U.S. Food and Drug Administration approval by 30%.[9]

Procter & Gamble ⊛ began augmenting its internal, proprietary R&D groups by creating and participating in multiple external innovation networks in 2000. Innovations from networks outside of P&G

now account for 35% of new products that have been brought to market.

A June 2006 seminar at Bentley College in Waltham, Massachusetts brought together businesspeople from a spectrum of industries with academics and network practitioners to talk about the issues in building and sustaining networks. My notes from that seminar highlighted a number of areas where companies are looking to get tangible value from working in a network approach:[10]

- Increased market share;
- Time-to-market;
- Competitiveness;
- Net present value;
- Lost opportunity cost from not partnering.

Collaborating through networks is a business goal today; however, companies that declare strategic collaboration initiatives are learning that it takes time to collaborate. Time spent in developing relationships or working in networks to develop ideas and implement new practices is not always part of a person's "day job." For knowledge workers who allocate their time to projects and clients, there is no charge code for relationship or knowledge development. When it's time to demonstrate a return on investment for collaboration, many experienced knowledge managers use a chart similar to that shown in Table 6.2. Table 6.2 summarizes the value of community of practice work to key constituents, the individuals, the community itself, and the company.

The measurements that sustained the development of communities of practice in their early days were based, said KM guru Tom Davenport, on "serious anecdote management."[11] It did not take many stories—anecdotal evidence—about how communites of practice saved $2 million in rework for the COP approach to become relevant. ROI? Case (often) closed.

Today, knowledge management and network practitioners collect measures of time saved and improvement in quality as key ROI measures. In Chapter 2, we heard about Caterpillar's Knowledge Network ; that network has demonstrated returns between 200%–700% on its infrastructure costs.

Table 6.2
The Value of a Community of Practice

Type of Value	Individual	Group	Company
Tangible	Contributions to body of knowledge Acknowledgment (rewards, plaques) for contributions Improved productivity	Growth of knowledge base Process for maintaining standards and content Rapid diffusion of knowledge Improved performance	Consistent set of practices and procedures that enhance efficiency and effectiveness Identification of expertise and production of reusable artifacts Improved efficiency
Intangible	Relationships with other community members Deeper learning through dialogue and problem solving Experience of working in, leading, and/or facilitating communities Satisfaction with work	Influx of new ideas Higher quality Learning about managing communities Increased social capital	Improved effectiveness Improved capability of managers Organizational memory

Impact

Stories have become a part of the new language of networks and communities, and some of the richest stories demonstrate how networks expand the reach of their members. Consider that over time we see the ability of a network to extend beyond the bounds of its own design. Recall the WWB 🕸 example: By growing the organization into a network and expanding its model to include additional networks, WWB reached 18,000,000 clients. City Year's 🕸 model, extended to AmeriCorps, has put 330,000 volunteers in service to millions.

Some network visions start with an ambitious goal. P&G 🕸 , for example, created its innovation networks in the context of a corporate imperative to grow 4%–6% a year. For P&G, that can represent $4 billion a year. The impact of this web of networks reaches a broad list of stakeholders: ourselves, as consumers; the many small entrepreneurs who participate in the innovation networks; and P&G's entire corporate network, including its own R&D operations.

Few network initiatives are quite as large in scope, but network creation does require an openness and flexibility that address how the components of purpose, structure, and style can be combined to shape both the network's capacity to produce value and the value it produces. What it requires is a design perspective, which I introduce in Chapter 7.

Notes

1. Verna Allee, *The Knowledge Evolution: Expanding Organizational Intelligence* (Burlington, MA: Butterworth-Heinemann, 1997).
2. www.identitygang.org/.
3. en.wikipedia.org/wiki/Open_source.
4. From the National Cooperative Business Association, www.ncba .org/.
5. www.cityyear.org/about/who/mission.cfm.
6. Verna Allee, *The Future of Knowledge: Increasing Prosperity through Value Networks* (Burlington, MA: Butterworth-Heinemann, 2003).
7. Mark Bonchek and Robert Howard, "The Power to Convene," in *The Firm as a Collaborative Community: The Reconstruction of Trust in the Knowledge Economy,* ed. C. Heckscher and P.S. Adler (Oxford: Oxford University Press, 2006).
8. "AmeriCorps Longitudinal Study: Impacts of Service on Members" (issue brief, Corporation for National and Community Service, December 2004), www.americorps.org.
9. "The Benefits Are Mutual in New Wave of Biotech/Pharma Alliances," Knowledge@Wharton, March 13, 2002, knowledge.wharton.upenn .edu.
10. Author's notes from "Collaborative Networks are the Organization" (symposium in conjunction with The Rhythm of Business at Bentley College, Waltham, MA, June 2006).
11. Author's notes from presentation by Tom Davenport.

Chapter 7

NET WORK: DESIGN

The first part of this book introduced networks, their facets of purpose, structure, style, and value and described attributes of each facet. This chapter discusses the developmental tasks for creating sustainable networks. Chapter 8 looks at key network sense-making tools that provide insight into the relationships among network members and examines how those relationships affect the network's potential. Chapter 9 answers the "Now what?" question that follows a network examination: It summarizes and provides examples of methods that support changing, repairing, and revitalizing networks.

CREATION BY INTENT OR DISCOVERY

A network results from a conversation among individuals or groups (organizations) who see the potential for uniting in a common purpose to create value. The development of the network proceeds through adaptive stages during which its unique structure and style evolve. Figure 7.1 shows a common network growth model.

- The network may be convened intentionally by one or more constituents who have a clear purpose in mind. Or the potential for a network may be discovered when a shared interest or concern surfaces in a conversation.

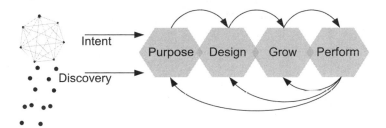

Figure 7.1
Growth model for networks

■ In the design phase, the activities are focused on defining the network's purpose, identifying stakeholders, and initiating or strengthening relationships. Organizational tasks include putting in place a structure and governance model, establishing norms for participation and setting up the network's pace and its presence in real place and virtual space.

■ During the growth phase, the network works to build its capabilities, including structural, human, and relational capital, creates connections, and enhances its tensile strength as members work together toward the network's purpose and establish core values.

■ During its performance phase, the network maintains its momentum and equilibrium as members interact in value-producing activities and conversations, communicating across the network, managing problems and responding to new possibilities and opportunities as they arise.

Growth does not proceed in an unwavering upward pattern. There are setbacks and disruptions, external events and internal struggles, and breakdowns that occur naturally over time in a long-lived network. Chapter 9 picks up the topic of how to manage a network through these types of transition and disruption.

The growth pattern shown in Figure 7.1 is one that is demonstrably repeatable in natural and human systems. It is completely consistent with the general systems pattern of growth first identified by George Land and augmented by August Jacacci and John Gowan as the Metamatrix. In the Metamatrix (introduced to me by Gus Jacacci in 1994), the stages of growth are Gather, Repeat, Share, and Transform. At each transformation, the stages are repeated at a new order of growth.[1]

In the context of networks, an initial network may go through its cycle (in my terminology) of Create, Organize, Grow, and Perform, at which time a transformation may create a network at a new level, for example, a "network of networks."

In their work on communities of practice, Wenger, McDermott, and Snyder described the stages of growth as Potential, Coalesce, Mature, Sustain, and Transform,[2] a model that I have drawn on heavily in my work on collaborative practices and network development.

Intentional Design

Consider the intentional act of creating the New England Healthcare Institute 🏵 . The founders wanted to bring a diverse set of minds and perspectives together to solve some of the most perplexing problems in healthcare. They knew that they would need to bring together people representing the diverse segments of the healthcare ecosystem. To *be a network* and to *create networks to solve problems* were core principles of the founding strategy. They designed the organizational and functional models of the network carefully and grew the membership, focusing on the stakeholder groups that they wanted to include: hospitals, insurance companies, medical device manufacturers, pharmaceutical and hospital supply companies, and so on. There was a large substrate of potential members in the Boston healthcare community; candidates were interviewed in-depth to determine their capacity to contribute and their acceptance of the norms. When NEHI reached the right level of membership, it was ready to begin creating value.

🏵   *Dow Chemical formed the SiLKnet Alliance, a nine-member group of chip materials suppliers, many of whom were competitors, in 2001. Dow's goal in creating SiLKnet was to provide these suppliers with advance information and test wafers for a new semiconductor dielectric resin (SiLK and related films). Because the adoption of SiLK would ultimately require suppliers to change their manufacturing processes, Dow created this collaborative community so its*

members could work in parallel to develop SiLK-compatible pro-
cesses, products, and technologies. By the end of 2004, SiLKnet had
28 members.

Discovery

NEHI 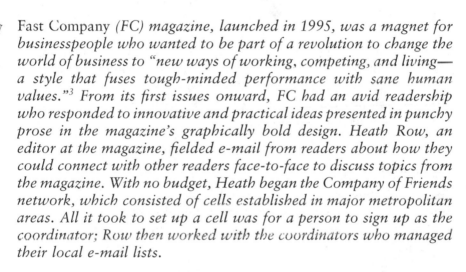 and SiLKnet 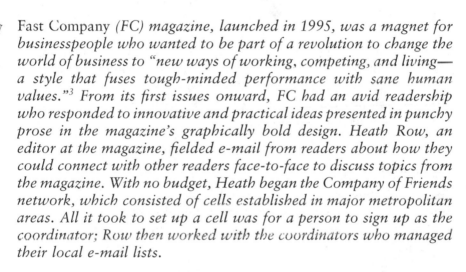 provide examples of networks that began
with the intention of an explicit design process. Networks can also
emerge when a number of people unknown to each other are attracted
to an idea and look for a means of connection.

Fast Company (FC) magazine, launched in 1995, was a magnet for
businesspeople who wanted to be part of a revolution to change the
world of business to "new ways of working, competing, and living—
a style that fuses tough-minded performance with sane human
values."[3] From its first issues onward, FC had an avid readership
who responded to innovative and practical ideas presented in punchy
prose in the magazine's graphically bold design. Heath Row, an
editor at the magazine, fielded e-mail from readers about how they
could connect with other readers face-to-face to discuss topics from
the magazine. With no budget, Heath began the Company of Friends
network, which consisted of cells established in major metropolitan
areas. All it took to set up a cell was for a person to sign up as the
coordinator; Row then worked with the coordinators who managed
their local e-mail lists.

The *Fast Company* magazine publishers contributed eventually a
small budget to manage the computing infrastructure needed for a
simple website and the mailing lists for the Company of Friends
coordinators and the cells. Row took on the critical role of network
organizer, but in all other respects Company of Friends became a
self-managed network whose design emerged from the commitments
that members were able to make. It actually grew as a function of
the value perceived by those who joined: the personal growth and
exchange of ideas afforded by meeting like-minded people. The
Company of Friends grew to over 100 cells in North America, with
an additional 40 scattered around the world.

Networks of networks, like the CoF, are also developing among
nonprofits. Steve Waddell's research on global action networks

(GANs) has shown that these multi-stakeholder NGO groups emerge in a number of ways. They may emerge after several years of conversations and consultations; they may form following a global conference on a topic that brings the stakeholders together; or they may arise from the "imagination" or discovery of synergies across groups.[4]

Roles in Design, Discovery, Development

However a network forms, it takes shape through the work of an organizer. In the preceding examples, the organizers all became committed members of the networks that they put into (or helped put into) motion. In a business or large nonprofit network, managing the startup of the network may fall to resident or consultant experts in strategic alliance or network design. During the design and startup development process, the organizer works with those who will guide the network during its growth.

Stakeholders

In a single-business context, stakeholders are normally associated with the following six roles: customers, employees, investors, suppliers, the environment, and society as a whole. In network terms, these become:

- Members of the network;
- The network's core group members;
- Network sponsors, funders, or investors;
- Partners;
- The environment;
- Society as a whole;
- The network as a whole.

Not every network will have stakeholders in all of these categories, but it's important during the startup design phase to list the stakeholders, how the purpose of the network relates to their needs and aspirations, and what value they will receive from participation.

Choreographers and orchestrators

Two analogies that describe the work of creating and sustaining networks are those of orchestrator and choreographer. Both roles carry the connotation of artistic design with an attention to relationships, among musicians or dancers. Both work from a musical score but interpret it according to the nuances required of a specific production based on the attributes and skills of the performers. For networks to succeed, the orchestrator or choreographer must "stay with the show," to continue to make adjustments as the repertoire changes, members arrive, leave, or are replaced, and so on. A successful orchestrator/choreographer[5] is:

- An entrepreneur;
- A business advocate;
- A coach and mentor;
- A tireless communicator.

Responsibility for orchestration may fall to a company or individual network within a network of networks. When the European Union funds research projects, it requires that there be multiple stakeholders, with one company managing the overall research alliance. The extent to which a company is orchestrator, manager, or participant in an alliance depends on how critical the work is to its core business.

In a structured alliance or partnership, the choreographer's role may include traditional management responsibilities and duties, such as due diligence and project management, entailing periodic review/ resetting of goals, measuring performance, and so on. But the choreographer also is the one who engages the members of the alliance in building trusting relationships, hammering out intellectual property agreements, and developing personal relationships with individuals in the member companies.

 Greg Bauer performed this role as the developer and manager of the SiLKnet Alliance. As he brought companies into the alliance and nurtured their participation, he needed to build a governance framework that protected each company's trade secrets while at the same time building their confidence in working within the alliance. As he developed the alliance, Bauer was conscious that each relationship

was different and reached commitment to the alliance at a different pace. He had to manage these multiple levels of readiness while continually moving the alliance forward.[6]

Business networks are more likely to begin with an intentional desire to seek partnership for a particular purpose: product innovation, creating integrated solutions, expanding markets, and so on. It is during this stage that the orchestrator must play the role of weaver in the network, paying close attention to bridging across groups that need to be connected and bonding—creating closer ties—with those who need to collaborate closely.

Prior to undertaking formal partner agreements, there are a number of necessary due diligence tasks that traditionally involve looking at a company's profile, the reputations of key executives and board members, and the strategic fit for both parties. Increasingly, the task of due diligence is expanding to include a look at a company's structure and style. Robert Schmid, director of Eli Lilly and Company's office of alliance management, for example, uses the term *cultural diligence* to describe the additional assessment that Eli Lilly makes prior to committing to an alliance. This cultural diligence includes looking at the size of the organization, its geographical reach, how decisions are made in the organization, and so on. The diligence process includes interviewing senior executives and employees at all levels in the organization to ensure that there is a consistency between what executives say and what employees say.[7]

Structural capital

The importance of establishing roles and responsibilities within a network cannot be overemphasized. The norms by which members can act and interact without coming into conflict or performing redundant work rely on the clarity of the commitments that members have made to the network. The clarification of key tasks and roles helps ensure that all can contribute to their maximum capacity.[8] Whether and how specific roles are filled depends of course on the network, but there are two essential categories of roles that contribute to a network's structural capital:

- Governance roles;
- Infrastructure roles.

Table 7.1

Structural Roles: Governance

Role	Functions
Sponsor or champion	Provides top-level support for and commitment to the network and its strategic purpose, tying the benefits of the community to a larger organization. Without such sponsorship, members in a corporate setting may find it difficult to allocate time to spend on the network, or the network overall may not have an impact.
Leader or leaders	Manages the network on a daily basis, ensuring that members are able to contribute and participate and that they have the resources they need, including connections to other networks.
Steering group or council	Reviews the work of the network on an ongoing basis to guide changes in strategy, bring in external ideas and insights, and encourage and challenge the network.
Core members	Commit to the work of the network and participate fully in the life of the community, stepping in and out of stewardship roles as needed.
Peripheral members	Occasionally participate in and contribute to network activities because they are vested in the goals of the network and may expect to make more significant commitments in the future.

Table 7.1 summarizes the first set of roles, those that provide a functional view of the network's structure and governance.

Functional services to the network may be provided by network members themselves or by external agents. These horizontal functions are commonly found in any hierarchical organization: financial administration and business development, operations, communications, technology infrastructure, and (in very large network organizations) human resources and organizational development. Such functions can scale down to reflect the needs of small, local, and informal networks. For example, small informal networks identify functional roles such as treasurer, webmaster, meeting planner, and so on. Table 7.2 summarizes a minimal set of infrastructure roles require to get a network started.

Roles are rarely unique to an individual, and individuals often fulfill multiple roles. It's natural for people to volunteer for or step into roles that fit their natural talents and skills, but also natural for individuals to tire of being in specific roles for long periods of time. A network that creates an open, collaborative environment provides

Table 7.2
Structural Roles: Infrastructure

Role	Tasks
Meeting coordinator	Maintain the schedule, logistics, agendas, and arrangements for network events and meetings.
Facilitator	Design the network's conversations, either in face-to-face meetings, in online discussions, or in virtual team spaces.
Communicator	Develop and publish news, announcements, and general information about the network via e-mail mailings, newsletters, websites, and so on.
Technologist	Set up, maintain, and support network members in their use of information technology.
Treasurer	Collect dues and fees and manage the network's cash flow.

individuals with the ability to express their needs and to change their roles according to their time and ability to contribute.

The KM Leaders 🕸 Philadelphia network identifies the owners of its infrastructure tasks at an annual board meeting, which is usually open to anyone who wants to attend. Members who attend these meetings are those who want to be engaged in the life of the community, so the volunteering process goes quite smoothly. Leaders often take on tasks for which there are no volunteers. Some tasks that require special skills or relationships are carried over from year to year, for example, mailing lists or scheduling logistics with a permanent venue.

These tasks may be shared by a small core group when a formalized network is primarily virtual, that is, is not driven by face-to-face meetings. In large funded networks outside of organizations, hired staff (as small as possible) perform administrative tasks required to provide this "process glue" that maintains the network's structure, while other tasks are a normal facet of the network leadership roles. In a federated model, many specific roles are then replicated to the chapters.

The fluidity of these roles depends very much on the formality of the network's governance model. In informal networks with shared leadership, members will rotate in and out of the leadership core. People whose lives become too busy to participate regularly shift to the extended periphery for a while, and so on.

Table 7.3
Design Tensions and Questions

Tension	Questions for Design and Examination
Network vs. the individual	How will the network and its leaders balance the need to produce value in support of the network's purpose and at the same time provide value to each of the individual members? Is the network's purpose sufficient to maintain the commitment of all its members? Is the benefit to each of the individual members sufficient to hold them in the network?
Top-down vs. emergent	Is there sufficient structure (including governance) in place to ensure efficient organization of resources to meet communications, logistics, and operational stability? Is the structure sufficiently flexible to manage the unpredictable? Does it support dialogue?
Closed vs. open	Does the network easily admit new members and new ideas? Are there times when the network must close and focus and times when it must make itself open for expansion? Does the network know how to tell the difference?
Outcome vs. discovery	Is the network intended to create a tangible outcome? Or is its purpose primarily to provide an environment in which ideas are exchanged and created? Are the members of the network conscious of this distinction?
Transaction vs. knowledge-based interactions	Has the network become overly focused on one form of transaction over another and failed to meet its own needs of growing knowledge and experience at the expense of its future?
Tangibles vs. intangibles	Has an emphasis on creating tangible value harmed the network's potential for creating positive relational value, reputation, and emotional well-being?

Design Tensions

Through the stages of development of the network, there are always tensions at play. It's important to consider network design as a work in progress even when the network is in its performance maturity. The design process itself is one of dialogue among the network's creators, organizers, and developers, with a continuing dialogue among all stakeholders through the life of the network. Table 7.3 summarizes the tensions inherent in networks and provides questions that can prompt these dialogues.

These tensions are present all the time; both leaders and members of a network should be aware of how these tensions impact the health of the network. All networks will shift along these lines of tension as they respond to changes in the environment, changes in the demographics of their members, and changes in purpose, structure, or style.

Gennova ✿ as a group grappled with finding a balance between "doing" and "talking" for almost two years. While it experimented with designing go-to-market professional services, none of the experiments proved fruitful. Meanwhile, the monthly meetings provided rich dialogue about the ideas behind networks and the ways to create and generate them. But what was it to be, if not in business? Why did people keep showing up? There is possibly a stage in all network formation the balance has not yet been struck and agreed to: How much do we do vs. how much do we talk about doing vs. how much do we just let the conversations happen and allow what the network *is* to emerge?

DEVELOPMENT ROADMAP

Preceding chapters have provided detail on purpose, structure, style, and value that we can now look at in the context of developmental tasks required during network design:

- Negotiating an expression of the purpose of the network and the basis of connectivity that has sparked interest in developing a network;
- Defining the basis of the organizational, structural, and membership attributes that provide coherence for the activities of the network;
- Laying the groundwork for the operational style, value-producing activities, and change management work that will ensure the success of the network.

These activities lead to the network's proper launch, an occasion for announcing and articulating the result of these development tasks while engaging members in the co-creation of the network's future.

Expressing a Purpose from the Potential

The most important artifact from the design stage of a network's development is the document, either formal or informal, that states the network's purpose. Purpose statements or mission statements both serve. "Purpose," for example, is one of the required sections of legal documents of incorporation for either profits or nonprofits.

The drafting of the mission statement is best placed in the hands of a small but representative set of members. (I once participated in a two-day meeting in which 40 people, most of them unknown to each other, tried to write a mission statement collaboratively. I don't recommend this approach.) The pithiest mission statements have only a few simple elements:

- What the network is for;
- Who or what the network is in service of;
- How the network is going to achieve its purpose (optionally).

The Knowledge Management Group 爵 of Philadelphia provides an example of a short purpose statement:

The purpose of the group is to provide a forum for understanding and applying the ideas of Knowledge Management.[9]

As does the Scottish Enterprise:

Our mission is to help the people and businesses of Scotland succeed.[10]

The Women's World Banking network 爵 shows precision in stating how it is going to achieve its purpose:

The Women's World Banking network aims to have a major impact on expanding the economic assets, participation and power of low-income women as entrepreneurs and economic agents by opening their access to finance, knowledge and markets.[11]

Mission statements are best when they are pithy and specific. Mission statements provide the context and language for working on organizational tasks.

Getting Organized

From stating the purpose, it follows that the network must describe the means by which it will accomplish that purpose and organize to do the work. That means in most cases establishing a governing body that will take the form of a board of directors, a council, a steering committee, and so on (as described in Chapter 4). The degree of formality required may be a function of the design tensions listed in Table 7.3. For example, a network designed to produce a concrete outcome with a carefully selected set of individuals (or companies) for whom financial and/or personal assets may be at risk will need to select a governance document.

Chapter 4 described some of the types of formal governance documents, including membership agreements, charters, and letters of intent. A charter document provides the simplest framework for engaging network members in a spirit of collaboration while responding to the need for accountability. Table 7.4 lists the components that are often included in a charter document in the left-hand column; the right-hand column suggests questions that will generate content for each component.

Guiding principles

Guiding principles do not need to be elaborate, but do require the benefit of dialogue before being written into a charter agreement. The following examples illustrate how different networks have positioned and stated guiding principles.

The Gennova Group 🕸 wrote a constitution[12] that included the following elements in Article 1, Section 1.02:

- To provide support, development, and sharing among members;
- To apply principles of democratic rule and self-organization;

Table 7.4
Elements of a Network Charter

Part/Element	Guiding Questions
Part 1. The Network	
Purpose	What will the network create, and who it will benefit?
Scope or criteria	What are the boundaries of membership in the network?
Deliverables	What specific tangible and intangible values will the network create? How will the values be measured?
Duration/Timeline	Are there specific activities that must be completed by certain dates? Will the network's charter expire automatically at a given future date? How does the network intend to renew itself?
Stakeholders	Who are the stakeholders in the network? What role will each play?
Part 2. The Membership	
Membership criteria	Is there a focused domain of knowledge or range of domains? A specific geographical area or region? Must groups, companies, or individuals hold a minimum asset value?
Potential members to enroll	What is the diverse mix of membership required to make the network viable and successful? Who in particular should be part of this network? What is the value proposition that will encourage these potential members to enroll?

Part 3. Guiding Principles
Guiding principles are a first draft of the elements of style for a network, providing norms by which the network will operate, resolve conflicts, and manage risk.
Part 4. Acceptance (Signatures)

- To operate as peers, working together with mutual respect;
- To enhance members' activities outside Gennova Group;
- To take actions that ultimately benefit the greatest number with the greatest good;
- To find innovative solutions to complex problems;
- To use the least infrastructure or overhead possible;
- To never compromise integrity or jeopardize trust;
- To practice reciprocity and generosity.

The SAS Institute has created a powerful innovation network that encompasses all of its stakeholders, including its customers, software developers, managers, and support staff. To harness creativity, it established the following guiding principles:

- Help employees do their best work by keeping them intellectually engaged and by removing distractions;
- Make managers responsible for sparking creativity and eliminate arbitrary distinctions between "suits" and "creatives";
- Engage customers as creative partners so you can deliver superior products.[13]

Principles often include protocols, for example statements about key resources, the protection of intellectual property, or the privacy of individuals who join a network. For example, when ten nonprofit organizations in Maine formed a network to conserve 48,000 acres of land, their protocols included a provision that they would not share information about potential donors.[14]

Similarly, intellectual property (IP) agreements that protect trade secrets, patents, and work in progress are a traditional element in research partnerships. Many partners came into SiLKnet⬠ very slowly, accepting collaboration only after they were sure that their IP would be adequately protected.

Some of the confidentiality issues can be assuaged by referring to guiding principles, nondisclosure statements, or other charter documents. Experts in convening networks, like Truman Company⬠, recommend the Chatham house rule:

> *When a meeting, or part thereof, is held under the Chatham house rule, participants are free to use the information received, but neither the identity nor the affiliation of the speaker(s), nor that of any other participant, may be revealed.*[15]

This agreement makes it possible for the ideas created and discussed during a meeting to be captured and written up without attribution of any specific comment to an individual. A modified version of this rule allows for listing the participants but not ascribing specific comments to individuals.

Growing Membership

Growth patterns of networks can be looked at from two perspectives:

- The growth of membership, which is either completely open or intended to cap at a specific number;
- The growth of social capital among the membership.

Let's look first at how successful network orchestrators attract the membership that they need to fulfill the network's goals. Finding and vetting members requires a close attention to the following qualitative criteria:

- Required diversity in knowledge domains, points of view, operating styles;
- Required commonality;
- Collaborative potential.

Required diversity

The first step is to establish the domains of knowledge that are important to the network's work, whether it be innovation, problem solving, creating new lines of business, managing the logistics of delivering aid, and so on. Invited members must have something to contribute to the knowledge domain; ideally, they also have passion for the work. Diversity is vital if the conversations are to be open, encompassing, and generative, particularly if the problems to be solved or opportunities to be addressed are complex and systemic. For instance, research healthcare networks—like NEHI 🏛 — typically include members from federal and local government agencies, hospitals and clinics, insurance companies, businesses that provide insurance for their employees, businesses that are suppliers to the healthcare industry, pharmaceutical companies, and so on.

Creating networks inside large corporations means looking across business unit, functional, and geographic boundaries. In the early 1990s, "concurrent engineering" was a term applied to a novel notion of product creation networks that included representatives from research, engineering, manufacturing, marketing, distribution, and sales as full participants in the development process, from the very beginning of a project. Quality function deployment techniques went the next step and brought customers into the design process. Today, networks such as SiLKnet ♔ extend across the supply network to engage equipment manufacturers in testing and providing feedback on new materials.

Within networks, demographic diversity—cultural background, gender, age—accompanies differences in professions, personal interests, and areas of expertise. There is also the matter of communication, cognitive, and personality styles. We each have specific, sometimes innate, ways that we perceive and process information, engage in discussions, debate, and dialogue, and interact with others. We play different roles at different times.

Required commonality

The next key criterion is to meet the expectations of those invited to the network that they will have something in common with all the other members:

- Shared uniting passion in a network's mission;
- Interest in the same knowledge domain;
- Equivalent level of expertise in a shared or related knowledge domain;
- Similar level of hierarchy or authority.

The last of these, peer parity, is important for building trust in a network, as it provides the basis for a common language to support dialogue and also is the basis for reciprocity.

Not all networks require alignment of members by hierarchical position. Often, what is most required is the commitment to an idea or a reputation for being a good thinker. Richard Saul Wurman, who initiated the multidisciplinary Technology, Entertainment, Design conferences, likens the invitation process to that of creating a good dinner party. You want people who can spark interesting conversations, connect ideas across disciplines, and neither proselytize nor perorate.

Note the design tension between diversity and peer parity: There needs to be enough commonality to support interaction and the generation of ideas, but sufficient parity to enable trust and reciprocity.

Collaborative potential

The third important criterion is to determine whether the prospective members would be committed to collaboration in the face of conflicting commitments. In some networks, a guiding principle is to balance the "whole good" of the network's purpose against the individual gain or value. NEHI🕸 , for example, is particularly careful to screen invited members. Members must be able to "check their industry hats" at the door, says NEHI's chief operating officer Valerie Fleishman. NEHI expects its members to have a broad view of systemic problems in the healthcare system and to work together to identify areas where research can be brought to bear on solutions. This means that a representative from a healthcare products manufacturer, for example, must participate without bias—and with commitment—in a discussion about how to reduce waste in hospitals and clinics.

Finding the "right" people

In a closed network, such as executive networks, or NEHI🕸 , finding a set of members who can be committed to the network, capable of collaboration, and being peers at some level, takes time and attention. Leaders and orchestrators combine to leverage their networks:

1. Looking first to their own active connections;
2. Looking next to their own latent connections;
3. Leveraging these personal ties for connections that are just "one more degree of separation";
4. Looking for other, related networks to invite into the network.

The base of existing social capital can be very important. A study of NGO networks[16] found that networks that evolved organically from existing relationships and a history of working together were much more likely to last than those that were created from the top down.

Truman Company orchestrates networks only for C-level (CEO, CIO, CMO, etc.) executives. When they identify participants, they know that they can't base selection on title alone (as these can vary significantly across companies of different sizes), but they can gauge the scope of responsibility. For example, criteria in identifying potential network members might include a phrase like "the senior-most executive responsible for purchasing decisions." For example, Ayava has a network called the customer contact council, an advisory group for their business in-call center and customer service operations. The primary criterion for membership in the council is that the member be the individual most responsible for setting the member company's strategy as to how technology can be used to improve customer contact. Some members are from their IT organizations, some from lines of business, some in customer service organizations. Titles range from general manager to V.P. to S.V.P. But all are peers in each other's eyes—people from whom they can learn and to whom they can contribute.

Idea and practice networks may have a more selective approach to acquiring members; the process may involve what I call the "thousand cups of coffee" approach. In the early 1990s at a convention on collaboration software systems, I heard a consultant speak about the trials of introducing the idea of using computer-based tools in meetings for decision support. When asked how he convinced managers to adopt the tools, he smiled and said, "A thousand cups of coffee." Enrolling people in a new idea or concept—like the impact that the Internet might have on IBM's business—requires leveraging and expanding one's personal network, one cup of coffee at a time.

 The Defense Intelligence Agency (DIA) is an important member of the U.S. intelligence community. During its post-9/11 transformation, the agency set a strategic objective to become a knowledge-based organization. Adrian (Zeke) Wolfberg, then chief of staff to the agency director, was assigned to design and implement a series of programs based on learning from outside the DIA, to work with a small team inside the DIA to identify areas for innovation, and to develop a voluntary network of people from across the organization committed to change. The initial core group of 27 volunteers was created by a forcing function: each line and staff organization was asked to nominate two or three people to participate. Wolfberg then

proceeded to interview each of the candidates twice in hour-long sessions to determine a fit for their ability to support the work of the network, called the Knowledge Lab, as well as to establish a basis of social capital.[17]

Attracting members

Networks whose membership is open for self-selection based on membership criteria grow in a number of ways:

- Announcements, postings, or advertisements in corporate or public resources on intranets or the Internet such as e-mail discussion groups;
- Viral word-of-mouth marketing;
- Seminars, conferences, and conventions;
- Personal network building.

Online networks that exist in virtual space naturally use the first of these, and word of mouth (or mail-to-mail) follows. If someone posts a question to a list that isn't relevant to that list, the poster may be referred to other lists. A particularly apt or humorous posting from a list may be forwarded via e-mails from person to person, stimulating people to join the list.

Businesses and nonprofit networks are more likely to use industry media or conferences to generate interest among potential members. They may deliver presentations, set up exhibits, or create opportunities for private meetings during large events that they sponsor uniquely for the purpose of generating the network. Or they may convene special conferences or "webinar" series to develop awareness and create connectivity.

Building social capital

Whenever people gather face-to-face with a common purpose, the network achieves a secondary purpose: It expands and enhances the set of relationships within it. When members work together toward a shared goal, they establish a relationship and a set of norms for working together. The more often they work together, the more likely they are to trust each other and want to work together in the future. The design of a network must both build on existing social capital and provide an environment in which more social capital can be created. NEHI 🕸 has succeeded in creating more value for its members than they had signed up for. A 2005 survey asked members what they felt was the primary value of NEHI. "Connections and collaborations" across a diverse set of people was either #1 or #2 on everyone's list.

It is now common for people to attend conferences and seminars with a specific goal of expanding their professional networks, and conference designers are taking note. Some event planners will collect photographs and biographies of all attendees prior to the event and get these to attendees beforehand. This helps attendees create a list of people that they want to be sure to connect with. A conference or one-time event is very much a "network-for-a-day" and, if conceived as such, can generate the social capital for the emergence of new networks.

If the development stage of the network has created a ground of social capital, then it is much easier to launch the network in a way that accelerates its path to creating value.

Build Trust

"Trust frees people," says Robert Galford.[18] He provides some general "to-dos" that are a good starting point for building trust:

- Allow, where possible, inclusion in visioning and goal setting;
- Be consistent about public recognition;
- Foster alternative viewpoints;
- Create healthy competition.

Trust and social capital are created through shared experience. This may begin with a carefully planned launch event, but it must be embedded in the processes and means of interaction among members. The founding intention for the Gennova 🕸 network, for example, was to create professional services partnerships—for people to work together on client projects. However, Gennova realized that in order for people to be able to refer clients to one another and work together professionally, there had to be a high level of trust between them. But in order for that trust to be present, there had to be some past experience of working together. Gennova's response to this "chicken-and-egg" problem was to build in its constitution a requirement for members to participate in subgroups that would focus on value creation. (This book is the ultimate product of one of those groups, which we called value networks.)

NETWORK LAUNCH

Launch is a discrete transition point ending the formal design of a network. It is a declaration of the network's purpose and structure, and it sets the style with which the network will operate. Launch preparation includes:

- Stakeholder enrollment;
- Technology infrastructure readiness;
- A well-paced and engaging kick-off event;
- Participant capability development.

The overarching goal of a network launch event is to establish the basis of relatedness, to articulate guiding principles and core values, to provide network members an opportunity to meet and create social ties, and to engage the network in its own design and definition.

In many cases, a network launch event is preceded by individual meetings or phone calls with the intended participants. These conversations provide a way to surface individual concerns, understand the expectations of the intended participants, and establish the basis for developing trust.

For a primarily face-to-face network, the most important infrastructure is the e-mail distribution list and possibly a website for posting announcements, maintaining the calendar, and distributing newsletters, reports, and links and documents of interest to the network. The website can also be an informational marketing tool. If the network will be using a collaborative platform for ongoing dialogue, then the workspace should be set up ahead of time, tested, and pre-populated with content.

Networks whose primary work is online must pay attention to the accessibility, robustness, and ease of use of the platforms they select. Knowledge sharing and community initiatives can be quickly derailed or distracted when members have difficulty getting access to a tool, can't figure out how to use its basic functions, or can't find what they are looking for.

Creating Engaging Events

We all know about network events that fizzle, networks that just don't quite "take off," or conferences that leave people cold; and we have all (hopefully) participated in events that are so well designed that we can't imagine a better experience. The launch experience should match the expectations of the participants as well as produce value consistent with the value that the network wants to create. Table 7.5 summarizes a range of models for launch events.

Each of these models has different potential for creating social bonds, exposing people to ideas, solidifying commitment to action, and so on. The problem-solving and conference forms are the ones we are most used to. Traditional meeting facilitation techniques offer a wide variety of methods for approaching problem solving and decision making.

A conference may be the best form for a large and mature practice network, like an association or industry convention. An "unconfer-

Table 7.5
Event Models

Model	Provides
Problem solving	Context-setting and facilitated discussion of topics intended to produce course-setting outcomes and decisions
Conference or symposium	Dissemination of information in predefined categories prepared in advance
"Unconference"	Open-ended agenda in which topics are driven by the participants with no materials planned in advance
Dialogue	Conversations that enable time for participants to engage deeply with a topic
Whole-system methods	Facilitated process for achieving common understanding of a problem or opportunity and mobilizing for action

ence" turns this model on its head by providing spaces for people to connect and talk about ideas of their own choosing. It may have invited speakers to establish an overarching theme, but will in the main work on providing the maximum number of ways for people to self-organize ("swarm") around topics and capture notes springing from their conversations through conference blogs or visual annotation.

A dialogue, or dialogue circle, is appropriate for the kick-off of a small (under 30) network that is personal or practice-oriented. Using a "check-in" process, members can each talk about their individual motivations and goals for being in the network. The starting conversation can be heightened by asking members to respond to a challenging or difficult question (such as "What is the most surprising thing you've learned in the past two days?" or "What is the question that is top-of-mind for you right now?") Dialogue, like the strategic design methods, provides the greatest opportunity for the emergence of the innovative or unexpected.

Whole-system methods are designed to include the collective insights and experiences of all the stakeholders in a system so that participants self-organize for action. These methods—including open space, the world café, and future search—are discussed as methods for network transformation in Chapter 9, but they are equally valuable for a network launch.

Attention to event place and space

Network members get their initial impressions of a network's style from the first event, so it is naturally important for face-to-face meetings to create attractive settings in convenient or desirable locations. The choice of venue is largely a matter of economics, convenience, or both. Professional meeting planners have an extremely broad network of contacts and shared resources that enable them to assist in all the details of site selection and setup.

Attention to physical place becomes more significant as the stakes—the costs of participation—grow higher. We all know that the executives get better hotels, better food, and more attention to their creature comforts in their normal business activities. When it comes to engaging executives in networks whose purpose is not directly related to their company's bottom line, the event logistics must be superb.

When Valerie Fleishman plans the quarterly meeting of NEHI 徽,
she doesn't overlook a detail. Months go into planning each day-long
meeting, including the meeting structure and flow and the comfort
of the attendees (right down to the lunch and dinner seating
charts).

On the other hand, kick-off events may be extremely modest—a
large enough room and enough chairs for everyone, flipcharts, adhe-
sive notes, markers. What matters is that the physical setup provides
comfort, adequate refreshment, room for conversation, and materials
for capturing what emerges. The event must be framed by setting
norms and closing actions. Norms establish the principles for the
network, including sensitivity to the intellectual capital that people
bring into the room. Closing actions assure people that the capital
created in the room will be fed into the future of the network.

It's not a question of whether technology infrastructure supports
the network, but of what tools will support the network most appropriately based on its tasks and the resources available to its members.
The technology that needs to be in place at the time a network is
launched depends on the expectations that the network's founders
have for the role of technology in the network's interaction style.
Appendix A includes a summary of the range of technologies available to support a network's ability to exchange and create information, ideas, and social capital.

Online networks

Online networks must balance a similar set of economic and social
factors to create an online event that will promote a sense of community and purpose. The critical steps required to prepare and
launch an online customer community, for example, include both a
clarity of purpose and the recruitment of members who represent a
diverse sample of the intended customers for a product. The virtual
space design is a critical element, as it has to be easy to use and
visually attractive. It must also provide a variety of mechanisms
for interaction, including polling and surveys, online discussions,
brainstorming, instant messaging, and chat, and the ability to post
photographs or graphics.

The launch or other events to support online communities have a
different set of planning challenges. An online launch event normally
takes place over two or three days and is planned to accommodate

global schedules, so there is opportunity for both real-time and off-line exchange. The launch of the CPsquare 🔯 community, for example, took place over several months. The founders put careful thought into the design of the launch of CPsquare, including:

- Identifying in advance members who would be interested in developing practice groups on topics such as technology, leadership, consulting, healthcare, and metrics;
- Holding a number of orientation sessions to introduce members to the core team, acquaint members with the community's norms, and provide a walk-through of the collaborative tools platform, discussion groups, and virtual team spaces;
- Scheduling a number of "hot topic" teleconferences that brought in invited speakers.

The ongoing success of such communities is predicated on the ability of coordinators to engage members in participating and also to provide coaching and support for using the technologies.

Capability Development

For a network to be effective, everyone in the network must have the capacity to participate, which means understanding and filling any gaps between existing capabilities and those required for being successful in a network. The three capability areas are summarized in Table 7.6.

Table 7.6 provides a starting point for thinking about what capabilities a network has at its beginning, what capabilities need to be grown or acquired, and how the capabilities can be built. Some writers refer to the sum of the capabilities in a network as its "collaborative capacity."

Creating the network culture

The style of a network will emerge from the interactions of the members, the way that the network was set up, the prior degree of social capital, members' commitments to both the network's purpose and its guiding principles, and so on. The infrastructure—place,

Table 7.6
Building Network Capabilities[19]

Capability	Consists of	Can Be Achieved Through
Building and working through connections and relationships	Placing a value on relationship capital Culture that embraces a network view Commitment to collaboration	Clarity of purpose Core group leadership Norms of trust and reciprocity Evolution of protocols for sharing and using intellectual property
Managing processes and deliverable outcomes through networks	Organizational competencies in structuring and governing networks Creating and managing lateral processes and value networks Accounting systems and management mechanisms appropriate to the network's task	Adopting and adapting best practices Learning and participation in communities of practice Knowledge management systems
Working collaboratively	Abilities in developing and sustaining individual relationships Using technologies that support collaboration and knowledge capture and exchange Dialogue skills	Training and orientation Documentation Collaborating on real projects Dialogue and reflective learning Coaching

space, and pace—will be dictated by the needs of the members and the resources of the network founders or sponsors. Once the structure and infrastructure are in place, development shifts to introducing or reinforcing behaviors that may be culturally new to many network members.

 At the DIA, Zeke Wolfberg worked with the core team in the Knowledge Lab to identify initiatives that could be piloted by individual members in their own organizations and then disseminated across DIA. However, as a network inside a larger network, it was clear that those who had volunteered for the Knowledge Lab did so

because they were already champions for the kind of change needed inside DIA. For Knowledge Lab initiatives to diffuse through the organization would require that the DIA as a whole be receptive to change and learning. Concurrently with the startup of the Knowledge Lab, Wolfberg commissioned a cultural assessment that revealed a significant barrier to knowledge transfer at the DIA: Analysts were often reluctant to advocate their positions when challenged by higher-ups. Accordingly, one of the first pilot projects undertaken by the Knowledge Lab was the introduction of a method for critical discourse, taught in workshops by the consultant Nancy Dixon. The pilots demonstrated the effectiveness of the workshops in making people more aware of the nature of their interactions with others and made them more ready to advocate their own positions more confidently.[20]

Even with good preparation, it can take a year or more for a network to reach a level of maturity at which both the network and its members are fully capable of working collaboratively in the context of that particular network.

DESIGN FOR EMERGENCE

In this chapter I've shared guidelines for designing networks, balancing the very tensions that I wrote about at the beginning. To create a successful network requires that you look for attractors that will draw people to the network and that you set boundaries for it. Planning is not anathema to networks, but over-planning is. Dave Snowden[21] often tells a story about a group of West Point graduates who were asked to manage the playtime of a kindergarten as a final assignment. "The cruel thing," he says, "is that they were given time to prepare." They planned a set of objectives for the children's play, including what activities at what time, and they determined backup and response plans, as they had been trained to do. When they tried to order the children's play, they were unable to manage to the plan and quickly lost control of the kids. The graduates were then given the opportunity to watch an experienced teacher manage a similar group. The teacher provided freedom within the boundaries of the materials available and let children choose what activities they would participate in. If a pattern became chaotic, the teacher would shift

Figure 7.2
Alignment, separation, and cohesion in nature

the children's attention to another activity to keep their behavior in bounds.

So it is with net work and the design of networks and events for networks. You can design structures, events, and activities that you believe will forward the work of the network based on your knowledge and understanding of what brings people together. These attractors (in the sense of complex adaptive systems) will draw people into patterns of interaction and conversation that will move the network in unexpected ways: preparing a network for such surprises is the principle of "designing for emergence."

Simple Rules

What needs to be reconciled is how to create networks in a way that acknowledges this complex property of emergence but also satisfies a need to provide direction and coherence. This happens in natural complex system behavior, like the flocking of birds, because the birds are programmed to following very simple rules of alignment, separation, and cohesion (see Figure 7.2). Within this set of rules, an extraordinary variety of network behaviors is possible. Table 7.7 suggests a way of thinking about these rules in the context of how our emergent human networks are guided.

Table 7.7
Simple Rules for Complex Organizations

Rule	Observable in a Flock of Birds	As Applied to Inner Guidance of Human Networks
Alignment	Steer toward average heading of neighbors	Focus on the shared purpose and value-creating activities
Separation	Avoid crowding neighbors	Maintain individuality within the style of the network; do those things that only you can do
Cohesion	Steer toward average position of neighbors	Pay attention to the texture and structure of the network

A good business architecture begins with principles that serve as rules that will guide the behavior of all those in the business. For example, if a company has a guiding principle of providing superior customer service, it can provide individual sales staff with the autonomy to make decisions. Fashion retailer Nordstrom, Inc.—the benchmark for customer service in retailing—asks its employees to conduct themselves according the company's core value: "Service to the customer above all else." Principles provide the basis for members of the network to organize themselves around specific tasks and programs without the obstruction of bureaucratic rules and processes.

When a network principle or its underlying rules are broken, the network may go off course. It will need intervention of some kind to either restore it to the state from which it veered or to take it in another direction altogether, but with purpose. Before deciding on an intervention, it's important to examine the network first, to find clues in its structure, style, or value-producing mechanisms.

NOTES

1. August T. Jacacci and Susan B. Gault, *CEO: Chief Evolutionary Office* (Burlington, MA: Butterworth Heinemann, 1999).
2. Etienne Wenger, Richard McDermott, and William Snyder *Cultivating Communities of Practice* (Boston: Harvard Business School Press, 2002).

3. "Words to Magazine By," *Fast Company*, April 1996.
4. Steve Waddell, "Multi-Stakeholder Global Networks" (Amsterdam: Royal Netherlands Academy of Arts and Sciences, June 2006).
5. Jeffrey Shuman and Jan Twombly, *Collaborative Communities* (Chicago: Dearborn Trade, 2001).
6. Jeff Shuman and Jan Twombly, "Made in Heaven," *American Executive* April (2004).
7. n.a., "Tying the Knot," *American Executive* November (2004).
8. Charles Heckscher and Paul S. Adler, *The Firm as a Collaborative Community: The Reconstruction of Trust in the Knowledge Economy* (New York: Oxford University Press, 2006).
9. www.kmgphila.org/.
10. www.scottishenterprise.com/ (About).
11. www.swwb.org/ (What We Believe).
12. The Gennova Group, Constitution May 2003.
13. Richard Florida and Jim Goodnight, "Managing for Creativity," *Harvard Business Review* 83, no. 77 (2005).
14. Peter Plastrik and Madeleine Taylor, *Net Gains: A Handbook for Social Entrepreneurs Building Networks to Increase Impact* 2006.
15. www.chathamhouse.org.uk/ (Chatham House Rule).
16. Claudia Liebler and Marisa Ferri, "NGO Networks: Building Capacity in a Changing World," November 2004.
17. Patti Anklam and Adrian Wolfberg, "Creating Networks at the Defense Intelligence Agency," *KM Review* 9, no. 1 (2006).
18. Robert Galford and Anne Seibold Drapeau, *The Trusted Leader* (New York: Free Press, 2002).
19. The components of this table are based loosely on the "Mindset, Toolset, Skillset" model developed by The Rhythm of Business, Inc.
20. Patti Anklam and Adrian Wolfberg, "Creating Networks at the Defense Intelligence Agency," *KM Review* 9, no. 1 (2006).
21. C.F. Kurtz and D.J. Snowden, "The New Dynamics of Strategy: Sense-Making in a Complex and Complicated World," *IBM Systems Journal* 42, no. 3 (2003).

Chapter 8

NET WORK: EXAMINATION

This chapter describes examination methods that are evolving to meet the challenge of investigating the complex flows of tangible and intangible value across networks. These methods help make sense of the relationships and interactions within a network so as to diagnose specific problems and opportunities and identify target points for change. The chapter begins with a summary of questions being used in traditional survey- and interview-based assessments and then provides introductions to three emerging tools that are derived from the perspective of networks:

- *Organizational network analysis (ONA):* A method based on social network analysis methods for collecting relational information about people and organizations. This data is analyzed statistically and presented visually using software tools. ONA provides insight into the structural qualities of a network and gives both visual and data-derived views of the current state of relationships in the network;

- *Value network analysis (VNA):* A participative method that elicits information from stakeholders in a network about the tangible and intangible exchanges of value between and among them. VNA provides insight into the dynamics of value exchanges in a network;

- *Complexity-based sensemaking:* A framework and methods that draw on complexity theory to generate distinctions between the complex and the noncomplex to generate insights and aid in problem solving.

Each of these approaches is intended for use in a setting in which the relevant members of the network are present to interpret the results and produce insights that move the network to action. Chapter 9 describes methods and strategies to use when the examination reveals that it's time to make a change.

ASSESSMENT QUESTIONS

Common instruments and methods for assessing the health of an organization and the network(s) it comprises include surveys, interviews, document reviews, audits, and so on, which can be directed internally or by external consultants. Table 8.1 summarizes the questions that most commonly form the backbone of an assessment process, whether for business alliances and partnerships, nonprofit networks, large professional groups and associations, or even small learning communities.

ORGANIZATIONAL NETWORK ANALYSIS

Chapter 4 provided numerous diagrams of network patterns and introduced the concept of organizational network analysis (ONA) as a tool to uncover the informal patterns of interaction that may be very different from formal organizational relationships. As interest in networks has grown over recent years, communities of researchers, practitioners, and learners have developed in response to the challenge of mapping these patterns. This section describes how ONA can provide insights into the subtleties of a network's structure and style.

Methodology Overview

ONA begins with a problem statement, a list of names, and a set of survey questions. The questions are designed to elicit insights into

Table 8.1
Network Examination Questions

Network Facet	Common Questions
Purpose	Is the network meeting its strategic goals?
	Is it meeting the goals of its stakeholders, including its individual members?
	Do all the network members share the commitment to a common purpose?
Structure	Does the network's formal pattern of relationships and accountability support its purpose?
	Is the network able to make decisions quickly and easily?
	Are the cost of administration and related transaction costs impeding the network's ability to make progress?
	Is the membership of the network diverse enough to meet the challenges in its environment?
Style	Are the place, space, and pace of the network attuned to the comfort and energy levels of the members?
	Does the network support dialogue and inquiry that enhance trust and reciprocity as well as emergence?
	Does the network work toward continuous improvements in quality and efficiency?
	Is the network continuously creating leadership capacity?
Value	Does the network have adequate resources to create value, both tangible and intangible?
	Is the network producing appropriate value for its stage in its development cycle?
	Are there performance metrics for tangible value produced?
	Is the network's value-producing model sustainable?
	Are all stakeholders receiving the value that they expect, and more?

the current state of relationships of the people named. For example, ONA is becoming a useful tool for people who are establishing and managing communities of practice. The problem statement might be: "How easy is it for new members to overcome isolation?" Names would be the community list, and questions might include: "When, How often do each of these other members provide you with information to accomplish your work?", "How well do you know each of these members now?", and "How likely are you to call each of these people when you have an idea that you want to brainstorm?"

Your Name:	
Question 1. Information	
Please indicate the extent to which the people listed below provide you with information you use to accomplish your work using a scale of 0 to 6, where:	

0	means you do not know or have never heard of this person
1	Very infrequently
2	Infrequently
3	Somewhat infrequently
4	Somewhat frequently
5	Frequently
6	Very frequently

Name	Response
Gary Lefton (GL)	
Farah Anders (FA)	
Maureen Brady (MB)	
Happy Candell (HC)	
...	

Figure 8.1
A survey of network relationships

The ONA method includes a simple survey that asks people to indicate the presence, frequency, and quality of their interactions with others. Mapping tools process the survey data to produce a snapshot of the patterns of connection and knowledge flow in the network. Figure 8.1 shows a fragment from a typical ONA survey; Figure 8.2 shows a map produced from it. (Note that the names in all the examples in this chapter are disguised.)

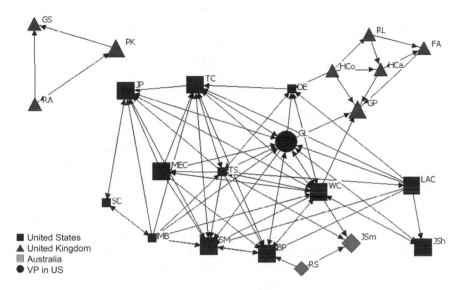

Figure 8.2
A network map of relationships

Surveys are most frequently written for online responses, but it's possible to collect the data from paper surveys as well. In the case shown here, the possible responses to the question include a "0" to indicate the absence of any tie. Figure 8.2 shows the map produced by the software that analyzes the results from the survey.

Reading network maps

Shapes, colors, and lines in a map all provide visual cues to the network's structure and information flow. In Figure 8.2, the large circle in the middle labeled GL is the vice president of the group; squares are people located in the United States (where the VP is also located); triangles are U.K.-based staff; and the diamonds represent the staff in Australia. The node's size is an indicator of job level. While this is a relatively flat organization structure, some of the second-level staff under the VP have their own direct reports (see GP and PK, for example).

The directional arrows indicate responses to the assertion "I frequently or very frequently receive information from [*other person*] that I need to do my job." The large number of arrows going directionally toward GL indicate that a number of people in the group get information from him frequently.

This map illustrates a number of important concepts about working with organizational network analysis.

Interpreting network maps

A network analysis doesn't provide answers. Rather, it aids in getting to the right questions quickly. It is very tempting to look at a map like that shown in Figure 8.2 and leap to assumptions about relationships; for example, the three triangles in the upper left-hand corner are separated from the rest of the group. Not only are they separate from the main cluster of U.S.-based staff, they appear to be separate as well from other U.K.-based staff. Similarly, while GL appears to be communicating regularly with the head of the U.K. group (GP), he is not exchanging information with the other people there. Disconnects like these can occur for a number of reasons. In this case, a look at this map enabled GL to reexamine his own communication patterns and exchanges:

- The group in the upper left was in an isolated city and, moreover, was part of a subgroup in the larger organization that was being spun off. Although the legalities of the spin-off took time, GL had neglected to think about these people as part of his group. On inspecting this map, he realized that the overall organization would benefit from continuing to include them in some group matters.

- Puzzled as to why the U.K.-based staff weren't acknowledging that he was a good communicator (he sent e-mails to his group a number of times each week), GL took a look at his e-mail distribution list. He realized that he had not been including the U.K. people on his electronic distribution.

An organizational leader will usually be able to develop a hypothesis quickly to explain a particular pattern that shows up on a map. Sometimes, though, an explanation will require more detailed and extensive interviewing of people who are isolated, overly central to a group, or serving as vital connectors between groups.

Each question in a survey provides insight into only one of many possible relationships. A question about information exchange can be extremely valuable for getting a sense of how information is flowing (or not) across a network, especially a network that draws members from multiple geographies.

Survey questions can also probe more sensitive issues of style, for example, by asking questions like:

- How much more effective could you be if you could communicate with this person more?

- How comfortable are you initiating a conversation with this person?

- How likely are you to go to this person when you need to make a decision?

An analysis needs to be interpreted in context. In the example I've used here, GL wanted to use the ONA as an organizational sensing mechanism. He was particularly concerned with the overall cohesiveness of his organization, and he immediately took steps on receiving the results of the analysis to improve the flaws in his own communication style.

ONA increasingly is seen by organizations as a method for measuring and providing a baseline for internal cohesion and connectivity. The data from the ONA provides insights into gaps and areas needing improvement that managers can use to target changes and address very specific aspects of an organizational situation.

Table 8.2 summarizes some of the major applications for network analysis.

Insights vary depending on the unit of analysis. The unit of analysis in an ONA is often the relationship among a group of individuals in a bounded network (as shown in the preceding examples), among groups within an organization, or among organizations within a large network or industry ecosystem. In the latter, the relationships can be activity with respect to partnering, mergers and acquisitions, or other publicly available data that describes a relationship between two companies.

What an ONA Can Reveal

The map in Figure 8.3 provides the basis for the subsequent discussion of how ONA can reveal the structural metrics of density, distance, centrality, openness, and value.

The group in Figure 8.3 consists of a senior vice president (KS, the round node in the middle), five vice presidents (the larger of each

Table 8.2

Sense-making Results from Examination by ONA

Probing Question	Provides Insights	Leading to Beneficial Network Actions
How well is information flowing across the organization/network? Who are the key people in the network?	Gaps in knowledge and information flow among groups based on geography, function, job role, or hierarchy often show up in an analysis Brokers, bottlenecks, and the "quiet" leaders in the network (people who hold the network together because of the number and strength of their individual relationships)	Implementing practices that improve communication (group meetings, newsletters, technologies) Repositioning or changing job roles and functions to reward sharing and to limit hoarding behaviors
Is our recent acquisition/merger/reorganization having the intended synergistic effects? How can we improve collaboration?	Extent to which groups are actually being integrated based on the nature of relationships that are developing A "baseline of connectivity" that illustrates how knowledge and ideas are likely to flow across the network	Targeted interventions to connect people and groups, improve communications, or reassign people to projects to enable them to learn each other's skills and knowledge Periodic measurements that indicate positive movement toward improvement
How can we measure the performance of our networks?	The realized value of relationships, expressed as time saved, responsiveness, or business results	Adoption of cultural changes and programs designed to improve individuals' capability to network more effectively
Do we have the right level of interaction inside and outside the organization to support innovation?	Discovery of isolated research or product development groups that are not benefiting from ideas from other locations, functions, or disciplines	Introduction of new channels of information exchange and stimulation of network connectivity

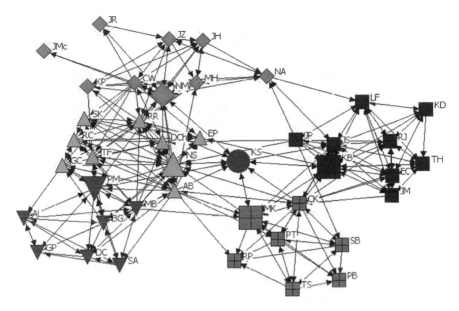

Figure 8.3
Frequency of interaction in an executive network

of the diamonds, squares, boxes, down and up triangles), and the people who report to the VPs. An arrow from one person to another indicates that the source reports receiving information "frequently or very frequently" from the target.

The visual impact of an ONA diagram can be stunning. The senior executives who saw this network map snapped to attention when they saw that their organizations were quite literally "stove pipes," contrary to what they believed. The immediate result was a collective insight about how separate their organizations were from each other, as well as their strong reliance on KS as the central connector keeping the network together. The visualization of the network in itself was very powerful, but there were even more interesting aspects of the network revealed by the metrics.

Revealing key people and structural holes

Notice from the diagram that KS, the senior vice president, seems to be the critical hub for this network. He is certainly connected by virtue of his interactions with each of the vice presidents (KB, NM,

MK, PM, and NS), who are each pretty well connected into their own groups. What you cannot tell easily from the diagram is that there are really a couple of other people who are better connected across the network who may play a role in keeping the network together.

Figure 8.3 indicates that there is one person, NA, who conveys information between the two groups depicted by diamonds and squares, and that there are no other direct ties between these groups. In his research into people in such positions, Ron Burt called these people "structural holes" because they are filling in the holes where the network might otherwise be disconnected.[1]

A structural hole is an opportunity for someone who understands how to benefit from it personally. It is also a good place from which a network weaver, orchestrator, or choreographer can start making introductions.

The map produced by an analysis reveals only part of the data. One of the most exciting aspects of organizational network analysis is the way that we can apply the mathematical calculations developed by social network research for analyzing large organizations or groups. In large networks, it's not always possible to discern all the connectors visually, but the mathematical analyses available make it possible to get insight into the actual texture of a network and several elements of its style.

Using metrics to uncover texture and openness

Chapter 4 introduced some of the structural metrics that reveal the texture of a network; these included density, distance, and the external/internal (or E/I) ratio. ONA metrics for this network (including the infrastructure groups) showed a density of 16%. That means that of the available and possible ties of frequent exchange of information among this group of 54 people, 16% were being utilized. The average distance between any two people in the network was 2 (that is, no one was on average more than one step away from anyone else in the network). These are reasonable numbers for a network of this type.

But there was more behind the patterns that attracted attention. As we have discussed in previous chapters, the balance between being open and closed is a matter of both structure and style. "Open" implies that there are connections to people and groups outside the current task group, organizational unit, or geographic location.

Table 8.3
Networks Open and Closed

	■	+	▼	◆	▲
■ (10)	72%	11%	0%	2%	5%
+ (8)	8%	77%	0%	1%	4%
▼ (8)	0%	2%	73%	0%	17%
◆ (9)	2%	1%	3%	54%	17%
▲ (10)	2%	5%	16%	12%	73%

Openness demonstrates that a network is available for ideas, input, and stimulation from diverse areas and is ready to receive and process divergent thinking. "Closed" implies a network that has deliberately chosen either to stay focused on a single task domain without disruption or to be constrained to the confines of what it already knows and is comfortable with.

One way to measure the openness of the groups within this network is to look more closely at the densities among and across each of the individual groups. Table 8.3 shows metrics from this ONA analysis that provide insight into how open each of these groups is to the others.

The symbols in Table 8.3 correspond to the symbols used to represent the different groups in Figure 8.3: Numbers in parentheses next to the symbols in the left-most column indicate the number of people in each group. The percentages in each of the cells are density calculations that represent, horizontally for each group, the percentage of relationships of high-frequency information exchange reported by members of each group. (When the numbers don't correspond across groups, it means that a person in one group may report frequent interactions with someone else, but the other person doesn't indicate the same level of frequency.)

The gray cells on the diagonal provide the internal density for each group; thus, the first group (represented by squares) has an internal density of 72%. That means that among the 10 people in the group, 72% of the possible ties are used. These internal densities of each of the groups are similar, with the exception of the fourth group, represented by diamonds. Such a discrepancy is cause to ask a question like, "What's different about the interactions in this group?"

Outside the diagonals you can see that there are relatively high numbers, 17%, 16%, 12%, and so on, but also cells containing lower numbers, 1%, 2%, and 0%. These numbers do not indicate that there are no transactions at all, only that there are no frequent or very frequent interactions. However, given the context of the organization, low numbers almost always raise interesting and cogent questions.

Review of an ONA provides a network with many views into how information really flows, the rigidity of its hierarchy (despite the best of intentions), the gaps between groups, and so on. The most successful projects are those in which the network's leaders develop a story about the network from the maps and metrics and engage the whole network to raise questions about the results and work together on a response.

Metrics from an ONA can help to identify where to make connections that will be useful to individuals as well as to the overall health of the network.

Changes based on ONA results tend to be targeted, incremental changes appropriate for working in complex systems. Actions tend to fall into three general categories, summarized in Table 8.4.

 An ONA at the Defense Intelligence Agency (DIA) demonstrated a number of disconnects across the various directorates and across the

Table 8.4
Actions Resulting from an ONA

Focus of Change	Typical Actions
Structural	Changing the structure of the network in some way, such as by altering roles and responsibilities that create and/or reinforce channels of communication and exchange
Place, space, and pace	Creating face-to-face events or technology infrastructure that enables people to connect and build ties and exchange, share, and develop intellectual capital
Personal leadership	Commitments on the part of individuals to change their behavior to be more connective, to delegate decision making, and so on

same directorates based on the buildings and floors where workers sat in offices. When Zeke Wolfberg set up the Knowledge Lab, a volunteer network that grew to 27 core members over its first year, he had a goal of using these volunteers as network integrators to build connections across the DIA. To build network ties more efficiently, Wolfberg decided to use data from the ONA to identify the most central people in the organization and also to identify the most peripheral people—those on the edge of the network, who were not well connected. What if, he hypothesized, a mentoring program selected mentoring pairs based on how well connected two individuals are? Using some home-grown rules of thumb on the ONA metrics and applying personal knowledge about the context of 111 individuals from the ONA, Wolfberg identified an initial set of 12 mentors and 13 novices. The first results from this Knowledge Lab pilot, in October 2005, showed recent hires' increase in contextual knowledge and understanding of how the DIA worked based on the relationship provided through the program.[2]

Some people like numbers; some like diagrams. Managers and engineers, especially, are drawn to the metrics in an ONA, and appreciate it when the numbers all tie together. But the discussion of numbers and metrics in ONA always brings up the question, "What's a good number?" How do the metrics for an ONA tell you whether a network is "as it should be"? At present, while the methodology and practice are still growing, there are no set of published benchmark numbers. The survey and the data must always be put into context. This is especially true when the questions in an ONA drive toward understanding more subtle aspects of a network.

Challenges in organizational network analysis

There are significant challenges in using ONA, particularly because it is a new and evolving practice. Organizational consultants and practitioners maintain a high awareness of the challenges in designing and implementing projects and conveying these nuances to the groups being analyzed.

Individual responses to an ONA may be prejudiced in a climate that lacks trust. In particular, ONA cannot produce valid insights when there are downsizings, impending mergers or acquisitions, or reengineering projects that threaten people's jobs or positions. In these circumstances, an ONA will be perceived as an instrument to identify people to retain or let go, and people may answer in ways that they think will make them look good rather than responding honestly.

It is very difficult to analyze a network completely. The design of an ONA project requires that the network be "bounded" in some way, which is usually along organizational, hierarchical, or membership lines. Finding the right "cutoff" point can be difficult, particularly when networks are increasingly interconnected and interdependent. A person who appears to be barely connected within her own organizationally bounded network may be a bridge to one or more outside networks and play a vital role of knowledge transfer into the organization. Moreover, it is often difficult to get a good response rate to a survey instrument, and without a good response rate, the data may not be sufficient to do a useful analysis.

Those who participate in a survey must have the right of privacy. If one or more people participating in a survey express a desire to remain anonymous, then the survey results must be shown in networkwide settings without displaying names. Given that the ONA is looking for broad patterns, anonymous results often spark more useful conversations than those in which individuals are identified.

The ONA represents a snapshot in time. There can be several weeks or longer between the collection of the ONA data from a survey and the time that the people in the network have the opportunity to examine and interpret the data for themselves. Given their nature, networks are constantly changing as people shift their relationships with one another, change jobs, meet new people, and connect with new organizations. It is therefore important in presenting the results of a survey to point out that the results may not appear to be accurate because of such shifts.

There are no "right" patterns or metrics that can be used to allege "goodness" of a network. While all networks can be described using a common language for different structural patterns and textures, all networks are unique. What matters is how comfortable the people in a network are with what they see during the examination of the network and the conversations that follow. The goal of the ONA is to prompt good questions that generate conversations that lead to action.

VALUE NETWORK ANALYSIS

Value networks, introduced in Chapter 6, represent webs of relationships through which resources or interactions work together to produce value in the form of products, services, or social good. Verna Allee's research and work in value networks and value network analysis has focused attention on the need to understand the intangible as well as tangible assets that are used and created throughout an enterprise and across the relationships in its value chain.

Value network analysis (VNA) is a method that creates a visual map of all exchanges that take place in the everyday life of a network. This way of looking at organizational and relational processes represents a major shift in perspective from a supply chain view of the world, as VNA extends the idea of value to include both tangibles (products, services, and so on) and intangibles (ideas, insights, relational capital, goodwill, and so on).

Methodology Overview

Like an ONA, a value network analysis begins with an objective for examining the network, an understanding of the current climate and environment in the network, and a commitment from stakeholders to act on the results of the VNA. VNA is effective in addressing a wide variety of network issues, including relationship management, business model and market strategies, process design, business web development, and understanding the interactions of networks of all types.

A VNA is a collaborative process in which the stakeholders themselves identify the boundaries of the network and its participants. The first step in the analysis work is to construct a map showing the participants and the exchanges among them. Figure 8.4 illustrates a map developed by the Australian Red Cross Blood Service as part of a strategic development process to enhance its services to patients.

In Figure 8.4, the nodes represent the participating groups and organizations that contribute to managing the blood supply and services. This map illustrates the key concepts of working with value network maps.

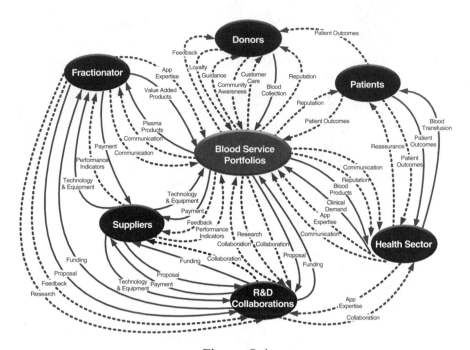

Figure 8.4
Value network map for the Australian Red Cross Blood Service
Reprinted by permission of Beverley Commings.

The nodes in a value network map represent roles in the value network and can be groups, companies, nations, or other networks as well as teams and (sometimes) individuals. This map includes the donors and patients as well as the suppliers of equipment, fractionators (who extract specialized medical supplies from plasma), R&D organizations, and the health sector itself that dispenses blood transfusions.

A map ideally is created as a collaborative effort, with all the key stakeholders in the room working together on a large canvas to identify the roles of the participants and to draw and label lines that show the exchanges among them.

A VNA maps both tangible and intangible exchanges. In Figure 8.4, the grey lines show the tangible exchanges: the blood and blood products, orders and payments for equipment and blood products, research proposals and funding, and so on. The mapping of the tangible exchanges is usually the first step in the process; working with tangibles grounds the map firmly in reality. Subsequently, the stakeholders start to add in the intangible exchanges, shown in Figure 8.4 as the segmented lines—communication, feedback, collaboration, guidance, reputation, and research (knowledge) that enrich the participants.

The construction of a value network map normally takes three to four hours, depending on the number of nodes in the network and the number of people assembled to work on the map. If people representing each of the constituent participants in the network collaborate on the creation of the map, the experience is enriched by the conversations that occur as people understand their interdependence.

The value network mapping process is only the first step in a detailed ValueNet Works Analysis, which is a complete business modeling methodology. Many groups and organizations find that the map alone provides insights and stimulates action that improves and enhances their own network behaviors. The full methodology, however, moves beyond insights into action plans that can help develop scorecards, conduct ROI and cost benefit analyses, and drive decision making.[3] Subsequent steps in the full analysis include the following:

- Sequencing the exchanges by numbering the order in which they occur provides a linear view of an overall process and puts each exchange in the context of "when, what, to whom, and from whom";
- An impact analysis takes a detailed look at each of the sequenced exchanges identifies and examines how inputs are actually (or could be) converted into building tangible and intangible assets;
- A value-creation analysis looks at the tangible and intangible assets to consider how well they are being used to create value for others in the network.

A map provides only one view of the network. The focus of creating a value network map must be scoped to a view that is manageable within the limits of a visual display. Therefore, VNA can be used to create multiple views of a network—different maps for different processes, different stakeholder groups, for "as is" and "current state" scenario analyses, and so forth.

What a Value Network Analysis Can Reveal

A major advantage of VNA is that it provides a platform that allows stakeholders to visualize their "value chain" in a nonlinear way. This nonlinear presentation allows for insight into network dynamics and discovery of key intangible value present in the network. Also, it allows for the entry of intangible values into the calculus of economic value; that is, how intangibles may be contributing to return on investment over time.

Structure and texture

Value network maps reveal the underlying structural patterns of the exchanges in a network. Figure 8.5 shows a map created by managers of a professional services organization who used VNA to examine their current and potential business models. Because this organization was embedded in a corporation that provided most of the equipment on which the services were based, the delivery of the actual services was contracted through the larger organization's customer

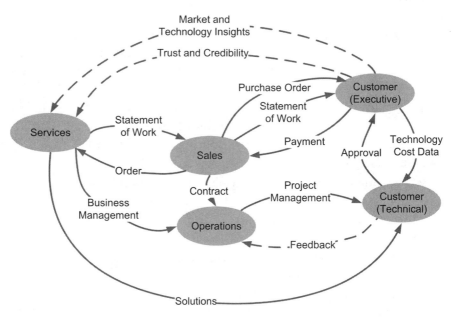

Figure 8.5
Missing the relationship value from customer services

services group. The map highlighted a structural gap in the flow of a major intangible: a relationship with the customer.

Style

A value network analysis demonstrates the balance of interaction style in a network between transactional and knowledge-based interactions. As you can see, Figure 8.5 shows a predominance of transactions that occur by exchanging documents. Where is the learning and knowledge transfer?

A map can also provide an indicator of the overall tone and culture of a network; for example, knowledge exchanges typically represent conversation and dialogue that occurs in the network—and a high degree of dialogue can be a good indicator of trust. Similarly, reciprocity will be evident when there are balancing exchanges—tangible, intangible, or both—between each pair of participants, or within the network as a whole.

Opportunities

During the creation of the value network map or in exchange analyses after, analysis can often point out:

- Central roles, potential beneficiaries of value, or important influencers who have not been taken into account during the mapping process;
- Potential scenarios for the introduction or removal of specific roles in the network;
- Value that is created but either not used or not reaching those who may need it most.

Figure 8.5 shows that the services group has direct contact with and develops relationships with the executives at senior business functions within their customer organizations. For the actual delivery of the services, however, they work through the sales and operations organizations to deliver proposals, business templates, and project resources. The services organization provides the services—actual solutions that integrate technologies into the customer's environment, training in those solutions, and so on—directly to the customer's technical infrastructure group. However, because the parent organization's operations group handled the actual project management with the technical group, it was also the recipient of customer feedback. The professional services group was receiving neither feedback about its work nor relational capital.

Advanced value networks visualization and analytics

These examples show how value network analysis can be used as a sense-making exercise to help people better understand their roles, expectations, interdependencies, and value interactions. For example, Cisco is pioneering this approach to help understand tangible and intangible value creation across its worldwide Customer Interaction Network, using contact center data and web usage patterns. Cisco is creating a one-touch customer contact network where knowledge flows are used to generate business intelligence and alert business units and Cisco partners to business, relationship, and technology opportunities.

COMPLEXITY-BASED SENSE MAKING

A framework and set of methods for distinguishing between complex and noncomplex states was developed by David Snowden,[4] who began his research in complexity theory during his work on organic knowledge management and storytelling. Snowden had developed ethnographic techniques for capturing stories of people at work that enabled him and his colleagues at IBM to develop models for knowledge management. The more he worked with stories, the more he was able to relate the concepts of complexity theory to the different ways that people and organizations perceive and make sense of their situations.

He discerned that truly complex problems and situations (and possible solutions) could be distinguished from those that are either straightforward, complicated, or even completely chaotic.

Using these distinctions, Snowden developed a sense-making framework—originally called "Cynefin" (pronounced *kun-ev'in*), based on a Welsh concept of belonging in multiple spaces—to help groups understand the underlying nature of a problem or a set of interactions. This framework provides a model for distinguishing complex problems from other types and so, often generates ideas for solving seemingly intractable problems.

Methodology Overview

Using the term *domain* to describe a specific state of relationships and the ways they are perceived, Snowden identified four domains using the following distinctions:

- The knowable and the unknowable;
- The ordered and the unordered.

The framework emerged from positioning the four possible combinations of these distinctions, as shown in Figure 8.6.

The Cynefin domains

Simple order is that in which a system, process, product, or set of tasks is routine, visible, and repeatable. The work is known and

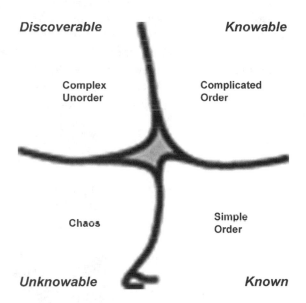

Figure 8.6
A framework for understanding complexity

visible. The relationships among people in this domain are usually hierarchical and ordered; the exchanges among them are purely transactional and procedure-based.

Complicated order is that in which there may be many relationships in a system or process, but the relationships and the intended results can be discovered. For example, a jetliner is a very complicated system with millions of parts; but if you take it apart, you can put it back together because you can know the relationships of each of the parts to one another.

Complex unorder is that in which relationships are changing too quickly for measurement. In human systems, it is impossible to predict with certainty how the system will behave because the free will of individuals transcends the control of any predetermined governance model. However, the behavior of complex systems can be discovered by looking at patterns and working with the underlying principles.

Chaotic unorder is the state in which there is no order to the relationships and neither patterns nor rules can be perceived. It's the place in which nothing makes sense and there is no known way to make sense of behavior.

These domains are never displayed in a square matrix because there are two additional dimensions: The center part represents the completely "unknown," the category of things about which you "don't know you don't know," and the twist between the domains of chaos and simple order represents the tendency of an ordered system to approach the edge of chaos—which, conventional wisdom says, is the source of innovation, change, and creativity.

Diagnostic insights

The goal of this brief discussion is to introduce the domains and provide brief descriptions of two key aspects of the framework that apply to net work:

1. Approach to problem solving
2. Network structures

The first aspect is simply a set of rules that help determine the current domain and with it the appropriate approach to problem solving.

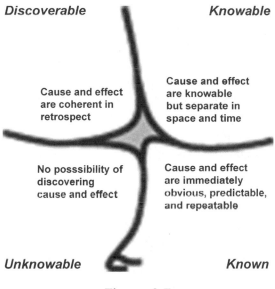

Figure 8.7
Cause and effect

You can use the statements in the specific domain areas shown in Figure 8.7 to compare with the pattern of activity in a network you are examining.

These patterns for comparison—intuitive rules of thumb, also called *heuristics*—become important in interpreting the style of a network if you want to understand the mechanisms by which it produces value:

- *Simple:* If the network has established a set of operational procedures to produce repeatable outcomes that can be measured, then it is most effective if its daily operations are managed as simple, ordered, and visible transactions. Problem diagnosis is a basic matter of looking for immediate cause related to effect and changing the causal condition;

- *Complicated:* When the operational activities of a network are more complicated, for example, in the management of supplies through a logistical chain, it may be more difficult to trace the source of the problem, but the problem and its solution can be researched, reported on, and implemented;

- *Complex:* The complex domain is the one that is the most important for net work, because the heuristic here reminds us that when there are human relationships at play, results cannot be predicted—but can almost always be understood in retrospect. For example, a decision result may be poor because a person with vital information wasn't present at a meeting, but that can't be known until after the fact;

- *Chaotic:* Events can throw unprepared networks into chaos, and although the cause may be known (a hurricane, for example, or the loss of a leader), the subsequent activities and actions within the network lose all coherence. Communication breaks down, individuals act without reference to others, and random actions yield unexpected results. You need only think of the Hurricane Katrina disaster in August of 2005 to understand what can happen when both networks (e.g., the Red Cross and local relief agencies) and hierarchies (federal, state, and local agencies) break down.

A sense-making workshop that uses collected anecdotes and the experiences of the people in the room can lead a network to distinguish its current situation as occurring in one these four domains. It's likely that a network will be solving problems in more than one domain at the same time, or that networks themselves will be positioned in one domain on the boundary of another. For example, if you think about the tasks of governing a network, you might see a number of activities, each addressing problems in different domains:

- Writing down the procedures for running meetings, generating monthly reports, or maintaining a mailing list is a codification exercise. How to do it is well known. It's simple, and there are examples and templates to follow.

- Making a decision about what policies to follow given policy from a local, national, or international regulatory body is a complicated problem. The answer can be found. Assign a few smart people to study the problem and make a recommendation.

- Collaborating on a project with another network on a specified task requires managing relationships at multiple levels—that of the network itself and that of each of the individuals or groups involved in the collaboration. It's a complex problem, and you must hope that you've set the expectations and principles so that people will self-organize to accomplish the work. All you can do is to make small changes, wait, and see what happens without expectation of a certain result.

■ When the network appears to have failed completely, someone needs to step in and take charge, make decisions, set boundaries on the relationships, and create structured conversations to re-create relationships, if only for the time it takes to shut the network down and give closure to its members.

These sense-making and problem-solving heuristics apply to organizations of all types, but are particularly important to the complexity inherent in networks.

The second aspect of the complex sense-making framework is the insight that the model gives into the constraints and opportunities of the network's underlying structure. Figure 8.8 shows another

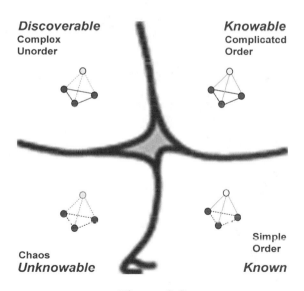

Figure 8.8
Network structures appropriate to different sense-making domains

iteration of the framework; this time, the patterns show what network structure is most representative of each of the domains.

The three-dimensional figures in each of the domains illustrate the strength of the hierarchically defined relationships (vertical ties) versus those of the informal networks. In the simple domain of the ordered, repeatable, and routine, the network's value comes from adhering to best practices and following procedure. In the complicated domain, however, the hierarchy and the network can work effectively in concert. This is the domain of problem-solving task forces and networks chartered within an organization to solve specific problems. Hierarchies and networks can coexist comfortably.

The complex domain is where the emergent and innovative networks thrive. Without the constraints of hierarchy, ideas flow freely among shifting patterns of relationships. The governance must be sufficient to provide infrastructure and perhaps guidance to the value-producing activities of the network, but the value of the network comes from its vitality.

In chaos, absence of any relationships represents the state in which no value can be produced.

When problems or challenges occur, examination can help make sense of the underlying dynamic context, and provide insight into whether to shift the problem from one domain to another.

EXAMINATION IS INTERVENTION

The examination methods presented in this chapter are proven useful diagnostic tools to target potential sources of problems in a network because they provide specific insights into the structure, style, and value-creating mechanisms of networks. You can use the concepts of these methods by yourself or with a few other people to make a sketch that will help you toward understanding a network. Once you start using the network lens, you may find that you become quick to make a sketch of what you know about relationships as you approach a new task or project.

A sketch can guide the way. For rigorous application to a key business problem or opportunity and to engage the network's stakeholders, these methods require forethought and design, a network champion or orchestrator, a leader/sponsor who will commit to the activity, and access to internal resources or external consultants who can facilitate the work.

Regardless of the motivation or the visibility of the examination, the examination begins the process of change in the network. If it is you as an individual who is looking at the network, your perceptions will change your behavior and ultimately will impact the behavior of those you work with in the network, the others they work with, and so on. You cannot examine the network without changing it.

Change, and the ways that experience, judgment, and a good toolkit can assist in solving network problems and moving networks from one state to another are the topics of the next chapter.

NOTES

1. Ron Burt, *Structural Holes* (Cambridge: Harvard University Press, 1995).
2. Patti Anklam and Adrian Wolfberg, "Creating Networks at the Defense Intelligence Agency," *KM Review* 9, no. 1 (2006).
3. Value Network Consortium www.vncluster.com/VNVAC.htm.
4. A description of the framework first appeared in C.F. Kurtz and D.J. Snowden, "The New Dynamics of Strategy: Sense-Making in a Complex and Complicated World," *IBM Systems Journal* 42, no. 3 (2003). Snowden will be completing his first book on this work in the summer of 2007.

Chapter 9

NET WORK: CHANGE AND TRANSITION

From the perspective of traditional hierarchies, managers can effect change and control outcomes by altering the hierarchical structure or processes in some ordered way: adding or removing parts, changing the rate of input, and so on. From the perspective of the network, however, the organization is organic, based on a complex set of relationships between individuals and among organizations and groups and the ways that they exchange value. In this perspective, traditional control mechanisms, while useful for many purposes, are not suitable, nor is the mindset that there is always a direct and knowable relationship between cause and effect.

We are learning to understand networks, to identify them by purpose, and to discern unique characteristics of their structures, styles, and value-producing processes. Within these facets there are adjustments within our power to make. This implies that while we cannot *manage* networks in the traditional sense, we can manage (or least influence) the *context* of the network and the environment in which it operates.

This chapter focuses on the ways that we can shift the context of networks in response to different types of events, or triggers, and on the leverage points for changing the context of a network for subtle course corrections, strategic changes, or transitions from one stage to another.

PROCESS

Chapter 7 introduced a growth model for networks in the context of designing a network to prepare for an organic set of transitions between stages of discovery and design through growth and performance maturity. These growth stages are common across living organisms and social and economic constructs. The network must cope with problems and opportunities at any stage during the process and be prepared to make changes. Figure 9.1 repeats the key elements of the network life cycle model introduced in Chapter 7, highlighting the fact that a transition at any stage of the life cycle may prompt a revitalization of the network that may alter or renew its purpose or adjust any of the aspects of its structural design.

We've seen that a network emerges from an act of creation, the result of conversations among people who identify a common purpose. In many cases, the momentum of those conversations will carry the network on a steady, generative path, but ultimately something will cause a network to halt, pause, or shift. It is at these points, or triggers, that net work is required.

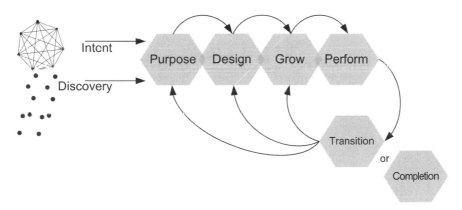

Figure 9.1
Pattern of network evolution

Triggers

Let's look at the context of change as occurring in response to one of the following types of triggers:

- Planned;
- Discovered;
- Dynamic;
- Asymmetric.

Planned triggers

A network that begins with a set of milestones for its own organizational evolution will have *planned* a set of triggers that prompt activity focused on change. Sometimes these are in conjunction with planned life cycle milestones, such as:

- Completion and signing of a proposal or a charter statement;
- Securing financial support;
- Reaching a specific goal for membership growth;
- Expanding outside a starting geography.

For example, it is common for an organizational charter to specify that there must be an annual, biennial, or five-year review that looks at various attributes of the network: the charter itself, operational efficiencies, actual vs. estimated value created, and so on. Many companies perform annual or biennial employee or customer satisfaction surveys and implement changes based on the results. Even informal networks convene a steering committee to periodically review the status of membership, commitments, and the network's overall vitality to determine if adjustments are needed.

Discovered triggers

The need for adjustment can be *discovered* when performance measures slip or when something is suddenly missing in the style or spirit of the network. Like the proverbial frog in a pot of cold water that is slowly warming to a boil, unnoticed changes may accumulate until discomfort reaches the boiling point. Donations may be drying up, or meeting attendance may be declining slowly. Or the network may grow beyond the point at which it can manage itself with volunteer staff and begin to require the addition of staff, new resources, new procedural documents, and so on.

Dynamic triggers

Dynamic change emerges from the shifting of relationships among the people and groups in the network. Within and across networks, any shift in one relationship can have a potentially large impact on the whole. Consider the impact of the loss of a leader and the resultant loss of multiple relationships that have held a network together and kept information flowing.

Dynamic, or organic, changes are not always immediately visible, and their effects are often both indirect and distant in time from their discovery. We understand dynamic triggers through sensing our environment.

Asymmetric changes

These three types of change triggers—planned, discovered, and dynamic—occur within the context of the network and its boundaries of membership, structure, style, and processes. A fourth type of trigger, the *asymmetric*, is one that is completely unanticipated given even the best of maps or plans. Storms, terrorist attacks, and economic collapse all present possibilities for huge events that can cause many networks and organizations to rethink and reshape themselves. For example, Peter Plastrik and Madeleine Taylor point to the strategic work underway at the American Red Cross since the depletion (physical and emotional) of its resources following hurricanes Katrina and Rita in 2005. Long a networked organization, the Red Cross has learned that it must—and can—rely on an extensive network of local organizations to support it in times of catastrophe. The Red Cross has responded by developing a formal, ongoing network of private companies—operating nationally and locally, coordinated but not centrally controlled.[1]

Asymmetric changes do not have to be catastrophic; sometimes it's a matter of demographics catching up with a group. Meeting attendance for local professional networks like the Company of Friends ⊕ was very high when its cells sprung up during the mid-1990s. By 2000, as the economy shifted, many members were either employed or working in their own small businesses. As the context shifted, so did the topics of interest, from job-hunting and career-development practices to broader and often more spiritual topics.

Responding to Triggers

From the network perspective, change is a constant, and these four triggers broadly describe contexts in which the need for change is noticed. The next question for net work is, "What is the process by which responses actually result in change? If we accept that we can't control the way a network will behave, how do we shift it, nudge it, shape it, alter its direction?"

Chapter 8 introduced various ways of examining networks. Certainly, one of these approaches may be useful if the trigger represents a challenge to the network or if it has surfaced a problem that needs diagnostic help. In most cases, however, the members of a network can engage in a conversation for sense making to reach a common understanding of what might be needed. Then, continuous incremental or small- and high-leverage changes are all that are required. Figure 9.2 shows a model for managing a network's context.

The labels at the steps—Probe, Sense, and Respond—provide a rule of thumb for effecting change in complex environments like networks. A "probe" is any small change that can cause a reaction; it can be to create a connection, highlight a specific element in the network, or even invite an unexpected guest to a meeting. The art is in making changes that are small enough to make a difference, but not so great as to alter the value-producing activities of the network.

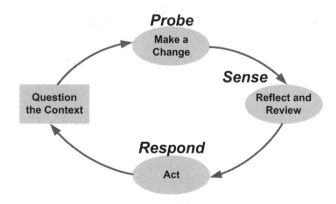

Figure 9.2
Managing a network's context

Each change is followed by analysis or review. Members see, or sense, what changed and decide if it shifted the context in a desirable direction. They can then respond to what they saw, make additional adjustments, or take some definitive action before they look at the next question. And start over. Probe. Sense. Respond.

Now that we've looked at the triggers of change and its fundamental process, we can look at the levers of change—the tools that help us to accomplish change, often to accomplish large change with a small amount of effort.

NET WORK LEVERAGE POINTS

Leverage points are any of the design elements of networks described in Part I of this book: purpose, structure, style, value, and each of their elements or component parts. The art of net work is practicing context management and learning to look for contextual clues to decide which levers to use, on which points, and when.

Therefore, the levers described in each of the sections that follow— methods, tools, and tips for intervention or change—are not limited for use at any specific point in the life cycle of a network. Nor are the levers described here in any way a full or complete set; consider them "probes" and you will, I hope, respond by creating ideas of your own.

Changing Purpose, Vision, Strategy

Revisiting or revising the core purpose, reframing its vision, or changing its underlying strategy for accomplishing the purpose is an activity that a network must do in times of transformation, for example, when two networks (or companies) merge, when a network has accomplished its goals and wants to recommit its purpose to something new or larger, or when a network has grown in size and diversity.

Whole-system methods

Within the last twenty years, many organizational development (OD) leaders have designed and matured processes that accommodate

Table 9.1
Facilitated Methods for Network Transformation

Method	Summary
Future Search	A structured step-by-step approach that brings all the stakeholders in a network together to map the path of their interactions to the present day, to establish common ground using the themes identified, and then to search for innovative strategies and build mutual commitment to a shared future.
Open Space	A theme-based conference that requires participants to identify topics that they want to talk about and provides break-out rooms for anyone interested in those topics to gather, engage with others on that topic, and understand what they are able to contribute and willing to commit to.
World Café	An orchestrated series of small-group dialogues focused on a common challenge question that enables the emergence of innovative ideas and insights by pulling wisdom from all participants.
Appreciative Inquiry	A process for working with all stakeholders that begins with the discovery of the positive core values as expressed by stories of the past, and goes on to use these values to envision a desired future state and co-constructing a strategy and action plan to achieve it.

"whole system" change, that is, change processes that include all the participants in a network—including as many as 1,000 people or more in a room at the same time, working collaboratively. Identified as one of the five disciplines of a learning organization in Peter Senge's *The Fifth Discipline*, "shared vision" represents the desired outcome of whole-system methodologies first explored by Marvin Weisbord and Kathleen Dannemiller in the 1980s and 1990s.[2]

The most widely used methods for summoning the whole system are summarized in Table 9.1. These methods leverage the diversity and breadth of a network by using collective intelligence, building scenarios, gathering stories, relying on principles of self-organization, and harnessing the power of effective conversation.

Tapping collective intelligence. In a Future Search, bringing all or a significant portion of a network's membership into a room creates an environment that draws on the collective intelligence of all the members of a network: The more stakeholders, including network members, who participate in the activities leading to changes in vision, strategy, and purpose, the more likely the activity will lead to specific, actionable work that network members volunteer to work on.

The World Café provides a structured setting for a large number of people to engage in small-group conversations that contribute to a whole-system response to a large, important question. Groups of four to six participants sit at café-style tables that are covered with butcher paper and furnished with markers to encourage the groups to capture the key themes and questions that arise as they discuss the topic. Every twenty minutes, all but one of the people at each table move to a different table. The cross-pollination and connection of ideas generates collective wisdom that leads to innovative approaches to creating a vision, developing strategic plans, or mapping out action.

Scenario mapping. For many years, scenarios have been used to examine alternate strategies for strategic development of purpose, positioning a network in its ecosystem, and innovations for producing value. A common method establishes one or more potential future states and constructs a set of hypothetical events that would lead from the present to one or more of those future states. Hypothetical events may include disruptions caused by the loss of a leader or a natural disaster, a shift in governmental policy, an innovation in technology, and so on. In a group setting, teams construct timelines by placing these event items on a wall and explaining how they are linked, why one must follow rather than precede another, and so on. People are free to create additional events as they build to a scenario that, in the end, must meet the tests of plausibility, relevance, and challenge.

Typical end-state scenarios for developing the strategy for a network or business development might include one that predicts a mega-merger or consolidation of all related networks into one large conglomerate, one that predicts the complete disruption of a value network into chaos, one that positions only one or two large networks controlling access to the key supplier networks, and so on. Scenario mapping lets stakeholders deconstruct assumptions about how their business works and where it is going and provides insights into how they might better shape business outcomes of today's initiatives.

Gathering stories. Many of these methods rely on the collection before or during a network event of stories or anecdotes from individuals' experiences of being in and working in the network. Analysis of the stories and the themes that emerge from grouping them provide a collective act of sense making that contributes to the richness of the shared vision and individuals' commitment to the common goals.

Anecdote collection is a key method for the sense making in complexity framework described in Chapter 8. Anecdotes, observations, and events are used to determine the nature (complex, simple, complicated, or chaotic) of a situation so it can be acted on appropriately. The review and refinement of anecdotes and observations can result in the development of archetypes or personas representing particular attitudes or patterns of behavior.

Appreciative Inquiry (AI) is a process that begins by eliciting positive statements or examples about the core values of the network or organization. The discovery phase for a change process, it's been found, takes negative energy that is focused on problems or difficulties and turns it into positive energy, which can then be focused on envisioning a future that leverages those positive qualities. These discovered values and dreams of the future provide the basis for a facilitated event that enables participants to design organizational processes that improve or transform the work.

Gervase Bushe at Simon Fraser University has been using Appreciative Inquiry with teams at many different points in their lifecycle and in a variety of ways. For example, he has used AI to help groups build relationships, either in new networks or in ongoing groups. He describes using his "best team" approach[3] for consulting with groups whose leadership teams had become ineffective. In a workshop setting, participants talk about their experiences working in high-performing groups and describe the characteristics of those groups. Because the focus of the stories is only on positive experiences, participants engage in deeper understanding of the ways that each can work together more effectively.

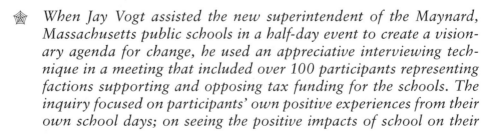

When Jay Vogt assisted the new superintendent of the Maynard, Massachusetts public schools in a half-day event to create a visionary agenda for change, he used an appreciative interviewing technique in a meeting that included over 100 participants representing factions supporting and opposing tax funding for the schools. The inquiry focused on participants' own positive experiences from their own school days; on seeing the positive impacts of school on their

*children, neighbors, or young relatives; or of hiring well-educated
employees. These conversations created a positive energy that led to
the creation of dozens of dreams for the future of the schools. After
the participants grouped the ideas into nine thematic aspirations, all
the participants voted to prioritize their choices.*[4]

Self-organizing. During facilitated events, participants are encouraged to generate topics of conversation and to self-organize into
groups for focused discussions on topics that interest them. In Open
Space Technology, for example, the facilitator frames a challenge to
the group and invites individuals who care passionately about an
issue to put a topic on the agenda. For a one- or two-day meeting,
the facilitator assigns a time and a meeting room for each topic, and
the person who suggested the topic convenes a group to discuss it.
Within the group, participants set their own schedules and are
responsible for exchanging and capturing ideas and any outcomes
that the group produces. At the end of the meeting, the results of all
the topic groups are collected and reviewed.

 *The Deputy Director of the State Planning Office in Maine, Sue
Inches, was challenged in the summer of 2005 to solicit feedback on
the state's Growth Management Act and development recommendations. She knew that to succeed she would need to include a variety
of stakeholders, including policy makers, planners, town officials,
consultants, developers, environmentalists, state agency staff, and
citizens interested in planning issues. Inches decided on an open-
space format and created an engaging invitation that was circulated
widely around the state. In August, 125 participants, many of whom
were antagonists in other settings, met for two days. They created
their agenda in sixty minutes and spent the rest of the two days debat-
ing, proposing, and creating proposals. The major themes that
emerged were refined through focus groups and became formal recommendations presented to the Maine legislature.*[5] *In addition to the
tangible outcome of ideas that led to recommendations, Inches noted
the equally important intangible outcomes: increased credibility for
the State Planning Office, improved relationships with previously
contentious groups, and the generation of many additional ideas.*

The methods I've described here and elsewhere in this book—ONA,
VNA, and complex sense making—have a unique and rich history

as methods in and of themselves, but they can also be used as building blocks to design specific interventions. For example, David Cooperrider, one of the inventors of Appreciative Inquiry, has used AI as a front end to a Future Search conference. In a Future Search, teams of participants create or analyze data that includes macro trends that will impact the organization, a report on AI interviews conducted prior to the event, and benchmarking information including novel or interesting practices being done in other organizations. The next major activity in the Future Search is the creative construction of a vision of the future that looks at the key organizational dimensions of purpose, organizational structure and roles, value-creating processes, technologies, strategy, and so on. The final activity consists of developing an action plan that will take the network to the vision it has co-created.

The design goal for a whole-system intervention using these methods is to involve as many people as possible. For example, a global "federated" network or organization can reach all of its members by first training a cadre of 1,000 people in each region to conduct interviews and then having these people each interview ten others. Regional events bring in these 1,000 and perhaps 1,000 others and so on, until everyone in an organization has participated in some way to the collective wisdom that generates an altered purpose, new goals, mission, or strategy.

These large transformational events do not—and perhaps need not—occur frequently in the life of a network. For launching a network into a common understanding of its purpose and what it wants to accomplish, however, such events are very effective. They also offer productive and useful ways to put a network back on track or onto a new course after a period of chaos while repurposing it.

At the heart of all the methods is the practice of effective conversations, that is, speaking and listening in a way that enables new ideas to emerge from among a diversity of perspectives and in a way that approaches problem solving without blame or fault. Such conversations require that people remain conscious of responding to ideas rather than personalities, that people see the conversation as collaboration rather than contest, and that they fully acknowledge that what each person brings is valuable.

In a network that supports "conversations that matter," it's possible to think about conversations as the core business process.[6] Conversations can initiate rapport, let possibilities emerge, generate opportunity, and manage activity. Conversations can also solve problems, often by creating small breakthroughs.

In the context of the network's structural elements, many levers can have positive impacts on the patterns of connectivity, the network's governance, and its texture.

Changing Structure

Chapter 4 provided examples of networks with both structured and organic patterns. The structured patterns, including hub-and-spoke, hierarchy, and federated models, represent common ways that networks establish lines of communication, decision making, and accountability. If a network grows through an evolution process of hub-and-spoke to hierarchy to federation, then those structural change points will alter the informal as well as the formal relationships within the network. Events that may require attention to the structure of the network include:

- Departure of key people;
- Sudden influx of many new members;
- Growth of cliques;
- Confusion about decision-making processes.

Chapter 8 demonstrated how an organizational network analysis can reveal disconnects or junctures in relationships in a network and suggested some possible responses.

Another way to think about a range of ways to change the patterns in the network is to think in terms of managing the connectivity.

Changing patterns and texture

The easiest way to think about how a change in connectivity can alter a network is to look at the simple case of A, B, and C (see Figure 9.3).

Starting with either a network map or an intuition about the existing connectivity across a network, anyone in the network can use a variety of tools—many of them on hand—to alter the structure. Table 9.2 provides a starting point for thinking about ways to alter the structure of networks.

Table 9.2
Changing Network Patterns[7]

Ways to Change Patterns in Networks	Techniques and Methods
Increase the number of ties (randomly)	Introduce people; hold seminars and knowledge fairs; make sure that face-to-face events provide time and facilitated methods that enable people to get acquainted
Increase the number of ties (selectively)	Establish roles for individuals to broker connections across groups; assign people to work on projects together
Open groups that are closed	Reassign members to new projects or locations; add new members with different perspectives
Fill in "structural holes" (see Chapter 8)	Institutionalize or expand the roles of people who are connecting different parts of a network
Increase the flow of information, ideas, and insights	Add communication channels (blogs, wikis, virtual team spaces, newsletters); increase the frequency of meetings or teleconferences
Enable discovery	Create member directories that give people an opportunity to let others know about their capabilities, talents, and experiences; use social networking software to help people make connections
Increase diversity	Add nodes by creating ties with people in different networks; bring in speakers who represent different disciplines or points of view
Leverage diversity	Create reward structures that reinforce working across expertise and geographical boundaries
Strengthen relationships	Assign people to work on projects together; use electronic tools like instant messaging to enable a sense of presence
Reduce cliques	Rotate network leadership
Increase the connective capacity of the network	Create awareness of the impact of an individual's place in a network; educate members on personal knowledge networking

Figure 9.4 shows the impact of taking specific actions to change the connectivity of a network. This example, from Rob Cross and Andrew Parker, shows a professional consulting group that sought to integrate highly technical specialists with organizational development experts to provide more holistic knowledge management solu-

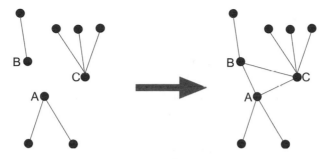

Figure 9.3
Making connections

tions. The map on the left shows the information flow between the two groups at the time that the integration was sought; the map on the left shows the interactions nine months later.

The specific activities that resulted in this change were generated by the people in the network themselves. They identified a number of internal projects, including writing white papers and building tools, that they could work on together that would enable them to build personal ties and become aware of each other's areas of skills and expertise. The partner added mixed-revenue sales goals for the managers of each of the two groups to make them accountable for selling solutions that included both domains of expertise. And they instituted a number of regular communication forums, including regular teleconferences and a joint project-tracking database.[8]

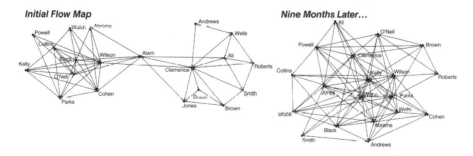

Figure 9.4
Changing connectivity
Source: Copyright © 2001, Elsevier Ltd.

Personal network analysis

When people see maps of networks that they participate in, they always look for their own names to see how they relate to the network as a whole. Within the data collected for an ONA are the individual network structures of each person in it. These "ego networks" can be augmented by people adding in the people they interact with who are outside the bounded network that is being mapped. When people see their personal networks, they are better able to understand how well positioned they are—not just with respect to their role in the network but also it terms of the resources (internal and external) to which they have access.

Clarify or change the governance model

Many networks experience problems when there is a lack of clarity about accountability and decision-making authority. Being able to work in networks implies the ability to work with a high degree of ambiguity, but sometimes trust just is not enough. The best way to position a network to deal with ambiguity is to agree on a charter statement and establish core principles.

Informal networks often start with little more than a mission statement (if that) and a sense of shared responsibility. However, as the network grows and the core group who started it becomes fatigued with procedural and logistic details, they see the need to:

- Define the network more carefully;
- Document guidelines and work practices;
- Clarify roles and responsibilities.

Language is extremely important in defining a network. Some terms are "alliance," "joint venture," "partnership," "coalition," "consortortium," and (of course) "network." Confusion between and among partners may exist at the simple level of naming. One company may call it an "alliance" and the other call it a "strategic relationship." It is only by spelling out the definitions and descriptions of measurable criteria that clarity and mutual understanding can be established.[9]

Changing Style

Dynamic changes in a network may be subtle or dramatic, a one-time crisis or a pattern or trend. Some of the signs that the network's style may need some work are:

- Fewer people show up for meetings;
- The network has stopped growing;
- Interactions are contentious;
- Morale is low and people are distrustful;
- No one posts messages in the online space.

This section reviews ways of probing a network when a malaise threatens its vibrancy.

Place, space, and pace

Discomfort with the physical and temporal aspects of a network—the space, place, and pace—is a discovered trigger that, among all the aspects of a network, is the easiest to change.

Surveys can be done on an annual (planned) basis, in response to an event, or on a regular basis. Many successful communities of learning distribute a brief survey after every meeting that requests feedback on:

- The content of the meeting;
- The physical venue and logistics;
- The way the meeting was run.

Sometimes it takes a crisis to realize how unhappy members are with a specific choice of location. Women in Networking ⬡ experienced several transitions in style, two of which coincided with changes in the settings of meetings. During its first two years, WIN meetings were held at a restaurant in a central location that provided a good meeting space, but the food was terrible. The context for the network changed as well. Whereas in the beginning WIN focused on helping women find jobs in a poor economy, as the economy shifted, it needed to change its focus. After a new leader stepped in and changed the meeting place and content focus, meeting attendance went back to its benchmark of 30 to 40 members attending each meeting.

Three years later, attendance had slowly dropped once again to about 15 women per meeting, and only two women showed up for the annual planning meeting. These two made a list of the tasks and core responsibilities, sent out a questionnaire, and used that to reshape and reconnect the women in the network. They arranged to have meetings in a jazz café that provided a comfortable and welcoming ambience and once again shifted the topics based on the questionnaire responses.

In virtual space, sometimes it's the technology that needs to change. CPsquare 🏵, the learning community for communities of practice, launched with a collaboration platform product that many members found difficult to understand and use. Despite the best efforts of the founders to prepare common discussion areas and virtual team spaces prior to the launch and to provide orientation sessions on how to use the software, it became apparent that the virtual space—which was to be the cornerstone for capturing the research, interactions, and community activities—would not succeed with that platform. Within six months, CPsquare leadership shifted to a different software platform that was easier to use, and has been communicating successfully with it ever since.

Pace is another important lever that is easy to change. The growth phase of a network may require more frequent and more intense interactions, but as the network shifts into its performance phase, the pace should adjust to the nature of the activities. Altering the frequency or duration of communications, events, and interactions is one way to probe the dynamics of the network and see what happens. In fact, the probe in this case needs only to be a question for discussion. A question such as "Should we shift our meeting schedule from bimonthly to quarterly?" will create a conversation that enables the network to self-organize into a response.

Cultural changes

Cultural change is often hardest at the second network transition, from design to growth, particularly if members of the network are not used to working across boundaries. To create a culture of openness, diversity, and transparency requires strong leadership that communicates and acts consistently with the norms required to create a collaborative network.

 MWH, a global leader in the areas of water, hydropower, and remediation, made a shift from geographic, hierarchically based business units to global, expertise-based groups in 2003. To facilitate the shift to collaborative virtual teamwork, MWH realized that it needed to help employees create individual ties and maintain a high level of awareness about the need to work across boundaries. It helped people establish personal connections and build trust by creating specific cross-functional teams, rotating people across geographies, and providing a generous travel budget. Creating and maintaining face-to-face contact was one of the primary success factors, as measured by an improved density metric across the geographies and expertise areas and the comments of managers.

The second major success factor was the consistency of messages. Corporate presentations and communications, including newsletters and group meetings, bridged the geographic and expertise boundaries of employees by repeating the message "We are not a regional company anymore." Most important, all levels of management were attuned to the composition of project teams and were quick to point out when a team was not including required expertise from other areas or geographies.[10]

Even well-established norms of trust and reciprocity are subject to erosion or disruption. Erosion occurs when the ties among individual members of a network are not refreshed and renewed through interactions or sustained by a communications infrastructure that maintains awareness and sustains members' identity with the network itself.

Networks of all types—even hierarchical networks—are prone to disruption when cultural norms are violated or broken. If a leader betrays the trust of the network, then it's vital for new leadership to step in and repair the network. In some cases, an individual member can introduce a level of toxicity into the network that breaks down the norms among other members as well.

Leadership

A change in leadership, for whatever reason, has the potential to alter the culture of a network. The business world is replete with examples

of how the character or personality of a CEO imprints an organization with specific values, and how a new CEO may disrupt them.
Sometimes the culture of the network can be the cause for a change
in leadership.

*Wikipedia.org—a worldwide knowledge base maintained by a
network—was shaped by its founders, entrepreneur Jimmy Wales
and "organizer-in-chief" Larry Sanger, who launched it as an experiment when their original product, Nupedia, was faltering. The
Wikipedia network grew to 350 people during its first year, January
through December of 2001. During that year, however, Sanger
found himself philosophically at odds with many members of the
community with respect to his editorial authority; a number of
major contributors felt that Wikipedia was best served by a fully
decentralized (nearly "anarchic") self-organizing and self-correcting
community. Sanger left in January 2002, having made "two great
contributions to Wikipedia: he built it, and he left it."[11] Wales
remained, a "benign ruler," and in 2003 transferred ownership of
Wikipedia to the Wikipedia Foundation and took a place on the
foundation's board.*

Whether through leadership, drift, or another reason, sometimes a
network starts to falter when it loses sight of whether and how it is
producing value for all of its stakeholders.

Value-Creating Processes

One of the most important norms that sustain networks is reciprocity, the "give and the get," as Jeff Shuman and Jan Twombly describe
it.[12] One sign that a network needs examination or a shift in its
value-creating processes is when it becomes clear that there is an
imbalance in the exchange of either or both tangible and intangible
values.

Other clues that the processes are out of balance may be the
failure to realize—or to communicate—the value expected of
stakeholders.

*The "Porter Question," as it is called at the U.S. Agency for Health-
care Research (AHRQ), altered the context within which AHRQ*

developed and measured its value. A U.S. House of Representatives subcommittee reviewed the agency's budget in 1998. The results of the agency's work was presented in terms of the number of the research reports it produced. Rep. John E. Porter commented, "What we really want to get at is not how many reports have been done, but how many people's lives have been bettered by what has been accomplished. In other words, is it being used, is it being followed, is it actually being given to patients?"[13] *Since this question was posed, the agency has worked to understand how it must operate to ensure that the research it funds does not end up unread and unreferenced, but that the learning from research is actually integrated into the daily practices of healthcare providers.*

Not all networks have such clear wake-up calls with respect to whether they are in fact focusing on producing value for the stakeholders who matter most. The network diagnostics described in Chapter 8 are powerful ways of creating understanding within a network of the ways that interactions among network members are enhancing or impeding value—and of generating new ways of looking at value.

Companies go out of business when they stop producing value for their shareholders, but networks increasingly can produce value only in the context of a web of stakeholders and partners. The equation is no longer simple, and the art of learning to find the right lever comes from finding the right method to make sense of the terrain. In a complex ecosystem of personal, organizational, corporate, and global relationships, those of us who are committed to working in networks need to approach the task of maintaining them and guiding them through transitions with strategies for sustainability. Let's call this creating the safety net.

THE RESILIENT SAFETY NET

Transitions and transformations in networks have the same origins as a network itself: emergence or intention. When it's time for change, a resilient network will be able to manage the context of a transition by leveraging its core strengths. These strengths, which can be either built into the design of the network or nurtured over time, include the following:

- Commitment to a common purpose that is well articulated but also a candidate for reflective and generative dialogue among members;

- A structure that is appropriate to its purpose and value-producing mechanisms, monitored on a regular basis to ensure inclusive and just governance protocols;

- Support for energetic, trusting, and balanced interactions;

- Clarity about its stakeholders, investments, and outcomes.

These strengths are not possible without the capacity for honest and engaging conversation. An infrastructure to support the conversational capacity includes the right technology and a core group of change agents.

Technology offers the means to create and manage large, ongoing conversations across a diverse set of people. Technologies can support network activities encompassing the tasks of communication, collaboration, connection, community building, content preparation, and review. In real time or after the fact, network members can understand the context of a situation and contribute in a way that makes sense. The Appendix gives a brief list and definitions of the mature and emerging technologies that provide infrastructure to support networks.

Creating a network and its infrastructure may be just the beginning of a long-term and systemic process of culture change. What if the goal is to make an entire organization more networked, open, and capable of learning and adapting? Sometimes there needs to be a network within a network, a core group or set of change agents like the analysts in the Knowledge Lab 🕸 at the Defense Intelligence Agency, or the Internet conspirators at IBM 🕸 .

When we have a network lens, we see what makes these strategies, which have been long in use, successful:

- Change agents connect to each other and reach across boundaries to recruit members from disparate groups and organizations. Often, good change agents both bridge across organizations and serve as central connectors within their own organizations. They keep information flowing.

- Working from a map, change agents will target specific groups or functions they want to bring into the network and identify individuals in those groups who are potentially strong central connectors.

- A change agent network must have at least one executive sponsor who is well connected, not just by formal ties but also by informal ties.

- Change agents need to be respectful of others' time and attention and provide reciprocal value as much as possible.

- Pilot programs work, not just because they provide proof of concept and learning, but also because they create strong ties between the people on the pilot teams and the change agent network.

A network of change agents is a powerful force within a network of any size, whether it is a core group, an authorized network like the Knowledge Lab 🏛, or an innovation network generating and building on ideas that may transform it into something altogether new.

Be Prepared for Closure

Although we design and join networks in the hope of vitality and longevity, we know that few networks last forever, and that all networks continue to change and evolve upon reaching maturity. As with family and tribal groups, organizational networks go through periods of growth, decline, subdivision, diaspora, and revitalization. To design a network today is to design with such eventualities in mind, to know that what is created today will change and may eventually reach closure.

Many collaborative networks form for the accomplishment of a specific goal and celebrate when the work is complete and the network's time comes to a close. Closure means celebrating accomplishments, acknowledging the work of others, and transitioning the value and results to a recipient. Many emergent networks, networks that arise from opportunity or in the context of a specific problem, also reach closure, though it's not always easy to see the end. Signs that a network has reached the end of its life include diminution of purpose, vision, and passion among a sufficient number of members. When a network is no longer meeting the expectations of its stakeholders and cannot find sufficient means to re-evaluate its outputs and outcomes, it's time to let members and stakeholders move on. Networks take time, time to create and sustain and also the time of individuals as measured in energy as well as clock-time. Freeing members and stakeholders enables them to recommit that energy to new networks, and to carry forward learning and relationships into new possibilities.

You have certainly realized while reading this book that there are many aspects of net work that you are already practicing. Over the past half-century, management science has built a store of good practices we can co-opt for net work—working with teams, knowledge management, change management, and human resources and workforce planning, to name the major ones. But the network lens helps us to see the application of these tools and methods in a new way, transforming much of our traditional work by adding a new component: net work.

NOTES

1. Peter Plastrik and Madeleine Taylor, *Net Gains: A Handbook for Social Entrepreneurs Building Networks to Increase Impact* (2006).
2. Peter Senge, *The Fifth Discipline* (New York: Doubleday Currency, 1990). Marvin R. Weisbord, *Productive Workplaces* (San Francisco: Jossey-Bass, 1987).
3. Gervase R. Bushe, "Appreciative Inquiry with Teams," *Organization Development Journal* 16, no. 3 (1988): 41–50.
4. Jay Vogt, "Unpredictable Ways to Release the Natural Intelligence of Your Organization," *Handbook of Business Strategy* 6, no. 1 (2005): 309–314.
5. Jay Vogt, "The Maine Land Use Planning Summit," *New England Planning*, March 2006.
6. Juanita Brown and David Isaacs, "Conversation as a Core Business Process," *Systems Thinker* 7, no. 10 (1996/1997).
7. Portions of this table first appeared in Patti Anklam, *The Social Network Toolkit* (London: Ark Group Publishing, 2005).
8. Rob Cross and Andrew Parker, "Making Invisible Work Visible," *California Management Review* 44, no. 2 (2002).
9. Ibid.
10. Patti Anklam, Rob Cross, and Vic Gulas, "Expanding the Field of Vision," *The Learning Organization* 12, no. 6 (2005): 539–551.

11. Marshall Poe, "The Hive," *Atlantic Monthly*, September 2006.
12. Jeffrey Shuman and Jan Twombly, *Collaborative Communities* (Chicago: Dearborn Trade, 2001).
13. John M. Eisenberg, "Putting Research to Work," *Health Services Research* June (2001).

Chapter 10

THE NET WORK OF LEADERSHIP

This book has offered models, examples, and techniques that are available to anyone who is noticing that our work, lives, and language now reflect the ways that we participate in multiple interdependent networks. I have provided a simple taxonomy of network types and a set of facets (structure, style, and value) that characterize and make each distinct, leading to design principles that puts the capacity to create and lead networks in our collective hands. I have shown how it is possible to examine networks using methods derived from principles of the sciences of networks and complexity, and I've offered a way of thinking about using these methods to guide networks through both dramatic and subtle transitions.

One of the assumptions I made in writing this book is that everyone in a network can influence the relationships in and thereby the outcomes of the network and that the work of leaders is primarily to create and maintain the conditions that enable relationships. This is the "net work" of leadership, for which this chapter offers the following prescriptions:

- Network intentionally;
- Practice network stewardship;
- Leverage technology;

- Create the capacity for net work;
- Use the network lens and net work tools to enhance the lives and contributions of individuals and the collective power of the network.

This chapter concludes with a summary of the challenges of net work and suggestions for practical first steps.

NETWORK INTENTIONALLY

Examples throughout this book have shown the results of careful nurturing of networks as well as organizational strategies based on building networks. There is nothing new about creating or using network strategies; it is just that we now have the insight and tools that enable us to be intentional about how we create and work in networks and to leverage and nurture emergent networks.

Networked Inside

For businesses that embrace networks to accomplish collaborative work, the question is not how to design "the network," but how to orchestrate multiple networks that may be designed quite differently. Jay Galbraith has looked at networks in Nestlé, IBM, and other multinational companies. He found that these companies have learned to manage multiple networks, with as many as nine different design models. While preserving their traditional hierarchical and divisional structures, these companies have created partnerships, task forces, global initiatives, and a host of other collaborative networks to address specific strategic dimensions of the business. For example, Nestlé creates a new network whenever it diversifies into a new business area.[1]

 When MWH reorganized in 2003 away from a hierarchical, regional-based structure to a global, expertise-based structure, Vic Gulas, MWH's Chief Knowledge Officer and CIO guided the transition process. He looked at the existing networks, formal and informal, and the ways in which MWH could rapidly start to knit new networks across regional boundaries that would connect people

based on expertise and common project affiliations. Using organizational network analysis to provide a baseline of interactions across regions and expertise areas, Gulas and the executive team at MWH began to design a program to ensure that projects would be designed and managed by tapping expertise, wherever it resided in the world.[2]

Gulas created communities of practice based on expertise groups, implemented a technology infrastructure to support collaboration, and maintained a regular pace of communication through face-to-face meetings and teleconferences. He also worked carefully with managers at all levels in the organization to ensure that they examined team and project structure with a network lens to ensure that internal and customer projects were staffed based on expertise, not locality.

Infrastructure to support networks—as for those in MWH—is now quite commonplace, as e-mail and intranet portals are augmented with collaboration platforms. Organizational infrastructure, including management support, is often found in knowledge management groups, a source of expertise for helping to create and manage communities of practices and learning networks.

The same communications infrastructure makes it possible for emergent networks led by persistent champions to create large-scale organizational change. The Internet group inside IBM, for example, created a profound shift in IBM strategy that would not have been possible without that infrastructure. MindTree Consulting actually uses the concept of community development as an attractor for innovation. As part of its knowledge management program, MindTree has provided an organizational infrastructure for communities and networks to self-organize around both short- and long-term projects and initiatives. MindTree's community efforts are based on the premise that social interactions lead to higher levels of trust and that a higher level of trust leads to a higher-performing and more innovative organization.[3]

Change agent networks may also be directed top-down, as in development of the Knowledge Lab at the Defense Intelligence Agency. This intentional network of change agents was able to demonstrate during its first two years of operation that it could have an impact on shifting behaviors to more productive, learning-based behaviors. It was renewed with a five-year commitment to execute a long-term roadmap that the DIA hopes will lead to transformation throughout the wider intelligence network.[4]

Network Outside

When Procter & Gamble 🏵 shifted its innovation strategy from internal invention to "connect and develop," it was setting itself up for tapping into the creative ideas of people both inside and outside P&G. Even in its proprietary internal R&D networks, P&G encouraged technology entrepreneurs located around the globe to reach outside of P&G to look at local markets and store shelves as well as scientific literature while building networks with local suppliers and research labs.

At the same time, P&G helped to create and/or join broker networks like NineSigma and InnoCentive. The overall strategy for P&G is to use networks to identify ideas that can be brought into the company to develop new products. This requires steady pressure on the culture at P&G to welcome innovation from the outside as opportunities for "solid business-building ideas."[5]

Previously, I've shown how the nonprofit network Guide Dogs for the Blind Association (GDBA) 🏵 adopted a strategy for growing through a network rather than enlarging their own operations. This ability— the flexibility to invent and adopt new business models—is seen as a primary challenge for businesses in the 21st century. IBM's *Global Innovation Outlook Report* for 2006 summarizes the collective insights of over 750 CEOs and concludes that innovation—the primary engine of business growth—will be dependent on a shift to new business models that look to networks outside proprietary R&D walls.[6]

Whether for innovation, enhanced productivity, access to new markets, creation of integrated solutions, or improved efficiency of the supply and distribution chains, the trend toward developing and managing partnerships and alliances will continue. Fortunately, there is a growing body of research and practice that supports organizations in their learning processes. There is no single form of network that works for any given situation. "If you've seen one alliance, you've seen one alliance," quips Michael Leonetti, Executive Director of Healthcare Partnerships at Boehringer Ingelheim Pharmaceuticals and Chairman of the Association of Strategic Alliance Professionals.[7] But there are evolving rules of thumb (also called criteria for success) that can guide sensible net work in the development of healthy partnerships:[8]

1. Select and manage the network of partners and stakeholders in the context of a well-formed value network, that is, one that has balanced tangible and intangible rewards based on the needs of each member

2. Build and manage trust

3. Manage expectations

4. Design appropriate but flexible governance mechanisms, being prepared to change the partnership agreement as it evolves

5. Set up regular, collaborative information exchange that is embedded in the work processes of those who work in the network on a daily basis

6. Make requisite relationship-specific asset investments, including continuity of boundary personnel, and resources and tools to enable learning while doing

7. Be prepared to manage conflict constructively

8. Practice the art of "give and get"

As anyone who has worked to set up alliances or partnerships knows, the creation and maintenance of such alliances is a delicate task of managing relationships between and among individuals at all levels of an organization. Network forms offer a range of operational styles that provide opportunities for networks to self-organize, self-manage, and self-direct. At the core of successful relationships, embodied in each of the above (and emphasized in point #8), is the practice of reciprocity.

Networks in the World

People participate in multiple, often overlapping networks. As individuals, we are may be formally members of (organizational, institutional) networks, but we are also able to act as free agents in other contexts. Those who work independently have already learned about how to work with networks "in the world," crossing the permeable boundaries of organizations for both short-term and long-term projects.

"Intensional" networks

The shape of industries and organizations has changed significantly over the past fifteen years. Few corporations or institutions offer employment for life and as a consequence may no longer provide individuals with career development opportunities or a sense of connectedness to a community. A study in 2000 identified a trend of workers looking to their relationships to access resources. The authors used the term "intensional" to describe these networks, and the manner of working through these intensional networks "NetWORK."[9] Within a geographical region or professional area of specialty, the networks of individuals tend to overlap in a way that provides that connectedness.

The fact that so many people are surviving and thriving in these networks outside the province of hierarchy suggests that these networks can be resilient over time.

Open-source communities

I have already described two open-source communities, Linux 🕸 and Higgins 🕸. These projects, and many like them, clearly demonstrate how it is possible for a single individual to create a network to produce software that is owned in common and accessible to anyone. The approach has been so successful that computer industry giants like IBM are now providing their proprietary frameworks to the open-source community—giving up ownership for the benefits that will come from having a larger and more diverse pool of software engineering talent. For example, IBM released its Eclipse platform for application development to a consortium (of which it was a member) in 2001. By the end of 2003, the consortium had over 80 members. In 2004, Eclipse was reorganized into a not-for-profit foundation that continues to use open-source methods for development and provides the software royalty-free.

Software engineers who participate in these communities do so because they enjoy working toward a large, complex, common goal with many others, because they can do so based on their own ability to contribute (hence selecting to do only the work that interests them), because they are part of a community of people who help each other in times of crisis, and because they receive acknowledgment from their peers when their code, corrections, and ideas are folded into the whole.

Guilds

The ages-old networked organizational structure called the guild is still with us, though not always called such. Research of MIT's Sloan School of Business into organizations of the 21st century looked at various responses to the collapse of the traditional employment contract and found three guild-like forms:

- Occupationally based groups, which include some unions and professional groups like the Screen Actor's Guild;
- Workforce brokers who match employers with workers, often through websites like the Freelancers Union;
- Regionally based organizations that partner public agencies with local employers to create jobs by building workers' skills.

Guilds, in whatever forms, have the potential to provide individuals in specific trades and professions with some of the benefits of working in large companies: economic security, health insurance and pensions, career advancement. They also provide—as for intensional networks—a means of daily social interaction and a sense of identity and belonging.

PRACTICE NETWORK STEWARDSHIP

I've said that networks, because they are complex systems, cannot be managed. I've also said that the most important quality in a network leader is stewardship. You must create the environment that "lets the network do its work," by building on traditional leadership skills.

Build on Traditional Leadership Skills

What I've found across all the types of networks is a recurring set of themes that describe a set of abilities that are not unique to network management, but that are more important for managing networks than hierarchies. These include:

- Convening diverse people and groups for the purpose of identifying common ground for action;
- Consensus decision making;
- Building social capital, with an emphasis on an environment of trust and reciprocity;
- Engaging network members in a shared vision;
- Managing conflict and generating cooperation through continuous dialogue and discourse.

Share Leadership

Shared, or collective, leadership comes naturally to many networks that are constituted primarily of cultural peers. People who speak the same natural and professional languages, share the same geographic cultural context, and have the occasion to meet and see each other frequently find it easy to slip in and out of leadership roles. For example, leadership in professional associations changes over the years as new members join the group, participate in special interest groups or service committees, and contribute their skills in managing and coordinating events and communications. These experiences bring them into the leadership arena, which both strengthens the core and keeps the network vibrant.

Many community networks face significant challenges in multicultural environments where the sustainability of the community is at risk. Since 2002, projects supported by the Kellogg Leadership for Community Change (KLCC) have developed a program in collective leadership development. The model for collective leadership that they have developed is based on the premise that leadership is relational: "The group as a whole is a leader just as members within the group can be leaders within the group." By practicing collective leadership, multicultural community groups from Buffalo, New York to the Flathead Reservation in Montana have created networks for social and policy change. They have found that "collective power—individuals working as partners to make a difference—is at the root of relevant and sustainable change efforts." Leaders, KLCC says:

- Must "learn new ways of thinking and doing";
- Are aware of "how to engage in respectful as well as critical collaborative processes";
- Network effectively to build alliances.[10]

The relational, community-based model that is this "root" comes from the principle that everyone works toward a common goal and develops strategy collectively.

LEVERAGE TECHNOLOGY

We are now so used to enterprise computer networks connected by the Internet providing the channel for transactions and transaction-based interactions that it's not even noteworthy. What is capturing interest is the way that technology is enabling relational interactions: It supports knowledge-based interactions by providing instant and immediate communication to all members of a network, a means to reach out to other networks and bring them into one's ecosystem, a way to capture and share knowledge artifacts, create and share connections among people around the world, and instantiate a network by providing it with a name and public space.

Contrary to the notion that the Internet is decreasing personal social ties, a Pew research study demonstrated that use of the Internet has expanded the social networks of those who use it and has become an information source and means to connect with others for help with critical life decisions.[11] Even family networks are enhanced and supported by e-mail, photo-sharing sites, and late-night chat sessions. As author David Weinberger, who started socializing the Internet in 1997, muses, the Web has become a vital part of the lives of hundreds of millions of people. It is about relationships in time, space, and knowledge, "where we can exist as social creatures in many ever expanding networks. [The Web reveals to us the] brute fact that we are creatures who care about ourselves and the world we share with others; we live within a context of meaning. The world is richer in meaning than we can possibly imagine."[12]

Social Software

The term "social software" predates by several years the social networking sites like Facebook and MySpace; it refers collectively to any software tool or application that facilitates social interaction. Before the World Wide Web, e-mail or computer-based applications for collaboration within organizations constituted the choices for people to connect and exchange information.

The technologies collectively referred to as "Web 2.0" comprise blogs and wikis, social networking sites, photo- and video-sharing sites, discussion boards, customer communities, virtual team spaces, web conference platforms, and so on. What distinguishes these applications individually and as a collection is that they are "universally available and *deeply participative.*"[13]

What the embracing of Web 2.0 technologies enables for net work is a completely self organizing and self-managed information infrastructure that can be tailored to support the purpose, structure, and style of a network in its value-producing capacity. It is wholly democratic and mirrors perfectly the needs of the networked organization for full participation of all members:

- Transparency;
- Diversity;
- Openness.

Inside a network, this astonishing infrastructure has the ability to make "an episode of knowledge work widely and permanently visible."[14] To those outside a network, the infrastructure that presents its public face provides an opening for expanding connections and collaboration. (See the Appendix for a summary of a network's activities that can be enabled or enhanced by the use of various technologies.)

The Network Mind

Technology provides much more than the enabling tools and applications for members of networks to connect and collaborate. Whole networks themselves are subject to market valuation and leverage. For example, in late 2006, social networking sites like MySpace and FaceBook had market values of $700 million and $2 billion, respectively. The value, of course, is not in the software but in the access to the participants in these networks, and in the enormous value of purchase power and influence of the demographic populations they represent.

Prediction markets offer another example of ways that networks are being prized for collective value. By creating stock market–like mechanisms for "buying" and "selling" potential decision choices (the winner of an election primary, the go-to-market price for a new product), companies are finding that the "winning" stock represents the collective wisdom of those who participate in trading and is often the most accurate and optimal choice. Technology makes it possible for us to be part of the collective intelligence that will contribute to the world that comes after.

That world is fast upon us. The Internet generation is upon us already; students entering the workforce today are more intensely networked through mobile devices than most of us could have imagined even ten years ago. They are learning to work collaboratively with others worldwide through games. They will expect to work in places that support their capacity for net work.

CREATING THE CAPACITY FOR NET WORK

"Capacity," as I am using it here, implies the development of capabilities as well as the absence of constraints on using those capabilities. The really foundational work for network success includes ensuring that:

- Individuals, managers, and organizations have developed specific competencies related to working with people in networks;
- The network has developed a style that includes conditions supporting the growth and use of those competencies.

Build Net Work Competencies

During the late 1980s, as "teamwork" entered the management sciences, corporate education groups began developing or bringing in special training to help managers and employees be more effective team members. We should not expect, therefore, that we can focus management attention on networks without thinking about what skills and competencies are required for people to be effective.

The skills required for successful collaboration within networks build on those collaboration skills that are currently part of personal and professional development curricula, including:

- Communications (speaking and listening, as well as effective writing);
- Facilitation;
- Collaborative problem solving;
- Team and project coordination;
- Influencing and negotiation;
- Group decision making and conflict management;
- Using collaboration tools.

However, conscious net work adds the requirement of becoming more aware of and able to manage the context of one's personal network and organizational networks.

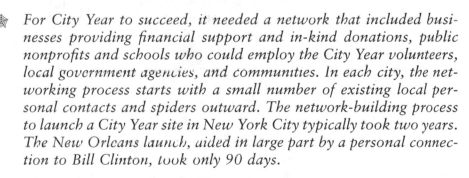

For City Year to succeed, it needed a network that included businesses providing financial support and in-kind donations, public nonprofits and schools who could employ the City Year volunteers, local government agencies, and communities. In each city, the networking process starts with a small number of existing local personal contacts and spiders outward. The network-building process to launch a City Year site in New York City typically took two years. The New Orleans launch, aided in large part by a personal connection to Bill Clinton, took only 90 days.

Personal network management

One of the research themes in social network analysis has been to examine the networks of top performers in organizations, both to understand how network structure contributes to performance and to develop guidance to improve the performance of other knowledge workers. What the researchers have found is that yes, indeed, top performers are effective at developing and using their social networks.[15] Networking for them is often an unconscious behavior; in fact, they might have an aversion to the term "networking," as it can be perceived as manipulative or exploitive behavior. However, successful people tend to:

- Be highly sought out for information;
- Be aware of the skills and expertise of a broader set of people across the network;
- Be positioned at key points in their networks;
- Be selective in establishing and maintaining high-quality relationships;
- Pay attention to reciprocity in relationships;
- Be far more likely to have connections outside their local groups and to provide connections between their own groups and others.[16]

Fannie Mae, the private shareholder-owned mortgage company, has been using the network lens to enhance collaboration at a number of levels within the company. One of their technology divisions has set up cohort groups consisting of roughly 25 participants from different hierarchical levels and departments. While these groups enrich the personal networks of each of the employees participating, participants also spend time analyzing their individual, personal networks and engaging with each other to understand what actions can improve and enrich their own networks and network capabilities.[17]

Tim DeMello, founder and CEO of Ziggs, Inc., an online search platform for businesspeople, and a self-professed serial entrepreneur, fosters the importance of connections among his employees by making a distinction between coworkers and fellow employees. A fellow employee is someone whose paycheck comes from the same bank account; a coworker is anyone who can assist you in the accomplishment of a task. The role of a leader, he says, is to make employees start to think in terms of their networks, to begin each day and each new task by thinking about their entire coworking network.

The awareness of this coworker network begins for DeMello at the hiring stage, where he thinks about the personal networks that people bring with them. He's not the only executive who makes hiring decisions based on the strength of the network that an individual can bring to the workplace. "We've always done this," he says, "but we didn't necessarily know it." (Although there was time in the not so distant past when sales or consulting executives were hired based on the size of their Rolodexes.)

DeMello believes so firmly that people must leverage their personal networks both inside and outside a company that he founded Ziggs on the notion that we should have personal expertise location tools on our personal computers—not just the company expertise locator, but one that includes all our personal contacts and directories from alumni and professional associations, past employers, and civic and religious organizations.[18]

On the other side of the employee entry/exit equation is the potential for new knowledge to come into a company or group when an employee leaves. Research at the Wharton School of Management has shown social capital dividends from ties created when employees leave a company. Once in a new environment, the worker's ties to former colleagues become weak ties into an entire new network—and an opportunity for knowledge access and potential partnership.[19]

Organizational competency

The network lens offers anyone in an organization the possibility to identify leverage points for improving the network's operational style or value-producing mechanisms, especially if that lens is accompanied by training in network analysis.

Ron Burt, who studied managerial networks at Raytheon Corporation, found that managers who worked to connect people across the company were better compensated and more likely to receive promotions.[20] Working with Don Ronchi, then Chief Learning Officer at Raytheon, Burt developed a program that taught executives to examine and work with social networks within their organizations. The Business Leadership Program they developed provides a three-month-long combination of instruction in organizational network analysis, field work within their own organizations within Raytheon, and a review of strategic initiatives with Raytheon's CEO. Burt and Ronchi used the program as a laboratory to understand whether this network competency would have an impact on the future success of the managers who took it. That is, they wanted to know whether managers who were more aware of and consciously managed the work of their organizations with an awareness of networks would be more successful.[21]

Given control groups of executives who did not attend the program but were similar in rank, position, and performance to those who did attend the program, Burt and Ronchi found that those who attended the program and learned how to use a network view to manage were ultimately more successful overall in terms of promotion and tenure in the organization.

Create the Conditions for Networks to Emerge and Succeed

Behavioral change doesn't just happen. It needs explicit changes in policy, processes, and programs in networks of all types. In a study of Sandia National Laboratories, Susan Mohrman and colleagues identified a number of enabling conditions that supported self-organizing collaborations across Sandia laboratories, other national labs, universities, and corporations.[22] While specific to the environment of the research laboratories, the findings provide insights for networks of all types. The enabling conditions include:

- Intermingling of sources of funding. Insight: *Find multiple sponsoring stakeholders who will bring different perspectives.*
- Flexible hiring systems and collaborative projects for interns and postdoctoral researchers. Insight: *Create opportunities for people to work together in new roles.*
- Changing norms and culture to support collaboration, in particular, aligning the reward system toward collaborative publication. Insight: *Create incentives for people to reach out and collaborate.*
- Organizational integration. Insight: *Create linkage mechanisms at a high enough organizational level to ensure cross-pollination.*
- Creating broad policy direction and furthering research across disciplinary fields. Insight: *Make the network goals broad and*

compelling enough to draw people from different areas to work together.

- Putting people to work together on projects in support of organizational goals. Insight: *Let people get to know each other in different roles.*

People are drawn into commitment to a network when they are in accord with its purpose and, especially, when they are able to care as much about the goals of the network—the scientific discovery in a laboratory, a social endeavor, product launch—as they do about their personal goals and to see the relationship between the two.

The leaders' work, then, is to maintain the context for the network to achieve its goals while maintaining and growing social capital that creates and enhance the ties among individuals.

Manage social capital

The ability to create and maintain social capital is an important organizational competency for the networked world. As an organizational competency, it touches and reaches all aspects of how people are put to work in an organization. Here's a short list of prescriptions:[23]

- *Social architecture:* Pay attention to facility design and location so that public workspaces afford people opportunities for serendipitous encounter and connections, comfortable conversations, and ad hoc collaborations;

- *Hiring and contracting processes:* Build an assessment of collaborative capacity into the hiring and contracting processes. Asking questions about how people solve problems or work on complex tasks and listening for the words "collaboration" or "network" in the responses often provides an opening for understanding how they would work in an open environment. Think about the extended networks that a person or contracted organization can bring into the company and how the company could leverage those connections;

- *Staffing projects:* Create project networks with a view toward introducing people from different disciplines, rotating people from one geographical location to another, or co-locating people on a project-by project basis;

- *Roles, not jobs:* Assign work to people based on their expertise, aptness for the work, and the network of experience that they can bring, providing opportunities for people to step out of rigidly defined job descriptions;

- *Formalized networks and communities:* Use communities of practice, management networks, task forces, and cross-functional initiatives to demonstrate a significant, visible commitment to using networks as an organizational structure, and as a way to help people build their personal networks;

- *Education:* Develop and institutionalize awareness of net work skills in formal and informal training and on-the-job work. Introduce the language of net work into existing training programs;

- *Rewards and incentives:* Integrate requirements of network participation and contribution into job descriptions; set goals and incentives based on working across boundaries; acknowledge those who work within networks to accomplish the good of the whole;

- *Trust and reciprocity:* To build a foundation of trust, demonstrate your own trustworthiness and acknowledge trust that others place in you. Acknowledge your own faults and mistakes. Always reciprocate. Do favors for others without expecting anything in return.

Use the Network Lens and Net Work Tools

One aspect of working in a complex environment is that we see each other in multiple roles at different times, in networks that are constantly shifting. The network lens comes with a language and a set of tools that help us better understand how we work with one another in complexity.

To Enhance Individuals' Performance

I believe that people are happiest and most able to contribute when they are in roles or are performing activities that utilize their natural talents and also enable them to work in the context of affiliation and trust. The insight that comes from an organizational network analysis can lead to placing an individual in a role that offers him or her the opportunity to use his or her unique combination of talent and trustworthiness. Consider the story of the University of Maryland's NCAA soccer team, the "Terps" (Terrapins). After sliding into a middling record in the 2000 season, the coach's brother, an HR vice president, recommended an organizational network analysis. The analysis revealed that a quiet sophomore, Scotty Buete (who had had to be convinced to play on the team), was the most respected among the team members for personal advice and opinions. After Buete was made the team's third co-captain, the team rallied that same day and over the next four years went on to four straight College Cup soccer appearances and a national championship.

The subtle change that occurred in the management of the team was the acknowledgment that one of the roles of leadership—even in a competitive sport—consists of being able to provide "glue," or social capital.[24]

In her research on social networks in R&D teams, Polly Rizova found a similar dynamic. She noticed that innovation across teams was more likely to succeed if existing positive relationships were converted into "prescribed," or formal relationships (as Buete's appointment to co-captain). The formula was the same: Identify the hubs—the central people in the network—and assign roles based on centrality.[25]

To Enhance Team Performance

Dennis Smith, an experienced project manager, has been using the network lens to understand how to structure and manage project teams in what he calls the "post-heroic" leadership model. In applying network terminology to the new, "Internetworked" team management model, he describes the structure of a large project team as a set of hubs. But instead of the hubs being hierarchical positions of authority, they are based on the roles that individuals play: There is a "deliverables hub," a "problem-solving hub," a "planning information hub," an "information on people hub," and so on.[26]

Surprisingly, there has been little formal research that brings formal network analysis and team studies together. Preliminary work suggests that managers who become network-aware can use team staffing and assignments (as in Smith's example) to build or leverage social capital.[27]

To Enhance Organizational Performance

Methods like organizational network analysis and value network analysis enable organizations to look at the relationships among people, roles, and groups. This higher-level view is being used in a variety of settings to solve a number of organizational performance challenges. Table 10.1 summarizes some ways that analysis tools support performance improvements.

Table 10.1
Benefits of the Network View

Challenge	Achieved By
Enhancing collaboration across networks and groups	Identifying the key areas where improved collaboration, communication, or knowledge exchange will have the most impact on internal effectiveness or customer relationships
Retention of people with vital corporate knowledge	Increasing the social capital in the organization so that people who are more connected are more likely to be satisfied with their work and more likely to stay
Increased innovation, productivity, and responsiveness	Understanding the flow of tangible and intangible work, knowledge, and artifacts in a value network
Smarter decisions about changing the formal organization structure or introducing new processes into organizations	Understanding the structure of the existing social and value networks
Insight into the challenges of integration following restructuring, mergers, or acquisitions	Identifying specific individuals or groups who are most likely to have the most influence across group borders and boundaries and network participants who have the most access to paths of knowledge flow

To Enhance the Collective

As human beings, we are always trying to "make sense" of the world around us, and there are various processes and means by which we do this.[28] Managers have historically used spreadsheets with columns of calculations as the primary tools of visualization. Concretely representing the business (number of trades, inventory, sales, and prices) to represent it to the organization and the outside once worked, but this single dimension cannot suffice in a multidimensional world. Models developed for business analysis, strategy, and decision making—like the classic 2 × 2 matrix we are so familiar with—also contribute to the sense making of the business.

Sense making in a complex world requires skills beyond these mechanical approaches; it must be deeply participatory. Strategy and sense making need to be collaborative, open, and transparent, using the diverse skills, talents, knowledge, and perspectives of all stakeholders.

Network analysis of various forms generates maps that let a network "see itself" in a way that leads to a process of inquiry. Value network maps and organizational (social) network maps described in Chapter 8 have tremendous power to hold a mirror up to an organization, not just to see a snapshot of its current state but also to draw interpretations and tell stories about what they see, and what it means for the future.

Discovering networks

Peter Gloor, who researches global networks of individuals pursuing innovation in common areas of interest called Collaborative Innovation Networks (COINs), has been watching the emergent behavior of groups of people, often unconnected and certainly unbounded, moving around the same idea or ideas. Gloor, and others who are using metaphors from the natural world to describe emergent network behavior, call these "swarms." Using software he developed that mines discussions on public discussion groups, Gloor has been able to map the patterns of idea exchanges among people in these swarms. Figure 10.1 is an example of the map created by the software.

Gloor foresees that this software will enable innovation seekers (also known as "coolhunters") to identify cutting-edge trends that

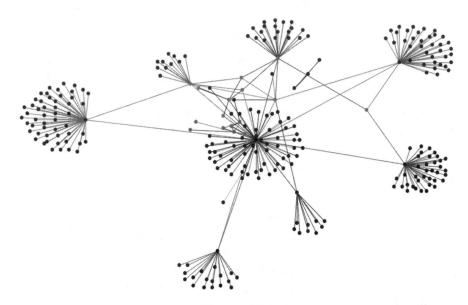

Figure 10.1
An innovation network swarm
Reprinted by Permission of iQuest Global.

emerge from the collective intelligence of collaborative activity among people who are motivated to share and collaborate out of shared interest, without regard to personal gain.[29]

Uniting networks

As we understand more and more about how networks emerge and self-organize, it will become second nature to reach for the tools that help us to map the relationships when multiple networks (as shown in Figure 10.1) emerge. For example, in New Orleans during the year after Hurricane Katrina, multiple organizations emerged in response to the vast number of social, infrastructural, and governance issues facing the city. One of the challenges following any disaster of this size is simply to maintain awareness of the large number of organizations and individuals who are contributing to the recovery. Multiple websites sprang up to identify work, but it was very difficult to see the overall effects and influences of the key participants in the recovery process.

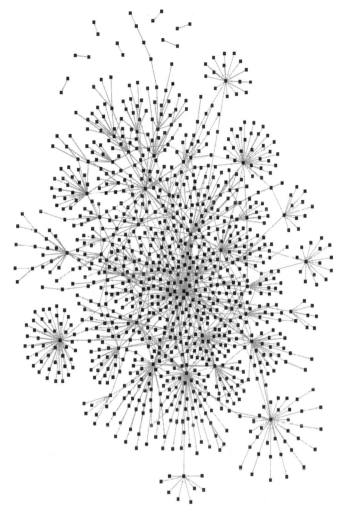

Figure 10.2
NOLA recovery networks
Reprinted by permission of Valdis Krebs.

Valdis Krebs, when queried about using organizational network analysis to map the relationships among groups working on recovery efforts, offered his time pro bono to help. Using data collected from the various websites and wikis, Valdis created the map shown in Figure 10.2.

As you can see, there are multiple network hubs; these represent social and organizational relationships of individuals and groups, including board members in the key recovery agencies, both governmental and quasi-governmental. Overall, the mapping shows how 1,000 organizations and individuals are connected in various recovery projects.

I see this image as holding the promise of net work: to bring to the forefront the underlying connections among people and groups and to use our understanding of networks to create collective knowledge and enjoin collaboration in purposeful shared work.

CHALLENGES

We are in the networked age. Our growing awareness comes from the symbiotic evolution of technology and new social structures: The more we use new technologies, the more possibility we see in how the technology can support us; the more the technology changes, the more ways we see how we can work together and fundamentally alter the nature of work and relationships.

But we are not there yet.

Making the Case

Net work takes time. It takes time to develop a large network to a level of performance maturity, time to acculturate people to collaborative behaviors and to establish work habits based on an integrated set of tools, time for a network to achieve results, time for a network to experiment with different structural and governance models before it settles into its rhythm, time to build trust.

It can, in fact, take time for a generation of managers to understand not just that networks are important, but that net work skills can be learned. Working in uncertainty, giving up status and economic power to a network, and committing to partnership without proof of return are not situations most managers have been trained to handle. NGO networks often have had to face donors requesting results who were not ready to "trust that the network will do its job."[30]

The case is making itself; the language of networks is creeping into the business lexicon, and the science of management is starting to address the tasks required. Paul Adler and Charles Heckscher cite the following four difficult problems that must be addressed to support work as "collaborative communities":

1. Working across boundaries
2. Increasing diversification of knowledge and skills, especially at the technical level
3. Allowing for authority based on knowledge and expertise rather than positional role
4. Bringing values into the realm of public discussion[31]

This fourth item is particularly important: A discussion of values requires people to reveal themselves and often to speak from a personal voice.

Authentic Conversation

It is not easy for those who live and work in cultures of competition and control to unlearn the habits of veiling conversations and to learn to speak openly, truthfully, and respectfully with others, often on topics that touch on personal values. Fortunately, the increasing adoption of methods such as World Café, Open Space, and others like those described in Chapter 9 are providing practice fields that enable leaders to demonstrate their commitment to listen and to work collaboratively. In these settings, simple rules that guide the conversation and process make it easy for people to learn to relax and be fully themselves when they participate.

Managers or leaders who are used to hierarchical patterns of communication and decision making may not be comfortable with a shift to working through a network and even more uncomfortable with the skills of dialogue.

 The LEArning Project, a partnership between a group of local authorities in England, the National College for School Leadership,

and the Department of Education and Skills Innovation Unit, was designed as a network of people learning how to use networks among schools, local services, and governmental agencies in policy, resource, and practice reform. They wanted to explore the role that local authorities could play in developing partnerships in a way that would enhance both learning and the well-being of young people. The NCSL and the Innovation Unit took the lead in brokering the beginning of the network by identifying local authorities who had a history of innovative local approaches to collaboration and bringing them together. They also created a separate learning group consisting of the chief officers from the authorities to create a "think tank." What they found was that local officers, trained in top-down policy mandates, had difficulty making the transition to an environment in which trust and open dialogue fostered real learning. The breakthrough occurred for this group of officers when they were able, one said, to speak honestly "without thinking that we were boasting or whining or being damned."[32]

Honest dialogue does not always come easy for senior executives schooled in command and control who must at all costs always "look good." However, those who coach executives and who create and manage executive networks are finding ways to create a trusting environment in which people can tackle hard issues. One of the first assessments in the Defense Intelligence Agency's Knowledge Lab was a cultural assessment of behaviors needed to develop a collaborative environment. Work with consultant Nancy Dixon revealed that analysts were reluctant to advocate their positions when challenged by higher-ups. As a result, one of the first programs initiated in the lab was the delivery of a three-day workshop and follow-on coaching to help the intelligence agents in the DIA understand the nature of their interactions with others and how they could become more confident in advocating their positions.[33]

Speaking authentically, being accountable for what we say, and listening as if something is at stake are all acts of personal risk, but they also help each of us individually toward expanding our abilities at sense making and being good "network persons." We cannot survive without learning to exist in networks, and as those networks are all about relationships, we must always be challenged to practice authentic conversation and above all in a network, to practice the rule of choosing voice over exit.

Managing Changes That Cannot be Managed

Another significant challenge for leaders of networks is to accept that in the realm of knowledge work, and even in transactional and transformational work that relies on the collaboration of teams of people, there are a large number of activities that cannot be overly controlled. One of the earliest management consultants to notice the trend toward networks in the early 1990s was Ram Charan, who observed that to be able to use network forms effectively, senior managers needed to work on shaping processes that allow the members of the network to make decisions.[34]

Sense making precedes decision making and it must above all be a collaborative effort, ideally based in the articulated principles and values set forth in a charter or member agreement. A good leader needs to be able to frame external pressures or internal shifts in the context of the impact on the network's purpose, and to use those shifts as opportunities for innovation, drawing on the insights, expertise, and experience of all who will be affected by the decision.

To work in complexity is not to abandon all the rules and principles of management science; there are many organizational, research, production, sales and marketing, and information systems that require structured discipline and leadership craft. What's important is to recognize that there are domains of work that are now heavily influenced by relationships, so the management tasks *must* be approached from the combined lens of complexity and networks.

SIX USEFUL FIRST STEPS

Net work is really about doing things you already know how to do; you are already embedded in networks of all types and sizes. You have learned to navigate in them. Here are six simple ideas for how you can stretch your net work limbs and start to walk in this new world.

Practice the Language

This book is full of memes, that is words and phrases that have entered my language through my interactions with people, in person and online. I am now passing these on to you and ask you to practice them and pass them on.

Be conscious of the words you choose to describe your work and collaborative activities when you write e-mail or talk with others. When you use the words "network," "complexity," "value," "pattern," "reciprocity," "dynamic," "discovery," "value network," "emergence," and "diversity," be intentional about how you are weave them into your sentences. Use them as if they matter.

Shift Your Mindset

Let go of needing to be in control. Look for rules that will help you navigate in complex situations. For example, follow the Open Space rules for conversation when you have a difficult meeting to facilitate:

1. Whoever comes are the right people.
2. Whatever happens is all that could have.
3. Whenever it starts is the right time.
4. When it's over, it's over.

(Note that these rules are accompanied by one law, the Law of Two Feet: Anyone who is neither learning nor contributing is responsible for using their two feet, and leaving after they make a gesture of acknowledgment to the group they are leaving.)[35]

Get Comfortable with a New Technology

Decide to participate in the universe of Web 2.0 (if you do not already). Create a blog, or comment on someone else's. Search for and join an online group exploring a topic that interests you. Talk to friends who use a social networking site and ask them to invite you to theirs and help you navigate through it. Contribute to Wikipedia. Put some of your digital photos on a photo-sharing site.

Sketch Networks in Your Notes

Get comfortable with the idea that you can draw a network any time, anywhere. Make a sketch of your personal network, the people you work with the most, and their connections. Draw a value network map of the project you are working on right now, and identify the tangible and intangible exchanges among the participant roles you identify.

Use a Network to Solve a Problem

The next time you have to solve a thorny problem that you would normally tackle by yourself, take out that sketch book or your address book. Ask yourself, "Who is in my network of support? Is a breakthrough beyond my own abilities possible if I open up to the insights, experience, and expertise accessible to me through my relationships?" Do not allow yourself to solve the problem on your own.

Connect People

A fundamental premise of this book is that we—as individuals—can influence the creation, growth, and usefulness of networks. Any individual, acting alone, alters the dynamics of a network, whatever the size. Make a phone call. Send an e-mail. Reach out. Make a new connection for yourself, or connect two people you know. Repair a network tie that may be broken, or renew an old acquaintance. Invite someone into a network; bring two networks together. Convene a group of like-minded people who may have much to offer each other and are not yet aware of the possibility that as a network, they multiply their abilities to make a difference at work, and in the world.

NOTES

1. Jay R. Galbraith, "Mastering the Law of Requisite Variety with Differentiated Networks," in *The Firm as Collaborative Community* (New York: Oxford University Press, 2006).

2. Patti Anklam, Rob Cross, and Vic Gulas, "Expanding the Field of Vision," *The Learning Organization* 12, no. 6 (2005): 539–551.
3. Jerry Ash, "Ideas Emerging: Case report on MindTree Consulting," *Inside Knowledge Magazine* 9, no. 10 (2006).
4. Adrian Wolfberg, "A Formula for Success," *GovExec.com*, September 13, 2006.
5. Larry Huston and Nabil Sakkab, "Connect and Develop: Inside Procter & Gamble's New Model for Innovation," *Harvard Business Review* 84, no. 33 (2006).
6. IBM, "Global Innovation Outlook 2.0," (New York: IBM, 2006).
7. Jeffrey Shuman and Jan Twombly, "Collaborating to Win" (White Paper Series, Vol. 1, The Rhythm of Business, Newton, MA, May 2006).
8. Ranjay Gulati, "Alliances and Networks," *Strategic Management Journal* 19 (1998); Shuman and Twombly, "Collaborating."
9. Bonnie A. Nardi, Steve Whittaker, and Heinrich Schwartz, "It's Not What You Know, It's Who You Know: Work in the Information Age," *firstmonday* 5, no. 5 (2000).
10. Kellogg Leadership for Community Change, "Crossing Boundaries, Changing Communities: Lessons in Collective Leadership" (Battle Creek, MI: Kellogg Foundation, 2006).
11. Jeffrey Boase, John Horrigan, Barry Wellman, and Lee Rainie, "The Strength of Internet Ties" (Washington, DC: Pew Internet & American Life Project, January 25, 2006).
12. David Weinberger, *Small Pieces Loosely Joined* (New York: Perseus Publishing, 2002).
13. Andrew P. McAfee, "Enterprise 2.0: The Dawn of Emergent Collaboration," *MIT Sloan Management Review* 47, no. 3 (2006). (Emphasis added.)
14. Ibid.
15. Rob Cross, Thomas H. Davenport, and Susan Cantrell, "The Social Side of Performance," *MIT Sloan Management Review* 45, no. 1 (2003).
16. Thomas H. Davenport, *Thinking for a Living* (Boston: Harvard Business School Press, 2005).
17. Rob Cross and Sally Colella, "Building Vibrant Employee Networks," *HR Magazine* December (2004).
18. Comments at "Collaborative Networks Are the Organization" (symposium at Bentley College, Waltham, MA, June 7, 2006).

19. n.a., "The Social Network Benefit: Losing an Employee Doesn't Have to Mean Losing Knowledge," *Knowledge@Wharton*, October 4, 2006.
20. Ronald S. Burt, *Brokerage and Closure* (New York: Oxford University Press, 2005).
21. Ronald S. Burt and Don Ronchi, "Teaching Executives to See Social Capital: Results from a Field Experiment" (Chicago: University of Chicago Graduate School of Business, August 2006).
22. Susan Mohrman, Jay R. Galbraith, and Peter Monge, "Network Attributes Impacting the Generation and Flow of Knowledge with and from the Basic Science Community" (research presentation at American Evaluation Association, Atlanta, GA, November 2004).
23. Many of these were taken directly from or are based on Wayne Baker's list "Ten Interventions for Building Social Capital as a Competence," in Wayne Baker, *Achieving Success Through Social Capital* (San Francisco: Jossey-Bass, 2000).
24. Jenna McGregor, "Game Plan: First Find the Leaders," *BusinessWeek*, August 21, 2006.
25. Polly Rizova, "Are You Networked for Successful Innovation?" *MIT Sloan Management Review* 47, no. 3 (2006).
26. Dennis Smith, *Team Transitions* (n.p.: Lulu 2006).
27. Nancy Katz and David Lazer, "Building Effective Intra-Organizational Networks: The Role of Teams" (working paper, Center for Public Leadership, John F. Kennedy School of Government, Harvard University, 2003).
28. See Karl Weick, *Sensemaking in Organizations* (Thousand Oaks, CA: Sage Publications, 2005).
29. Peter Gloor, "Zen and the Art of Coolhunting" (Rehobeth, MA: iQuest Analytics, March 2006).
30. Claudia Liebler and Marisa Ferri, "NGO Networks: Building Capacity in a Changing World," November 2004.
31. Charles Heckscher and Paul S. Adler, *The Firm as a Collaborative Community: The Reconstruction of Trust in the Knowledge Economy* (New York: Oxford University Press, 2006).
32. Maggie Farrar and Denis Mongon, "Spreading Innovation across Local Authorities: Creating a National Network" (Nottingham, UK: National College for School Leadership, 2005), www.ncsl.org.uk/
33. Patti Anklam, and Adrian Wolfberg, "Creating Networks at the Defense Intelligence Agency," *KM Review* 9, no. 1 (2006).

34. Ram Charan, "How Networks Reshape Organizations—for Results," *Harvard Business Review* 69, no. 5 (1991).
35. Harrison Owen, *Riding the Tiger: Doing Business in a Transforming World* (Missoula, MT: Abbott, 1991).

Afterword

The working title of this book was *The Gennova Conspiracy*, an acknowledgment of the influence that Gennova, a quiet, informal idea network—so often referenced in this book—has on the emerging practice of net work, but also a nod to *The Aquarian Conspiracy*, written by Marilyn Ferguson in 1980, which I came upon in 1992. I came by it through a network. I participated in a formal network of women at Digital Equipment Corporation who worked with the Stone Center at Wellesley College to explore the theme of women in the workplace. Some time later, one of the women in that network recommended to me a summer management program at Smith College, which I subsequently attended. A career counselor there recommended to me *The Aquarian Conspiracy*, by Marilyn Ferguson. Ferguson identified many currents in organizational development, integration of the spiritual into work life, and the awakening of the "new age." She intuited a change occurring at the end of the twentieth century, the Aquarian Revolution, that would come about as individuals and small groups made connections with one another, sharing ideas and joining hands in work.

Like the Aquarian Conspiracy, the Gennova Conspiracy is much wider than the small idea network that meets monthly only a few miles from the site of Henry David Thoreau's cabin. The world is catching on. It's a conspiracy about the power of networks. Pass it on.

Appendix

THE TECHNOLOGIES
OF NET WORK

Before the Internet, we worked in networks and communities, but our collaborations were constrained by the physical limits of geography, telephony, and paper documents, including letters. As the 20th century advanced, computers became workhorses of industry, academia, and the military. Vannebar Bush's 1945 article in the *Atlantic Monthly*, "As We May Think," envisioned a future of networked information, but it wasn't until 1962 that researchers at MIT and DARPA began seriously to collaborate on the underlying technology required to achieve that vision. From the time that the Arpanet—the result of that first collaboration—first connected four host computers in 1969 until the advent of the World Wide Web, the Internet became more and more robust, until by 1985 it was well established in the research and defense development community and was also being used in the business community for daily computer communications: e-mail.

In their 1993 book *Connections*, Lee Sproull and Sara Kiesler researched the impact of e-mail on organizations, specifically distinguishing first-level and second-level effects. The first-level effect is the impact on productivity and efficiency gains: Time savings, transaction costs, and reduction of paperwork were three of the key criteria used to justify the cost of investments.

Second-level effects come about "because new communication technology leads people to change how they spend their time and what they think is important, have contact with different people, and depend on one another differently."[1]

Since the early 1990s, technologies to support connections have danced a mutually reinforcing dance between the capabilities of technology and the ways that we use them. As we move into an increasingly networked world, they will be more and more important for creators and contributors of network to learn, adopt, and adapt.

Throughout this book, I've referenced different technologies and tools for communications and collaboration without defining each of them specifically. The technologies and the ways we use them continue to evolve. I have no doubt that between the time I've had my last chance to make edits to this appendix and the time that *Net Work* appears in print, there will be something new. But I am also quite sure that it will be built on the actual technology or concepts embedded in the technologies listed in Table A.1, as this table is structured according to the distinct types of activity pertinent to net work.

In my thirty years of working with collaborative technologies, I have often been surprised by the extent to which the key element of basic training is overlooked. Assumptions that we can make about skills using online tools are changing with the demographics of the culture, and it is probably safe to assume that a 20-year-old in the Western world knows how to use a chat room. But most of us, however, are in different states of learning and understanding. So if technology is a vital element in the knowledge management of the network, it's important that all network members can use it effectively.

Here are some basic rules for introducing collaboration software:

- Select and match technology to meet both business needs and those of the knowledge worker;
- Make sure that the use of the technology is embedded in the work practices of the network;
- Introduce the technology in the context of those work practices, and assign tasks that require people to use the technology;

Table A.1
Network Technologies for Net Work

Activity	Common Technologies
Content creation, access, discovery, and use	Portals, personalization
	Collaboration platforms
	Information repositories and document management systems
	Search engines, automatic categorization, filtering
	Blogs
	Wikis
	Social tagging, collaborative filtering
	Virtual team workspaces
Collaboration	Virtual team spaces
	Presence indication, instant messaging
	Video and electronic conferencing
	Threaded discussions
	Desktop sharing
Communication	E-mail
	Blogs
	RSS subscription services, podcasts
	Face-to-face, teleconference, videoconference
	Webinars
	Intranet portals and websites
	Traditional publications (including hardcopy newsletters and the like)
Coordination	Calendar management (including shared calendars, meeting scheduling)
	Project/schedule management
	Task management
	Meeting management
	Workflow integration
Connection	PDAs, web phones, text messaging
	Expertise location
	Member directories
	Online presence
	Online social networking
Community	Community portal
	Face-to-face and virtual events
	Social network mapping
	Social tagging, collaborative filtering
	Online social networking
	Shared distribution and contact lists

- Give individuals multiple ways to learn, and provide both online and face-to-face coaching as well as documentation and formal training, if required;
- Close down alternate or back-door communication channels;
- Identify and work with key knowledge brokers and opinion leaders who can be role models for using the technology.

All of these assume, of course, that the technology platform has been prepared and tested to make sure that it works properly—by an integrated project network.

NOTE

1. Lee Sproull, and Sara Kiesler, *Connections* (Cambridge, MA: MIT Press, 1993).

INDEX

About the Author

Patti Anklam is a professional consultant with over 25 years experience bringing innovative ideas and concepts into knowledge-intensive organizations and using those ideas and concepts to solve real problems. For the past ten years, Patti has focused on the structure and dynamics of collaborative networks: how networks form, how to examine them to understand their dynamics and directions, and how to lead within the context of networks.

Anklam has worked as a writer, information architect, software development manager, analyst, and as director of knowledge management in large computer and telecommunications enterprises. As a consultant, she has worked for clients across a range of industries in the public and private sector using the tools described in *Net Work*.

Her current work focuses on how relationships and informal networks in organizations can provide efficiency, effectiveness, and innovative breakthroughs in knowledge-intensive activities. Anklam is the author of several articles on knowledge management and social networks; she speaks, consults, and conducts workshops both domestically and internationally. She writes frequently on Net Work topics at: www.pattianklam.com